Pokémon™

Gotta catch 'em all!™

DELUXE ESSENTIAL HANDBOOK

The need-to-know stats and facts on over 700 Pokémon

Published by Scholastic India Pvt. Ltd. under licence from Dream Theatre Private Limited
Scholastic India Pvt. Ltd. is a subsidiary of Scholastic Inc., New York, 10012 (USA).

For information regarding permission, write to:
Scholastic India Pvt. Ltd.
A-27, Ground Floor, Bharti Sigma Centre
Infocity-1, Sector 34, Gurgaon-122001 (India)

First edition: June 2019
This reprint edition: November 2024

ISBN-13: 978-93-5275-785-5

Printed in India at MicroPrints India, New Delhi

Welcome to the World of Pokémon!

Kanto . . . Johto . . . Hoenn. . .
Sinnoh . . . Unova . . . Kalos . . .

There are six Pokémon regions bursting with fascinating Pokémon. And this book is bursting with information about them!

The key to success in raising, battling, and evolving your Pokémon is staying informed. Information about each Pokémon's type, species, height, and weight can make all the difference in Gym battles, in the wild, and anywhere else you might meet Pokémon.

In this book, you'll get all the stats and facts you need about over 700 Pokémon. You'll find out how each Pokémon evolves, which moves it uses, and learn which Pokémon can evolve into Mega-Evolved Pokémon during battle.

So get ready, Trainers: With this *Deluxe Essential Handbook*, you'll be ready to master almost any Pokémon challenge!

HOW TO USE THIS BOOK

Here are the basics you'll discover about each Pokémon:

NAME

HOW TO SAY IT

When it comes to Pokémon pronunciation, it's easy to get tongue-tied! There are many Pokémon with unusual names, so we'll help you sound them out. Soon you'll be saying Pokémon names so perfectly, you'll sound like a professor!

HEIGHT AND WEIGHT

How does each Pokémon measure up? Find out by checking its height and weight stats. And remember, good things come in all shapes and sizes. It's up to every Trainer to work with his/her Pokémon and play up its size.

POSSIBLE MOVES

Every Pokémon has its own unique combination of Moves. Before you hit the battlefield, we'll tell you all about each Pokémon's awesome attacks. And don't forget, with a good Trainer, they can always learn more!

DESCRIPTION

Knowledge is power! Pokémon Trainers have to know their stuff. Find out everything you need to know about your Pokémon here.

EVOLUTION

If your Pokémon has an evolved form or pre-evolved form, we'll show you its place in the chain and how it evolves.

MEGA EVOLUTION

Certain key Pokémon have an all-new skill—during battle, they can Mega Evolve. Mega-Evolved Pokémon can tap into strength far greater than anything they've ever experienced. Mega Pokémon can change height, weight, and even type. You'll get the new stats in this book.

TYPE

Each Pokémon has a type, and some even have two! (Pokémon with two types are called dual-type Pokémon.) Every type of Pokémon comes with its advantages and disadvantages. We'll break them all down for you here.

REGION

There are different regions in the Pokémon world, like Kanto, Johto, Hoenn, Sinnoh, Unova, and Kalos. Each region has Pokémon particular to it.

Curious about what Pokémon types you'll spot on your Pokémon journey? Find out about all eighteen types on the next page . . .

GUIDE TO POKÉMON TYPES

A Pokémon's type can tell you a lot about it—from where to find it in the wild to the Moves it'll be able to use on the battlefield. Type is the key to unlocking a Pokémon's power.

A clever Trainer should always consider type when picking a Pokémon for a match, because type shows a Pokémon's strengths and weaknesses. For example, a Fire-type may melt an Ice-type, but against a Water-type, it might find it's the one in hot water. And while a Water-type usually has the upper hand in battle with a Fire-type, a Water-type move would act like a sprinkler on a Grass-type Pokémon. But when that same Grass-type is battling a Fire-type, it just might get scorched.

Keep in mind that Moves can be mightier based on the location of the battle. Rock-type Pokémon rock at mountainside battles, Electric-types get charged up near power plants, and Ground-types like to get down and dirty right in the dirt. And if a Pokémon has two types—that is, if it's a dual type—well, then it's double trouble!

Here are the eighteen different Pokémon types:

Ready to discover more about each Pokémon? Then let's begin!

ABOMASNOW

Frost Tree Pokémon

REGIONS
KALOS (MOUNTAIN), SINNOH

TYPE: GRASS-ICE

Snow-covered mountains are Abomasnow's preferred habitat. It creates blizzards to hide itself and keep others away.

How to say it: ah-BOM-ah-snow

Height: 7' 03"
Weight: 298.7 lbs.

Possible Moves: Ice Punch, Powder Snow, Leer, Razor Leaf, Icy Wind, Grass Whistle, Swagger, Mist, Ice Shard, Ingrain, Wood Hammer, Blizzard, Sheer Cold

MEGA ABOMASNOW

Frost Tree Pokémon

TYPE: GRASS-ICE

Height: 8' 10"
Weight: 407.9 lbs.

REGIONS
KALOS (CENTRAL), KANTO

ABRA

Psi Pokémon

TYPE: PSYCHIC

Even while Abra is sleeping, which is most of the time, it can escape a foe by teleporting away. If it doesn't get enough sleep, its powers fade.

How to say it: AH-bra

Height: 2' 11"
Weight: 43.0 lbs.

Possible Move: Teleport

Abra → Kadabra → Alakazam → Mega Alakazam

ABSOL

Disaster Pokémon

REGIONS
HOENN, KALOS (COASTAL)

TYPE: DARK

Absol doesn't often appear to people, but when it does, they should pay attention. It leaves its mountain home to warn others of an approaching disaster.

How to say it: AB-sol

Height: 3' 11"
Weight: 103.6 lbs.

Possible Moves: Perish Song, Me First, Razor Wind, Detect, Taunt, Scratch, Feint, Leer, Quick Attack, Pursuit, Bite, Double Team, Slash, Swords Dance, Future Sight, Night Slash, Detect, Psycho Cut, Sucker Punch

MEGA ABSOL

Disaster Pokémon

TYPE: DARK

Height: 3' 11"
Weight: 108.0 lbs.

REGIONS
KALOS (MOUNTAIN), UNOVA

ACCELGOR

Shell Out Pokémon

TYPE: BUG

After coming out of its shell, Accelgor is light and quick, moving with the speed of a ninja. It wraps its body up to keep from drying out.

How to say it: ak-SELL-gohr

Height: 2' 07"
Weight: 55.8 lbs.

Possible Moves: Final Gambit, Power Swap, Leech Life, Acid Spray, Double Team, Quick Attack, Struggle Bug, Mega Drain, Swift, Me First, Agility, Giga Drain, U-turn, Bug Buzz, Recover

Shelmet Accelgor

Shield Forme

REGION
KALOS (CENTRAL)

AEGISLASH

Royal Sword Pokémon

TYPE: STEEL-GHOST

Aegislash has long been seen as a symbol of royalty. In olden days, these Pokémon often accompanied the king.

How to say it: EE-jih-SLASH

Height: 5' 07" **Weight:** 116.8 lbs.

Possible Moves: Fury Cutter, Pursuit, Autotomize, Shadow Sneak, Slash, Iron Defense, Night Slash, Power Trick, Iron Head, Head Smash, Swords Dance, Aerial Ace, King's Shield, Sacred Sword

Blade Forme

Honedge Doublade Aegislash

AERODACTYL

Fossil Pokémon

REGIONS
KALOS (COASTAL), KANTO

TYPE: ROCK-FLYING

This Pokémon was restored from a piece of fossilized amber. It's said that Aerodactyl ruled the skies in its ancient world.

How to say it: AIR-row-DACK-tull

Height: 5' 11"
Weight: 130.1 lbs.

Possible Moves: Iron Head, Ice Fang, Fire Fang, Thunder Fang, Wing Attack, Supersonic, Bite, Scary Face, Roar, Agility, Ancient Power, Crunch, Take Down, Sky Drop, Hyper Beam, Rock Slide, Giga Impact

MEGA AERODACTYL

Fossil Pokémon

TYPE: ROCK-FLYING

Height: 6' 11"
Weight: 174.2 lbs.

Aerodactyl → Mega Aerodactyl

TYPE: STEEL-ROCK

Aggron is extremely protective of the mountain it claims as its territory. After a natural disaster, it will work tirelessly to restore its mountain, rebuilding the topsoil and planting trees.

How to say it: AGG-ron

Height: 6' 11"
Weight: 793.7 lbs.

Possible Moves: Tackle, Harden, Mud-Slap, Headbutt, Metal Claw, Iron Defense, Roar, Take Down, Iron Head, Protect, Metal Sound, Iron Tail, Autotomize, Heavy Slam, Double-Edge, Metal Burst

REGIONS
HOENN, KALOS (MOUNTAIN)

AGGRON

Iron Armor Pokémon

MEGA AGGRON

Iron Armor Pokémon

TYPE: STEEL

Height: 7' 03"
Weight: 870.8 lbs.

AIPOM

Long Tail Pokémon

REGION
JOHTO

TYPE: NORMAL

Aipom uses the appendage at the end of its tail just like a hand. Its actual hands have lost their dexterity because it relies so much on its tail.

How to say it: AY-pom

Height: 2' 07" **Weight:** 25.4 lbs.

Possible Moves: Scratch, Tail Whip, Sand Attack, Astonish, Baton Pass, Tickle, Fury Swipes, Swift, Screech, Agility, Double Hit, Fling, Nasty Plot, Last Resort

Aipom → Ambipom

ALAKAZAM

Psi Pokémon

REGIONS
KALOS (CENTRAL), KANTO

TYPE: PSYCHIC

Because its brain never stops growing, Alakazam must use telekinesis to hold up its heavy head. On the plus side, its memory and intellect are amazing.

How to say it: AH-la-kuh-ZAM

Height: 4' 11"
Weight: 105.8 lbs.

Possible Moves: Teleport, Kinesis, Confusion, Disable, Miracle Eye, Ally Switch, Psybeam, Reflect, Telekinesis, Recover, Psycho Cut, Calm Mind, Psychic, Future Sight, Trick

MEGA ALAKAZAM

Psi Pokémon

TYPE: PSYCHIC

Height: 3' 11"
Weight: 105.8 lbs.

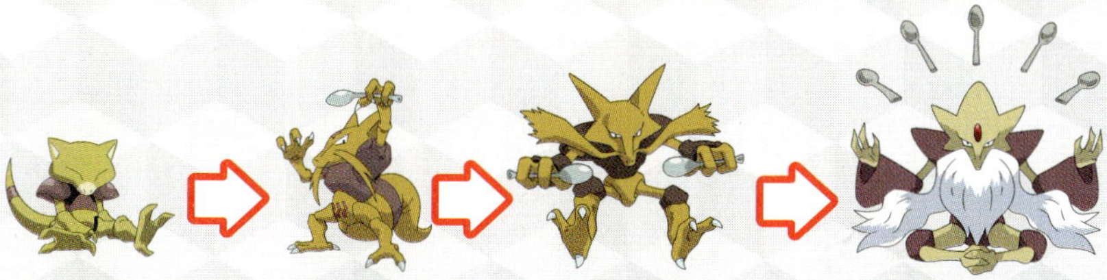

Abra → Kadabra → Alakazam → Mega Alakazam

ALOMOMOLA

Caring Pokémon

REGIONS
KALOS (COASTAL), UNOVA

TYPE: WATER

When Alomomola finds injured Pokémon in the open sea where it lives, it gently wraps its healing fins around them and guides them to shore.

How to say it: uh-LOH-muh-MOH-luh

Height: 3' 11" **Weight:** 69.7 lbs.

Possible Moves: Hydro Pump, Wide Guard, Healing Wish, Pound, Water Sport, Aqua Ring, Aqua Jet, Double Slap, Heal Pulse, Protect, Water Pulse, Wake-Up Slap, Soak, Wish, Brine, Safeguard, Helping Hand

Does not evolve

ALTARIA

Humming Pokémon

REGIONS
HOENN, KALOS (MOUNTAIN)

TYPE: DRAGON-FLYING

When Altaria sings through the sky in its beautiful soprano voice, anyone listening falls into a happy daydream. Its soft, cottony wings are perfect for catching updrafts.

How to say it: ahl-TAR-ee-uh

Height: 3' 07"
Weight: 45.4 lbs.

Possible Moves: Sky Attack, Pluck, Peck, Growl, Astonish, Sing, Fury Attack, Safeguard, Mist, Round, Natural Gift, Take Down, Refresh, Dragon Dance, Dragon Breath, Cotton Guard, Dragon Pulse, Perish Song, Moonblast

MEGA ALTARIA

Humming Pokémon

TYPE: DRAGON-FAIRY

Height: 4' 11"
Weight: 45.4 lbs.

Swablu Altaria Mega Altaria

AMAURA

Tundra Pokémon

REGION
KALOS (COASTAL)

TYPE: ROCK-ICE

In the ancient world, Amaura's cold habitat kept predators at bay. It was restored from a frozen fragment.

How to say it: ah-MORE-uh

Height: 4' 03" **Weight:** 55.6 lbs.

Possible Moves: Growl, Powder Snow, Thunder Wave, Rock Throw, Icy Wind, Take Down, Mist, Aurora Beam, Ancient Power, Round, Avalanche, Hail, Nature Power, Encore, Light Screen, Ice Beam, Hyper Beam, Blizzard

Amaura Aurorus

REGION
SINNOH

AMBIPOM

Long Tail Pokémon

TYPE: NORMAL

Because Ambipom's two tails are so dexterous, it rarely uses its arms after evolving. Groups of Ambipom will sometimes link tails as a sign of friendship.

How to say it: AM-bih-pom

Height: 3' 11"
Weight: 44.8 lbs.

Possible Moves: Scratch, Tail Whip, Sand Attack, Astonish, Baton Pass, Tickle, Fury Swipes, Swift, Screech, Agility, Double Hit, Fling, Nasty Plot, Last Resort

Aipom Ambipom

REGIONS
KALOS (MOUNTAIN), UNOVA

AMOONGUSS

Mushroom Pokémon

TYPE: GRASS-POISON

In a swaying dance, Amoonguss waves its arm caps, which look like Poké Balls, in an attempt to lure the unwary. It doesn't often work.

How to say it: uh-MOON-gus

Height: 2' 00"
Weight: 23.1 lbs.

Possible Moves: Absorb, Growth, Astonish, Bide, Mega Drain, Ingrain, Feint Attack, Sweet Scent, Giga Drain, Toxic, Synthesis, Clear Smog, Solar Beam, Rage Powder, Spore

Foongus Amoonguss

AMPHAROS

Light Pokémon

REGIONS
JOHTO, KALOS (COASTAL)

TYPE: ELECTRIC

Ampharos shines so brightly that its light can be seen over long distances. Long ago, people used this light to send signals from far away.

How to say it: AMF-fah-rahs

Height: 4' 07" **Weight:** 135.6 lbs.

Possible Moves: Zap Cannon, Magnetic Flux, Ion Deluge, Dragon Pulse, Fire Punch, Tackle, Growl, Thunder Wave, Thunder Shock, Cotton Spore, Charge, Take Down, Electro Ball, Confuse Ray, Thunder Punch, Power Gem, Discharge, Cotton Guard, Signal Beam, Light Screen, Thunder

MEGA AMPHAROS

Light Pokémon

TYPE: ELECTRIC-DRAGON

Height: 4' 07"
Weight: 135.6 lbs.

Mareep Flaaffy Ampharos Mega Ampharos

REGION
HOENN

ANORITH

Old Shrimp Pokémon

TYPE: ROCK-BUG

The eight wings along Anorith's body wave in sequence to propel it through the warm seas where it lives. It was restored from a fossil.

How to say it: AN-no-rith

Height: 2' 04"
Weight: 27.6 lbs.

Possible Moves: Scratch, Harden, Mud Sport, Water Gun, Metal Claw, Protect, Ancient Power, Fury Cutter, Slash, Rock Blast, Crush Claw, X-Scissor

Anorith Armaldo

REGIONS
KALOS (MOUNTAIN), KANTO

ARBOK

Cobra Pokémon

TYPE: POISON

A powerful constrictor, Arbok can crush a steel barrel in its mighty coils. Getting out of its grip is no small feat.

How to say it: ARE-bock

Height: 11' 06"
Weight: 143.3 lbs.

Possible Moves: Ice Fang, Thunder Fang, Fire Fang, Wrap, Leer, Poison Sting, Bite, Glare, Screech, Acid, Crunch, Stockpile, Swallow, Spit Up, Acid Spray, Mud Bomb, Gastro Acid, Belch, Haze, Coil, Gunk Shot

Ekans Arbok

ARCANINE

Legendary Pokémon

REGION
KANTO

TYPE: FIRE

Arcanine's internal flame is the fuel for its amazing speed and endurance. If it runs for a whole day, it can cover more than 6,000 miles.

How to say it: ARE-ka-nine

Height: 6' 03" **Weight:** 341.7 lbs.

Possible Moves: Thunder Fang, Bite, Roar, Fire Fang, Odor Sleuth, Extreme Speed

Growlithe Arcanine

ARCEUS

Alpha Pokémon

REGION
SINNOH

TYPE: NORMAL

In the mythology of the Sinnoh region, Arceus emerged from its Egg into complete nothingness, and then shaped the world and everything in it.

How to say it: AR-key-us

Height: 10' 06" **Weight:** 705.5 lbs.

Possible Moves: Seismic Toss, Cosmic Power, Natural Gift, Punishment, Gravity, Earth Power, Hyper Voice, Extreme Speed, Refresh, Future Sight, Recover, Hyper Beam, Perish Song, Judgment

MYTHICAL POKÉMON

Does not evolve

REGION
UNOVA

ARCHEN

First Bird Pokémon

TYPE: ROCK-FLYING

It is believed that modern-day flying Pokémon descended from the ancient Archen, even though its wings aren't strong enough for flight. It was restored from a fossil.

How to say it: AR-ken

Height: 1' 08" **Weight:** 20.9 lbs.

Possible Moves: Quick Attack, Leer, Wing Attack, Rock Throw, Double Team, Scary Face, Pluck, Ancient Power, Agility, Quick Guard, Acrobatics, Dragon Breath, Crunch, Endeavor, U-turn, Rock Slide, Dragon Claw, Thrash

Archen Archeops

REGION
UNOVA

ARCHEOPS

First Bird Pokémon

TYPE: ROCK-FLYING

After evolving, Archeops can fly, though they aren't very good at it. They need a running start to get airborne and can generally get around more reliably by running.

How to say it: AR-kee-ops

Height: 4' 07" **Weight:** 70.5 lbs.

Possible Moves: Quick Attack, Leer, Wing Attack, Rock Throw, Double Team, Scary Face, Pluck, Ancient Power, Agility, Quick Guard, Acrobatics, Dragon Breath, Crunch, Endeavor, U-turn, Rock Slide, Dragon Claw, Thrash

Archen Archeops

ARIADOS

Long Leg Pokémon

REGIONS
JOHTO, KALOS (MOUNTAIN)

TYPE: BUG-POISON

The web Ariados spins is made of thin silk, strong enough to bind and hold an enemy. The tiny hooks on its feet make it an excellent climber.

How to say it: AIR-ree-uh-dose

Height: 3' 07" **Weight:** 73.9 lbs.

Possible Moves: Venom Drench, Fell Stinger, Bug Bite, Poison Sting, String Shot, Scary Face, Constrict, Leech Life, Night Shade, Shadow Sneak, Fury Swipes, Sucker Punch, Spider Web, Agility, Pin Missile, Psychic, Poison Jab, Cross Poison, Sticky Web

ARMALDO

Plate Pokémon

REGION
HOENN

TYPE: ROCK-BUG

With its huge claws and armored body, Armaldo is well equipped for battle. It has adapted to walk on its hind legs so it can live on land.

How to say it: ar-MAL-do

Height: 4' 11" **Weight:** 150.4 lbs.

Possible Moves: Scratch, Harden, Mud Sport, Water Gun, Metal Claw, Protect, Ancient Power, Fury Cutter, Slash, Rock Blast, Crush Claw, X-Scissor

AROMATISSE

REGION
KALOS (CENTRAL)

Fragrance Pokémon

TYPE: FAIRY

Aromatisse uses its powerful scent as a weapon in battle. It can overpower an opponent with a strategic stench.

How to say it: uh-ROME-uh-teece

Height: 2' 07"
Weight: 34.2 lbs.

Possible Moves: Aromatic Mist, Heal Pulse, Sweet Scent, Fairy Wind, Sweet Kiss, Odor Sleuth, Echoed Voice, Calm Mind, Draining Kiss, Aromatherapy, Attract, Moonblast, Charm, Flail, Misty Terrain, Skill Swap, Psychic, Disarming Voice, Reflect, Psych Up

ARON

REGIONS
HOENN, KALOS (MOUNTAIN)

Iron Armor Pokémon

TYPE: STEEL-ROCK

Aron chews up metal objects, from iron ore to steel bridges, and uses the metal to build up its body. It can destroy a heavy truck with a full-speed charge.

How to say it: AIR-ron

Height: 1' 04" **Weight:** 132.3 lbs.

Possible Moves: Tackle, Harden, Mud-Slap, Headbutt, Metal Claw, Iron Defense, Roar, Take Down, Iron Head, Protect, Metal Sound, Iron Tail, Autotomize, Heavy Slam, Double-Edge, Metal Burst

ARTICUNO

Freeze Pokémon

REGIONS
KALOS (COASTAL), KANTO

LEGENDARY POKÉMON

TYPE: ICE-FLYING

When Articuno flaps its wings, the air turns chilly. This Legendary Pokémon often brings snowfall in its wake.

How to say it: ART-tick-COO-no

Height: 5' 07" **Weight:** 122.1 lbs.

Possible Moves: Roost, Hurricane, Freeze-Dry, Tailwind, Sheer Cold, Gust, Powder Snow, Mist, Ice Shard, Mind Reader, Ancient Power, Agility, Ice Beam, Reflect, Hail, Blizzard

Does not evolve

AUDINO

Hearing Pokémon

REGIONS
KALOS (CENTRAL), UNOVA

TYPE: NORMAL

With the sensitive feelers on their ears, Audino can listen to people's heartbeats to pick up on their current state. Egg hatching can be predicted as well.

How to say it: AW-dih-noh

Height: 3' 07"
Weight: 68.3 lbs.

Possible Moves: Last Resort, Play Nice, Pound, Growl, Helping Hand, Refresh, Double Slap, Attract, Secret Power, Entrainment, Take Down, Heal Pulse, After You, Simple Beam, Double-Edge

MEGA AUDINO

Light Pokémon

TYPE: NORMAL-FAIRY

Height: 4' 11"
Weight: 70.5 lbs.

Audino → Mega Audino

AURORUS
Tundra Pokémon

REGION
KALOS (COASTAL)

TYPE: ROCK-ICE

With the icy crystals that line its sides, Aurorus can freeze the surrounding air and trap its foes in ice.

How to say it: ah-ROAR-us

Height: 8' 10"
Weight: 496.0 lbs.

Possible Moves: Freeze-Dry, Growl, Powder Snow, Thunder Wave, Rock Throw, Icy Wind, Take Down, Mist, Aurora Beam, Ancient Power, Round, Avalanche, Hail, Nature Power, Encore, Light Screen, Ice Beam, Hyper Beam, Blizzard

AVALUGG
Iceberg Pokémon

REGION
KALOS (MOUNTAIN)

TYPE: ICE

Avalugg's broad, flat back is a common resting place for groups of Bergmite. Its big, bulky body can crush obstacles in its path.

How to say it: AV-uh-lug

Height: 6' 07"
Weight: 1,113.3 lbs.

Possible Moves: Iron Defense, Crunch, Skull Bash, Tackle, Bite, Harden, Powder Snow, Icy Wind, Take Down, Sharpen, Curse, Ice Fang, Ice Ball, Rapid Spin, Avalanche, Blizzard, Recover, Double-Edge

AXEW
Tusk Pokémon

REGIONS
KALOS (CENTRAL), UNOVA

TYPE: DRAGON

If one of Axew's tusks breaks off, it quickly regrows, even stronger and sharper than before. It uses its tusks to crush berries and mark territory.

How to say it: AKS-yoo

Height: 2' 00"
Weight: 39.7 lbs.

Possible Moves: Scratch, Leer, Assurance, Dragon Rage, Dual Chop, Scary Face, Slash, False Swipe, Dragon Claw, Dragon Dance, Taunt, Dragon Pulse, Swords Dance, Guillotine, Outrage, Giga Impact

Axew Fraxure Haxorus

AZELF
Willpower Pokémon

REGION
SINNOH

TYPE: PSYCHIC

According to legend, Azelf brought a lasting balance to the world. It is known as "the Being of Willpower."

How to say it: AZ-elf

Height: 1' 00" **Weight:** 0.7 lbs.

Possible Moves: Rest, Confusion, Imprison, Detect, Swift, Uproar, Future Sight, Nasty Plot, Extrasensory, Last Resort, Natural Gift, Explosion

Does not evolve

LEGENDARY POKÉMON

AZUMARILL
Aqua Rabbit Pokémon

REGIONS
JOHTO, KALOS (CENTRAL)

TYPE: WATER-FAIRY

When Azumarill spots a Pokémon struggling in the water, it creates a balloon of air so the other Pokémon can breathe. It has excellent hearing.

How to say it: ah-ZU-mare-rill

Height: 2' 07"
Weight: 62.8 lbs.

Possible Moves: Tackle, Water Gun, Tail Whip, Water Sport, Bubble, Defense Curl, Rollout, Bubble Beam, Helping Hand, Aqua Tail, Double-Edge, Aqua Ring, Rain Dance, Superpower, Hydro Pump, Play Rough

AZURILL
Polka Dot Pokémon

REGIONS
HOENN, KALOS (CENTRAL)

TYPE: NORMAL-FAIRY

Azurill can fling itself more than ten yards by spinning the large ball at the end of its tail and then throwing it. It can also use the tail to bounce around.

How to say it: uh-ZOO-rill

Height: 0' 08"
Weight: 4.4 lbs.

Possible Moves: Splash, Water Gun, Tail Whip, Water Sport, Bubble, Charm, Bubble Beam, Helping Hand, Slam, Bounce

REGIONS
HOENN, KALOS (COASTAL)

BAGON

Rock Head Pokémon

TYPE: DRAGON

Chasing its dream of flight, Bagon practices by jumping from high places. To protect it during these leaps, its head has become hard enough to smash boulders.

How to say it: BAY-gon

Height: 2' 00" **Weight:** 92.8 lbs.

Possible Moves: Rage, Bite, Leer, Headbutt, Focus Energy, Ember, Dragon Breath, Zen Headbutt, Scary Face, Crunch, Dragon Claw, Double-Edge

Bagon → Shelgon → Salamence → Mega Salamence

REGION
HOENN

BALTOY

Clay Doll Pokémon

TYPE: GROUND-PSYCHIC

Baltoy can spin on its single foot to keep itself upright when moving or sleeping. Apparently, these Pokémon lived among people in ancient times.

How to say it: BAL-toy

Height: 1' 08" **Weight:** 47.4 lbs.

Possible Moves: Confusion, Harden, Rapid Spin, Mud-Slap, Psybeam, Rock Tomb, Self-Destruct, Ancient Power, Power Trick, Sandstorm, Cosmic Power, Extrasensory, Guard Split, Power Split, Earth Power, Heal Block, Explosion

Baltoy → Claydol

BANETTE

Marionette Pokémon

REGIONS
HOENN, KALOS (MOUNTAIN)

TYPE: GHOST

Banette keeps its mouth zipped tightly shut so its energy doesn't escape. It sticks itself with pins to curse others.

How to say it: bane-NETT

Height: 3' 07"
Weight: 27.6 lbs.

Possible Moves: Knock Off, Screech, Night Shade, Curse, Spite, Will-O-Wisp, Shadow Sneak, Feint Attack, Hex, Shadow Ball, Sucker Punch, Embargo, Snatch, Grudge, Trick

MEGA BANETTE

Marionette Pokémon

TYPE: GHOST

Height: 3' 11"
Weight: 28.7 lbs.

REGION
KALOS (COASTAL)

BARBARACLE

Collective Pokémon

TYPE: ROCK-WATER

When seven Binacle come together to fight as one, a Barbaracle is formed. The head gives the orders, but the limbs don't always listen.

How to say it: bar-BARE-uh-kull

Height: 4' 03" **Weight:** 211.6 lbs.

Possible Moves: Stone Edge, Skull Bash, Shell Smash, Scratch, Sand Attack, Water Gun, Withdraw, Fury Swipes, Slash, Mud-Slap, Clamp, Rock Polish, Ancient Power, Hone Claws, Fury Cutter, Night Slash, Razor Shell, Cross Chop

Binacle Barbaracle

BARBOACH

Whiskers Pokémon

REGIONS
HOENN, KALOS (MOUNTAIN)

TYPE: WATER-GROUND

Barboach buries itself in the mud, leaving its whiskers exposed to sense when something is moving nearby. The slimy coating on its body makes it very hard to grab.

How to say it: bar-BOACH

Height: 1' 04"
Weight: 4.2 lbs.

Possible Moves: Mud-Slap, Mud Sport, Water Sport, Water Gun, Mud Bomb, Amnesia, Water Pulse, Magnitude, Rest, Snore, Aqua Tail, Earthquake, Future Sight, Fissure

Barboach Whiscash

BASCULIN

Hostile Pokémon

REGIONS
KALOS (MOUNTAIN), UNOVA

TYPE: WATER

An ongoing feud exists between Basculin with blue stripes and Basculin with red stripes. Because they're constantly fighting, they are rarely found in the same place.

How to say it: BASS-kyoo-lin

Height: 3' 03"
Weight: 39.7 lbs.

Possible Moves: Thrash, Flail, Tail Whip, Tackle, Water Gun, Uproar, Headbutt, Bite, Aqua Jet, Chip Away, Take Down, Crunch, Aqua Tail, Soak, Double-Edge, Scary Face, Final Gambit

Red Stripe

Blue Stripe

Does not evolve

REGION
SINNOH

BASTIODON

Shield Pokémon

TYPE: ROCK-STEEL

When several Bastiodon stand shoulder to shoulder, no attack can penetrate the shield wall formed by their rocky faces. Despite their imposing appearance, they are quite gentle.

How to say it: BAS-tee-oh-donn

Height: 4' 03" **Weight:** 329.6 lbs.

Possible Moves: Tackle, Protect, Taunt, Metal Sound, Take Down, Iron Defense, Swagger, Ancient Power, Block, Endure, Metal Burst, Iron Head, Heavy Slam

Shieldon → Bastiodon

REGION
JOHTO

BAYLEEF

Leaf Pokémon

TYPE: GRASS

The tree shoots that form a wreath around Bayleef's neck give off an invigorating fragrance. A tube-shaped leaf protects each shoot.

How to say it: BAY-leaf

Height: 3' 11" **Weight:** 34.8 lbs.

Possible Moves: Tackle, Growl, Razor Leaf, Poison Powder, Synthesis, Reflect, Magical Leaf, Natural Gift, Sweet Scent, Light Screen, Body Slam, Safeguard, Aromatherapy, Solar Beam

Chikorita → Bayleef → Meganium

BEARTIC

Freezing Pokémon

REGIONS
KALOS (MOUNTAIN), UNOVA

TYPE: ICE

Beartic live in the far north, where the seas are very cold. Their fangs and claws are made of ice formed by their own freezing breath.

How to say it: BAIR-tick

Height: 8' 06"
Weight: 573.2 lbs.

Possible Moves: Sheer Cold, Thrash, Superpower, Aqua Jet, Growl, Powder Snow, Bide, Icy Wind, Play Nice, Fury Swipes, Brine, Endure, Swagger, Slash, Flail, Icicle Crash, Rest, Blizzard, Hail

Cubchoo → Beartic

BEAUTIFLY

Butterfly Pokémon

REGION
HOENN

TYPE: BUG-FLYING

To attract a Beautifly, plant flowers near your windows. This Pokémon uncoils its long mouth to gather pollen from flowers.

How to say it: BUE-tee-fly

Height: 3' 03"
Weight: 62.6 lbs.

Possible Moves: Absorb, Gust, Stun Spore, Morning Sun, Mega Drain, Whirlwind, Attract, Silver Wind, Giga Drain, Bug Buzz, Quiver Dance

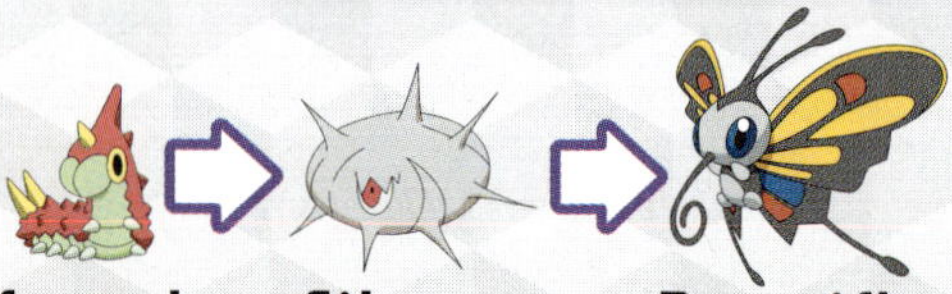

Wurmple → Silcoon → Beautifly

REGIONS
KALOS (CENTRAL), KANTO

BEEDRILL

Poison Bee Pokémon

TYPE: BUG-POISON

Stay far away from a Beedrill nest. These territorial Pokémon will swarm any intruder in a furious attack.

How to say it: BEE-dril

Height: 3' 03" **Weight:** 65.0 lbs.

Possible Moves: Fury Attack, Focus Energy, Twineedle, Rage, Pursuit, Toxic Spikes, Pin Missile, Agility, Assurance, Poison Jab, Endeavor, Fell Stinger

MEGA BEEDRILL

Poison Bee Pokémon

TYPE: BUG-POISON

Height: 4' 07"
Weight: 89.4 lbs.

BEHEEYEM

Cerebral Pokémon

REGION
UNOVA

TYPE: PSYCHIC

Beheeyem flashes its fingers in three different colors to communicate, but the patterns aren't yet understood. With its psychic power, it can take control of an opponent's mind.

How to say it: BEE-hee-ehm

Height: 3' 03"
Weight: 76.1 lbs.

Possible Moves: Confusion, Growl, Heal Block, Miracle Eye, Psybeam, Headbutt, Hidden Power, Imprison, Simple Beam, Zen Headbutt, Psych Up, Psychic, Calm Mind, Recover, Guard Split, Power Split, Synchronoise, Wonder Room

Elgyem → Beheeyem

REGION
HOENN

BELDUM
Iron Ball Pokémon

TYPE: STEEL-PSYCHIC

The magnetic force that runs through Beldum's body keeps it hovering in midair. It can send magnetic pulses to communicate with others.

How to say it: BELL-dum

Height: 2' 00" **Weight:** 209.9 lbs.

Possible Move: Take Down

REGIONS
JOHTO,
KALOS
(CENTRAL)

BELLOSSOM
Flower Pokémon

TYPE: GRASS

In strong sunlight, this Pokémon's leaves spin in a joyful dance. Bellossom that evolve from a particularly stinky Gloom will grow the most beautiful flowers.

How to say it: bell-LAHS-um

Height: 1' 04" **Weight:** 12.8 lbs.

Possible Moves: Leaf Storm, Leaf Blade, Mega Drain, Sweet Scent, Stun Spore, Sunny Day, Magical Leaf, Petal Blizzard

BELLSPROUT
Flower Pokémon

REGIONS
KALOS (MOUNTAIN), KANTO

TYPE: GRASS-POISON

Bellsprout's long, thin body can bend in any direction, so it's good at dodging attacks. The liquid it spits is highly corrosive.

How to say it: BELL-sprout

Height: 2' 04"
Weight: 8.8 lbs.

Possible Moves: Vine Whip, Growth, Wrap, Sleep Powder, Poison Powder, Stun Spore, Acid, Knock Off, Sweet Scent, Gastro Acid, Razor Leaf, Slam, Wring Out

BERGMITE
Ice Chunk Pokémon

REGION
KALOS (MOUNTAIN)

TYPE: ICE

When cracks form in Bergmite's icy body, it uses freezing air to patch itself up with new ice. It lives high in the mountains.

How to say it: BERG-mite

Height: 3' 03"
Weight: 219.4 lbs.

Possible Moves: Tackle, Bite, Harden, Powder Snow, Icy Wind, Take Down, Sharpen, Curse, Ice Fang, Ice Ball, Rapid Spin, Avalanche, Blizzard, Recover, Double-Edge

BIBAREL

Beaver Pokémon

REGIONS
KALOS (CENTRAL), SINNOH

TYPE: NORMAL-WATER

With their large, sharp teeth, Bibarel busily cut up trees to build nests. Sometimes these nests block small streams and divert the flow of the water.

How to say it: bee-BER-rel

Height: 3' 03"
Weight: 69.4 lbs.

Possible Moves: Rototiller, Tackle, Growl, Defense Curl, Rollout, Water Gun, Headbutt, Hyper Fang, Yawn, Amnesia, Take Down, Super Fang, Superpower, Curse

BIDOOF

Plump Mouse Pokémon

REGIONS
KALOS (CENTRAL), SINNOH

TYPE: NORMAL

Bidoof live beside the water, where they gnaw on rock or wood to keep their front teeth worn down. They have a steady nature and are not easily upset.

How to say it: BEE-doof

Height: 1' 08"
Weight: 44.1 lbs.

Possible Moves: Tackle, Growl, Defense Curl, Rollout, Headbutt, Hyper Fang, Yawn, Amnesia, Take Down, Super Fang, Superpower, Curse

BINACLE

Two-Handed Pokémon

REGION
KALOS (COASTAL)

TYPE: ROCK-WATER

Binacle live in pairs, two on the same rock. They comb the beach for seaweed to eat.

How to say it: BY-nuh-kull

Height: 1' 08"
Weight: 68.3 lbs.

Possible Moves: Shell Smash, Scratch, Sand Attack, Water Gun, Withdraw, Fury Swipes, Slash, Mud-Slap, Clamp, Rock Polish, Ancient Power, Hone Claws, Fury Cutter, Night Slash, Razor Shell, Cross Chop

BISHARP

Sword Blade Pokémon

REGIONS
KALOS (MOUNTAIN), UNOVA

TYPE: DARK-STEEL

When Pawniard hunt in a pack, Bisharp leads them and gives the orders. It's often the one that deals the final blow.

How to say it: BIH-sharp

Height: 5' 03"
Weight: 154.3 lbs.

Possible Moves: Guillotine, Iron Head, Metal Burst, Scratch, Leer, Fury Cutter, Torment, Feint Attack, Scary Face, Metal Claw, Slash, Assurance, Metal Sound, Embargo, Iron Defense, Night Slash, Swords Dance

REGIONS
KALOS (CENTRAL), KANTO

BLASTOISE

Shellfish Pokémon

TYPE: WATER

From the spouts on its shell, Blastoise can fire water bullets with amazing accuracy. It can hit a target more than one hundred sixty feet away!

How to say it: BLAS-toyce

Height: 5' 03"
Weight: 188.5 lbs.

Possible Moves: Flash Cannon, Tackle, Tail Whip, Water Gun, Withdraw, Bubble, Bite, Rapid Spin, Protect, Water Pulse, Aqua Tail, Skull Bash, Iron Defense, Rain Dance, Hydro Pump

MEGA BLASTOISE

Shellfish Pokémon

TYPE: WATER

Height: 5' 03"
Weight: 222.9 lbs.

Squirtle Wartortle Blastoise Mega Blastoise

BLAZIKEN

Blaze Pokémon

REGION
HOENN

TYPE: FIRE-FIGHTING

With continued strengthening of its legs, Blaziken can leap over a thirty-story building. The flames that flare from its wrists burn hotter against a worthy foe.

How to say it: BLAZE-uh-ken

Height: 6' 03"
Weight: 114.6 lbs.

Possible Moves: Fire Punch, High Jump Kick, Scratch, Growl, Focus Energy, Ember, Double Kick, Peck, Sand Attack, Bulk Up, Quick Attack, Blaze Kick, Slash, Brave Bird, Sky Uppercut, Flare Blitz

MEGA BLAZIKEN

Blaze Pokémon

TYPE: FIRE-FIGHTING

Height: 6' 03"
Weight: 114.6 lbs.

REGION JOHTO

BLISSEY

Happiness Pokémon

TYPE: NORMAL

Blissey is extremely sensitive to people's emotions. If it senses sorrow, it leaps into action, rushing to the sad person's side with the gift of a special egg.

How to say it: BLISS-sey

Height: 4' 11" **Weight:** 103.2 lbs.

Possible Moves: Defense Curl, Pound, Growl, Tail Whip, Refresh, Double Slap, Softboiled, Bestow, Minimize, Take Down, Sing, Fling, Heal Pulse, Egg Bomb, Light Screen, Healing Wish, Double-Edge

BLITZLE

Electrified Pokémon

REGION
UNOVA

TYPE: ELECTRIC

Blitzle's mane attracts lightning and stores the electricity. It can discharge this electricity in controlled flashes to communicate with others.

How to say it: BLIT-zul

Height: 2' 07" **Weight:** 65.7 lbs.

Possible Moves: Quick Attack, Tail Whip, Charge, Shock Wave, Thunder Wave, Flame Charge, Pursuit, Spark, Stomp, Discharge, Agility, Wild Charge, Thrash

BOLDORE

Ore Pokémon

REGIONS
KALOS (COASTAL), UNOVA

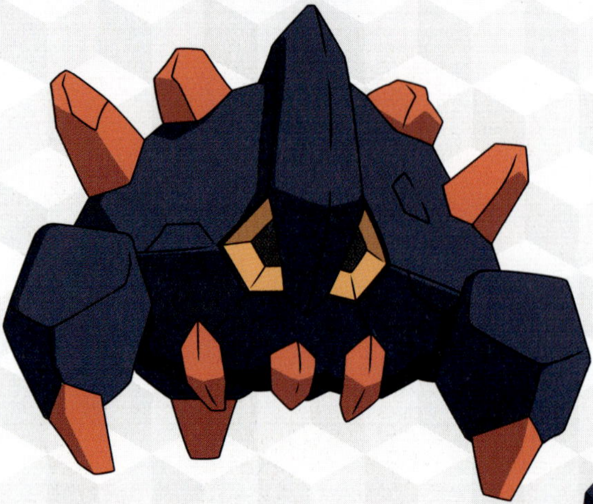

TYPE: ROCK

The energy within Boldore's body overflows, leaks out, and forms into orange crystals. Though its head always points in the same direction, it can quickly move sideways and backward.

How to say it: BOHL-dohr

Height: 2' 11" **Weight:** 224.9 lbs.

Possible Moves: Tackle, Harden, Sand Attack, Headbutt, Rock Blast, Mud-Slap, Iron Defense, Smack Down, Power Gem, Rock Slide, Stealth Rock, Sandstorm, Stone Edge, Explosion

BONSLY
Bonsai Pokémon

REGIONS
KALOS (MOUNTAIN), SINNOH

TYPE: ROCK

Bonsly prefers to live in dry places. When its body stores excess moisture, it releases water from its eyes, making it look like it's crying.

How to say it: BON-slye

Height: 1' 08"
Weight: 33.1 lbs.

Possible Moves: Fake Tears, Copycat, Flail, Low Kick, Rock Throw, Mimic, Feint Attack, Rock Tomb, Block, Rock Slide, Counter, Sucker Punch, Double-Edge

Bonsly → Sudowoodo

BOUFFALANT
Bash Buffalo Pokémon

REGION
UNOVA

TYPE: NORMAL

Though Bouffalant can knock a train off the rails with the force of its headbutt, it doesn't worry about hurting itself, because its fluffy fur absorbs the impact.

How to say it: BOO-fuh-lahnt

Height: 5' 03"
Weight: 208.6 lbs.

Possible Moves: Pursuit, Leer, Rage, Fury Attack, Horn Attack, Scary Face, Revenge, Head Charge, Focus Energy, Megahorn, Reversal, Thrash, Swords Dance, Giga Impact

Does not evolve

BRAIXEN

Fox Pokémon

REGION
KALOS (CENTRAL)

TYPE: FIRE

When Braixen pulls the twig out of its tail, the friction from its fur sets the wood on fire. It can use this flaming twig as a tool or a weapon.

How to say it: BRAKE-sen

Height: 3' 03"
Weight: 32.0 lbs.

Possible Moves: Scratch, Tail Whip, Ember, Howl, Flame Charge, Psybeam, Fire Spin, Lucky Chant, Light Screen, Psyshock, Flamethrower, Will-O-Wisp, Psychic, Sunny Day, Magic Room, Fire Blast

Fennekin Braixen Delphox

BRAVIARY

Valiant Pokémon

REGION
UNOVA

TYPE: NORMAL-FLYING

To protect its friends, Braviary will keep battling even when it's hurt. Its wings and talons are so strong that it can carry a car through the air.

How to say it: BRAY-vee-air-ee

Height: 4' 11"
Weight: 90.4 lbs.

Possible Moves: Peck, Leer, Fury Attack, Wing Attach, Hone Claws, Scary Face, Aerial Ace, Slash, Defog, Tailwind, Air Slash, Crush Claw, Sky Drop, Superpower, Whirlwind, Brave Bird, Thrash

Rufflet Braviary

BRELOOM
Mushroom Pokémon

REGION
HOENN

TYPE: GRASS-FIGHTING

If a seed falls from Breloom's tail, you really shouldn't eat it. The seeds are toxic and taste terrible. Its arms stretch to throw impressive punches.

How to say it: BRELL-loom

Height: 3' 11" **Weight:** 86.4 lbs.

Possible Moves: Absorb, Tackle, Stun Spore, Leech Seed, Mega Drain, Headbutt, Mach Punch, Counter, Force Palm, Sky Uppercut, Mind Reader, Seed Bomb, Dynamic Punch

Shroomish Breloom

BRONZONG
Bronze Bell Pokémon

REGION
SINNOH

TYPE: STEEL-PSYCHIC

In ancient times, people thought Bronzong was responsible for making the rain fall, so they often asked it for help to make their crops flourish.

How to say it: brawn-ZONG

Height: 4' 03" **Weight:** 412.3 lbs.

Possible Moves: Sunny Day, Rain Dance, Tackle, Confusion, Hypnosis, Imprison, Confuse Ray, Extrasensory, Iron Defense, Safeguard, Block, Gyro Ball, Future Sight, Feint Attack, Payback, Heal Block, Heavy Slam

Bronzor Bronzong

BRONZOR

Bronze Pokémon

REGION
SINNOH

TYPE: STEEL-PSYCHIC

In ancient times, people thought a mystical power was contained within Bronzor's back pattern. Artifacts matching its shape have been discovered in tombs from that era.

How to say it: BRAWN-zorr

Height: 1' 08"
Weight: 133.4 lbs.

Possible Moves: Tackle, Confusion, Hypnosis, Imprison, Confuse Ray, Extrasensory, Iron Defense, Safeguard, Gyro Ball, Future Sight, Feint Attack, Payback, Heal Block, Heavy Slam

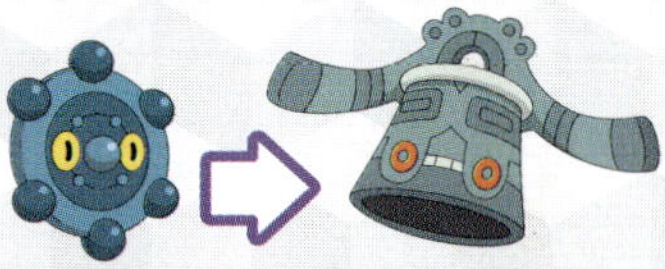

Bronzor Bronzong

BUDEW

Bud Pokémon

REGIONS
KALOS (CENTRAL), SINNOH

TYPE: GRASS-POISON

When the weather turns cold, Budew's bud is tightly closed. In the springtime, it opens up again and gives off its pollen.

How to say it: buh-DOO

Height: 0' 08"
Weight: 2.6 lbs.

Possible Moves: Absorb, Growth, Water Sport, Stun Spore, Mega Drain, Worry Seed

Budew Roselia Roserade

BUIZEL

Sea Weasel Pokémon

REGIONS
KALOS (MOUNTAIN), SINNOH

TYPE: WATER

Buizel rapidly spins its two tails to propel itself through the water. The flotation sac around its neck keeps its head up without effort, and it can deflate the sac to dive.

How to say it: BWEE-zul

Height: 2' 04"
Weight: 65.0 lbs.

Possible Moves: Sonic Boom, Growl, Water Sport, Quick Attack, Water Gun, Pursuit, Swift, Aqua Jet, Double Hit, Whirlpool, Razor Wind, Aqua Tail, Agility, Hydro Pump

Buizel   Floatzel

BULBASAUR

Seed Pokémon

REGIONS
KALOS (CENTRAL), KANTO

TYPE: GRASS-POISON

Bulbasaur likes to take a nap in the sunshine. While it sleeps, the seed on its back catches the rays and uses the energy to grow.

How to say it: BUL-ba-sore

Height: 2' 04"   **Weight:** 15.2 lbs.

Possible Moves: Tackle, Growl, Leech Seed, Vine Whip, Poison Powder, Sleep Powder, Take Down, Razor Leaf, Sweet Scent, Growth, Double-Edge, Worry Seed, Synthesis, Seed Bomb

Bulbasaur   Ivysaur   Venusaur   Mega Venusaur

BUNEARY
Rabbit Pokémon

REGION
SINNOH

TYPE: NORMAL

Buneary keeps its ears rolled up except when attacking or scouting for danger. It can extend its ears with enough force to pulverize a boulder.

How to say it: buh-NEER-ree

Height: 1' 04"
Weight: 12.1 lbs.

Possible Moves: Splash, Pound, Defense Curl, Foresight, Endure, Frustration, Quick Attack, Jump Kick, Baton Pass, Agility, Dizzy Punch, After You, Charm, Entrainment, Bounce, Healing Wish

BUNNELBY
Digging Pokémon

REGION
KALOS
(CENTRAL)

TYPE: NORMAL

Bunnelby can use its ears like shovels to dig holes in the ground. Eventually, its ears become strong enough to cut through thick tree roots while it digs.

How to say it: BUN-ell-bee

Height: 1' 04" **Weight:** 11.0 lbs.

Possible Moves: Tackle, Agility, Leer, Quick Attack, Double Slap, Mud-Slap, Take Down, Mud Shot, Double Kick, Odor Sleuth, Flail, Dig, Bounce, Super Fang, Facade, Earthquake

REGIONS
KALOS (CENTRAL), SINNOH

BURMY (GRASS CLOAK)

Bagworm Pokémon

TYPE: BUG

Burmy creates a cloak for itself out of whatever materials it can find. The cloak protects it from chilly temperatures and shields it in battle.

How to say it: BURR-mee

Height: 0' 08" **Weight:** 7.5 lbs.

Possible Moves: Protect, Tackle, Bug Bite, Hidden Power

REGIONS
KALOS (CENTRAL), SINNOH

BURMY (SANDY CLOAK)

Bagworm Pokémon

TYPE: BUG

Did you know that each Burmy covers up with the objects around it? This Burmy uses rocks and sand for protection.

How to say it: BURR-mee

Height: 0' 08" **Weight:** 7.5 lbs.

Possible Moves: Protect, Tackle, Bug Bite, Hidden Power

BURMY (TRASH CLOAK)

Bagworm Pokémon

REGIONS
KALOS (CENTRAL), SINNOH

TYPE: BUG

If you're looking for Burmy with a Trash Cloak, try poking around inside a few buildings. You might get lucky!

How to say it: BURR-mee

Height: 0' 08" **Weight:** 7.5 lbs.

Possible Moves: Protect, Tackle, Bug Bite, Hidden Power

BUTTERFREE

Butterfly Pokémon

REGIONS
KALOS (CENTRAL), KANTO

TYPE: BUG-FLYING

Butterfree is excellent at seeking out flowers with the most delicious nectar. It sometimes flies more than six miles to locate its favorite food.

How to say it: BUT-er-free

Height: 3' 07"
Weight: 70.5 lbs.

Possible Moves: Confusion, Poison Powder, Stun Spore, Sleep Powder, Gust, Supersonic, Whirlwind, Psybeam, Silver Wind, Tailwind, Rage Powder, Safeguard, Captivate, Bug Buzz, Quiver Dance

REGION
HOENN

CACNEA

Cactus Pokémon

TYPE: GRASS

Cacnea produce the most beautiful and fragrant flowers when they live in particularly harsh and dry environments. They can shoot their thorns to attack.

How to say it: CACK-nee-uh

Height: 1' 04" **Weight:** 113.1 lbs.

Possible Moves: Poison Sting, Leer, Absorb, Growth, Leech Seed, Sand Attack, Pin Missile, Ingrain, Feint Attack, Spikes, Sucker Punch, Payback, Needle Arm, Cotton Spore, Sandstorm, Destiny Bond

REGION
HOENN

CACTURNE

Scarecrow Pokémon

TYPE: GRASS-DARK

Cacturne stand very still during the day so as not to waste energy or moisture in the heat of the desert sun. After dark, they hunt in packs, often attacking travelers who weren't prepared for the environment.

How to say it: CACK-turn

Height: 4' 03" **Weight:** 170.6 lbs.

Possible Moves: Revenge, Poison Sting, Leer, Absorb, Growth, Leech Seed, Sand Attack, Pin Missile, Ingrain, Feint Attack, Spikes, Sucker Punch, Payback, Needle Arm, Cotton Spore, Sandstorm, Destiny Bond

CAMERUPT

Eruption Pokémon

REGION
HOENN

TYPE: FIRE-GROUND

When Camerupt gets angry, the volcanic humps on its back tend to erupt. The magma that sprays out is superheated and very dangerous.

How to say it: CAM-err-rupt

Height: 6' 03"
Weight: 485.0 lbs.

Possible Moves: Growl, Tackle, Ember, Magnitude, Focus Energy, Flame Burst, Take Down, Amnesia, Lava Plume, Rock Slide, Earth Power, Earthquake, Fissure

MEGA CAMERUPT

Eruption Pokémon

TYPE: FIRE-GROUND

Height: 8' 02"
Weight: 706.6 lbs.

CARBINK

REGION
KALOS (COASTAL)

Jewel Pokémon

TYPE: ROCK-FAIRY

While excavating caves, miners and archeologists sometimes stumble upon Carbink sleeping deep underground. The stone on top of its head can fire beams of energy.

How to say it: CAR-bink

Height: 1' 0"
Weight: 12.6 lbs.

Possible Moves: Tackle, Harden, Rock Throw, Sharpen, Smack Down, Reflect, Stealth Rock, Guard Split, Ancient Power, Flail, Skill Swap, Power Gem, Stone Edge, Moonblast, Light Screen, Safeguard

Does not evolve

CARNIVINE

REGIONS
KALOS (MOUNTAIN), SINNOH

Bug Catcher Pokémon

TYPE: GRASS

Carnivine wraps itself around trees in swampy areas. It gives off a sweet aroma that lures others close, then attacks.

How to say it: CAR-neh-vine

Height: 4' 07"
Weight: 59.5 lbs.

Possible Moves: Bind, Growth, Bite, Vine Whip, Sweet Scent, Ingrain, Feint Attack, Leaf Tornado, Stockpile, Spit Up, Swallow, Crunch, Wring Out, Power Whip

Does not evolve

CARRACOSTA

Prototurtle Pokémon

REGION
UNOVA

TYPE: WATER-ROCK

With its powerful jaws and massive front flippers, Carracosta is a formidable fighter. It can break through the hull of a tanker ship with a single slap.

How to say it: kar-ruh-KOSS-tuh

Height: 3' 11"
Weight: 178.6 lbs.

Possible Moves: Bide, Withdraw, Water Gun, Rollout, Bite, Protect, Aqua Jet, Ancient Power, Crunch, Wide Guard, Brine, Smack Down, Curse, Shell Smash, Aqua Tail, Rock Slide, Rain Dance, Hydro Pump

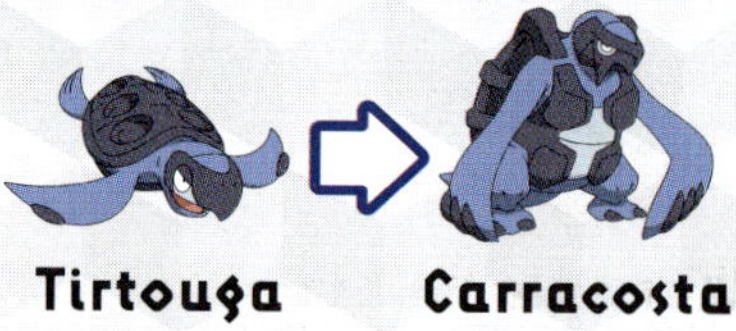

CARVANHA

Savage Pokémon

REGIONS
HOENN, KALOS (CENTRAL)

TYPE: WATER-DARK

Carvanha descend in a swarm to attack anything that enters their territory. When they work together, their strong jaws and sharp teeth can rip a hole in a boat's hull.

How to say it: car-VAH-na

Height: 2' 07" **Weight:** 45.9 lbs.

Possible Moves: Leer, Bite, Rage, Focus Energy, Scary Face, Ice Fang, Screech, Swagger, Assurance, Crunch, Aqua Jet, Agility, Take Down

REGION
HOENN

CASCOON

Cocoon Pokémon

TYPE: BUG

When Cascoon is ready to evolve, it wraps itself up in silk, which hardens around its body. If something attacks its cocoon, it takes the hit without moving so as not to use up energy . . . but it also remembers the attacker.

How to say it: CAS-koon

Height: 2' 04"
Weight: 25.4 lbs.

Possible Move: Harden

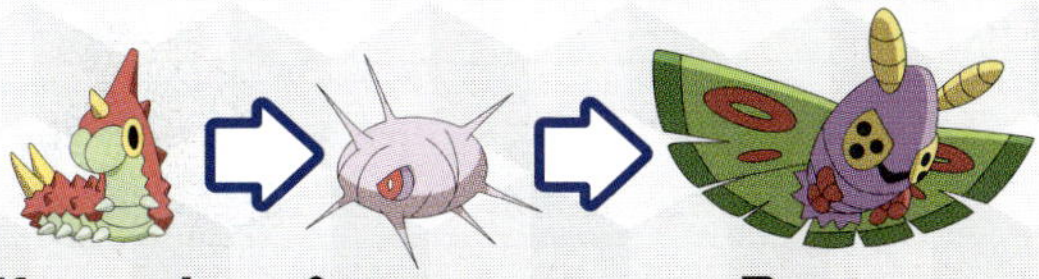

Wurmple Cascoon Dustox

REGION
HOENN

CASTFORM

Weather Pokémon

Regular Form

TYPE: NORMAL

Changes in the weather alter Castform's appearance and its mood. It draws on the power of nature to transform and protect itself from the elements.

How to say it: CAST-form

Height: 1' 00" **Weight:** 1.8 lbs.

Possible Moves: Tackle, Water Gun, Ember, Powder Snow, Headbutt, Rain Dance, Sunny Day, Hail, Weather Ball, Hydro Pump, Fire Blast, Blizzard

Snowy Form

Rainy Form

Sunny Form

Does not evolve

CATERPIE

Worm Pokémon

REGIONS
KALOS (CENTRAL), KANTO

TYPE: BUG

A ravenous Caterpie can quickly gobble up leaves that are bigger than itself. Its antenna can produce a terrible smell.

How to say it: CAT-ur-pee

Height: 1' 00"
Weight: 6.4 lbs.

Possible Moves: Tackle, String Shot, Bug Bite

CELEBI

Time Travel Pokémon

REGION
JOHTO

MYTHICAL POKÉMON

TYPE: PSYCHIC-GRASS

Celebi traveled back in time to come to this world. According to myth, its presence is a sign of a bright future.

How to say it: SEL-ih-bee

Height: 2' 00" **Weight:** 11.0 lbs.

Possible Moves: Leech Seed, Confusion, Recover, Heal Bell, Safeguard, Magical Leaf, Ancient Power, Baton Pass, Natural Gift, Heal Block, Future Sight, Healing Wish, Leaf Storm, Perish Song

Does not evolve

REGIONS
KALOS (MOUNTAIN), UNOVA

CHANDELURE

Luring Pokémon

TYPE: GHOST-FIRE

Chandelure's spooky flames can burn the spirit right out of someone. If that happens, the spirit becomes trapped in this world, endlessly wandering.

How to say it: shan-duh-LOOR

Height: 3' 03"
Weight: 75.6 lbs.

Possible Moves: Pain Split, Smog, Confuse Ray, Flame Burst, Hex

Litwick Lampent Chandelure

REGION
KANTO

CHANSEY

Egg Pokémon

TYPE: NORMAL

The eggs Chansey produces every day are full of nutrition and flavor. Even people suffering a loss of appetite eat them up with delight.

How to say it: CHAN-see

Height: 3' 07"
Weight: 76.3 lbs.

Possible Moves: Defense Curl, Pound, Growl, Tail Whip, Refresh, Double Slap, Softboiled, Bestow, Minimize, Take Down, Sing, Fling, Heal Pulse, Egg Bomb, Light Screen, Healing Wish, Double-Edge

Happiny Chansey Blissey

CHARIZARD

Flame Pokémon

REGIONS
KALOS (CENTRAL), KANTO

TYPE: FIRE-FLYING

Charizard seeks out stronger foes and only breathes fire during battles with worthy opponents. The fiery breath is so hot that it can turn any material to slag.

How to say it: CHAR-iz-ard

Height: 5' 07" **Weight:** 199.5 lbs.

Possible Moves: Flare Blitz, Heat Wave, Dragon Claw, Shadow Claw, Air Slash, Scratch, Growl, Ember, Smokescreen, Dragon Rage, Scary Face, Fire Fang, Flame Burst, Wing Attack, Slash, Flamethrower, Fire Spin, Inferno

MEGA CHARIZARD X

Flame Pokémon

TYPE: FIRE-DRAGON

Height: 5' 07" **Weight:** 243.6 lbs.

MEGA CHARIZARD Y

Flame Pokémon

TYPE: FIRE-FLYING

Height: 5' 07" **Weight:** 221.6 lbs.

REGIONS
KALOS (CENTRAL), KANTO

CHARMANDER

Lizard Pokémon

TYPE: FIRE

The flame on Charmander's tail tip indicates how the Pokémon is feeling. It flares up in a fury when Charmander is angry!

How to say it: CHAR-man-der

Height: 2' 00"
Weight: 18.7 lbs.

Possible Moves: Scratch, Growl, Ember, Smokescreen, Dragon Rage, Scary Face, Fire Fang, Flame Burst, Slash, Flamethrower, Fire Spin, Inferno

REGIONS
KALOS (CENTRAL), KANTO

CHARMELEON

Flame Pokémon

TYPE: FIRE

When Charmeleon takes on a powerful opponent in battle, its tail flame glows white-hot. Its claws are very sharp.

How to say it: char-MEE-lee-un

Height: 3' 07"
Weight: 41.9 lbs.

Possible Moves: Scratch, Growl, Ember, Smokescreen, Dragon Rage, Scary Face, Fire Fang, Flame Burst, Slash, Flamethrower, Fire Spin, Inferno

CHATOT

Music Note Pokémon

REGIONS
KALOS (COASTAL), SINNOH

TYPE: NORMAL-FLYING

Chatot can mimic other Pokémon's cries and even human speech. A group of them will often pick up the same phrase and keep repeating it among themselves.

How to say it: CHAT-tot

Height: 1' 08"
Weight: 4.2 lbs.

Possible Moves: Hyper Voice, Chatter, Confide, Taunt, Peck, Growl, Mirror Move, Sing, Fury Attack, Round, Mimic, Echoed Voice, Roost, Uproar, Synchronoise, Feather Dance

Does not evolve

CHERRIM

Blossom Pokémon

REGION
SINNOH

TYPE: GRASS

Cherrim keeps its petals folded around itself except in bright sunshine. When the weather is nice, its bloom opens wide to absorb as much sunlight as it can.

How to say it: chuh-RIM

Height: 1' 08" **Weight:** 20.5 lbs.

Possible Moves: Morning Sun, Tackle, Growth, Leech Seed, Helping Hand, Magical Leaf, Sunny Day, Petal Dance, Worry Seed, Take Down, Solar Beam, Lucky Chant

Cherubi Cherrim

REGION
SINNOH

CHERUBI

Cherry Pokémon

TYPE: GRASS

Cherubi stores nutrients in the small red ball attached to its head. When it's ready to evolve, it uses up all the nutrients at once, making the small ball wither.

How to say it: chuh-ROO-bee

Height: 1' 04"
Weight: 7.3 lbs.

Possible Moves: Morning Sun, Tackle, Growth, Leech Seed, Helping Hand, Magical Leaf, Sunny Day, Worry Seed, Take Down, Solar Beam, Lucky Chant

Cherubi → Cherrim

REGION
KALOS
(CENTRAL)

CHESNAUGHT

Spiny Armor Pokémon

TYPE: GRASS-FIGHTING

When its friends are in trouble, Chesnaught uses its own body as a shield. Its shell is tough enough to protect it from a powerful explosion.

How to say it: CHESS-nawt

Height: 5' 03" **Weight:** 198.4 lbs.

Possible Moves: Feint, Hammer Arm, Belly Drum, Tackle, Growl, Vine Whip, Rollout, Bite, Leech Seed, Pin Missile, Needle Arm, Take Down, Seed Bomb, Spiky Shield, Mud Shot, Bulk Up, Body Slam, Pain Split, Wood Hammer, Giga Impact

Chespin → Quilladin → Chesnaught

CHESPIN

Spiny Nut Pokémon

REGION
KALOS (CENTRAL)

TYPE: GRASS

When Chespin flexes its soft quills, they become tough spikes with sharp, piercing points. It relies on its nutlike shell for protection in battle.

How to say it: CHESS-pin

Height: 1' 04"
Weight: 19.8 lbs.

Possible Moves: Tackle, Growl, Vine Whip, Rollout, Bite, Leech Seed, Pin Missile, Take Down, Seed Bomb, Mud Shot, Bulk Up, Body Slam, Pain Split, Wood Hammer

Chespin Quilladin Chesnaught

CHIKORITA

Leaf Pokémon

REGION
JOHTO

TYPE: GRASS

Chikorita brandishes its leaf in battle to fend off a foe. When it does this, the leaf gives off a lovely aroma that calms everyone down.

How to say it: CHICK-oh-REE-ta

Height: 2' 11" **Weight:** 14.1 lbs.

Possible Moves: Tackle, Growl, Razor Leaf, Poison Powder, Synthesis, Reflect, Magical Leaf, Natural Gift, Sweet Scent, Light Screen, Body Slam, Safeguard, Aromatherapy, Solar Beam

Chikorita Bayleef Meganium

REGION
SINNOH

CHIMCHAR

Chimp Pokémon

TYPE: FIRE

Chimchar's rear is always on fire, even when it stands in the rain. If it's not feeling well, the flame flickers weakly.

How to say it: CHIM-char

Height: 1' 08"
Weight: 13.7 lbs.

Possible Moves: Scratch, Leer, Ember, Taunt, Fury Swipes, Flame Wheel, Nasty Plot, Torment, Facade, Fire Spin, Acrobatics, Slack Off, Flamethrower

Chimchar Monferno Infernape

REGIONS
HOENN, KALOS (COASTAL)

CHIMECHO

Wind Chime Pokémon

TYPE: PSYCHIC

The sucker on the top of Chimecho's head can attach to a tree branch or building. Its hollow body amplifies its chiming cries.

How to say it: chime-ECK-ko

Height: 2' 00"
Weight: 2.2 lbs.

Possible Moves: Healing Wish, Synchronoise, Wrap, Growl, Astonish, Confusion, Uproar, Take Down, Yawn, Psywave, Double-Edge, Heal Bell, Safeguard, Extrasensory, Heal Pulse

Chingling Chimecho

CHINCHOU
Angler Pokémon

REGIONS
JOHTO, KALOS (COASTAL)

TYPE: WATER-ELECTRIC

With its two antennae, Chinchou can release an electric charge for use as a weapon, or flash lights to communicate. It sometimes gets a tingly feeling if it generates too much electricity.

How to say it: CHIN-chow

Height: 1' 08" **Weight:** 26.5 lbs.

Possible Moves: Water Gun, Supersonic, Thunder Wave, Flail, Bubble, Confuse Ray, Spark, Take Down, Electro Ball, Bubble Beam, Signal Beam, Discharge, Aqua Ring, Hydro Pump, Ion Deluge, Charge

Chinchou Lanturn

CHINGLING
Bell Pokémon

REGIONS
KALOS (COASTAL), SINNOH

TYPE: PSYCHIC

When Chingling hops about, a small orb bounces around inside its mouth, producing a noise like the sound of bells. It uses high-pitched sounds to attack its opponents' hearing.

How to say it: CHING-ling

Height: 0' 08"
Weight: 1.3 lbs.

Possible Moves: Wrap, Growl, Astonish, Confusion, Uproar, Last Resort, Entrainment

Chingling Chimecho

CINCCINO

REGION UNOVA

Scarf Pokémon

TYPE: NORMAL

A special oil coats Cinccino's soft white fur. This oil repels dust and dirt, deflects enemy attacks, and keeps static electricity at bay.

How to say it: chin-CHEE-noh

Height: 1' 08"
Weight: 16.5 lbs.

Possible Moves: Bullet Seed, Rock Blast, Helping Hand, Tickle, Sing, Tail Slap

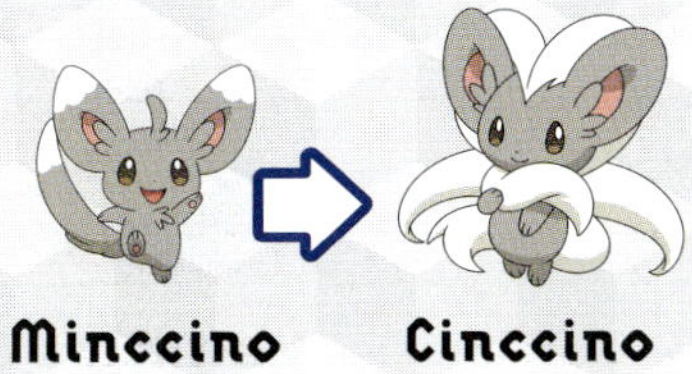

CLAMPERL

REGIONS HOENN, KALOS (COASTAL)

Bivalve Pokémon

TYPE: WATER

Even as Clamperl's soft body grows inside its hard shell, the shell stays the same size until it evolves. In addition to protecting itself, it uses the shell to catch food or to grab onto an opponent in battle.

How to say it: CLAM-perl

Height: 1' 04" **Weight:** 115.7 lbs.

Possible Moves: Clamp, Water Gun, Whirlpool, Iron Defense, Shell Smash

CLAUNCHER

Water Gun Pokémon

REGION
KALOS (COASTAL)

TYPE: WATER

Clauncher shoots water from its claws with a force that can pulverize rock. Its range is great enough to knock flying Pokémon out of the air.

How to say it: CLAWN-chur

Height: 1' 08"
Weight: 18.3 lbs.

Possible Moves: Splash, Water Gun, Water Sport, Vice Grip, Bubble, Flail, Bubble Beam, Swords Dance, Crabhammer, Water Pulse, Smack Down, Aqua Jet, Muddy Water

CLAWITZER

Howitzer Pokémon

REGION
KALOS (COASTAL)

TYPE: WATER

Clawitzer's giant claw can expel massive jets of water at high speed. It fires the water forward to attack, or backward to propel itself through the sea.

How to say it: CLOW-wit-zur

Height: 4' 03" **Weight:** 77.8 lbs.

Possible Moves: Heal Pulse, Dark Pulse, Dragon Pulse, Aura Sphere, Splash, Water Gun, Water Sport, Vice Grip, Bubble, Flail, Bubble Beam, Swords Dance, Crabhammer, Water Pulse, Smack Down, Aqua Jet, Muddy Water

CLAYDOL

REGION HOENN

Clay Doll Pokémon

TYPE: GROUND-PSYCHIC

Claydol is thought to have originated from an ancient clay statue. It levitates to move and can shoot energy beams from its hands.

How to say it: CLAY-doll

Height: 4' 11" **Weight:** 238.1 lbs.

Possible Moves: Teleport, Confusion, Harden, Rapid Spin, Mud-Slap, Psybeam, Rock Tomb, Self-Destruct, Ancient Power, Power Trick, Sandstorm, Hyper Beam, Extrasensory, Cosmic Power, Guard Split, Power Split, Earth Power, Heal Block, Explosion

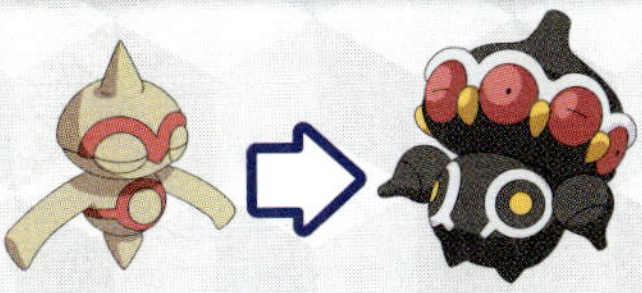

Baltoy Claydol

CLEFABLE

REGION KANTO

Fairy Pokémon

TYPE: FAIRY

Clefable moves with such lightness that it can skip across the water—perfect for a moonlight stroll on the surface of a lake.

How to say it: cluh-FAY-bull

Height: 4' 03"
Weight: 88.2 lbs.

Possible Moves: Sing, Double Slap, Minimize, Metronome

Cleffa Clefairy Clefable

CLEFAIRY
Fairy Pokémon

REGION
KANTO

TYPE: FAIRY

Groups of Clefairy gather to play under the full moon. When the sun rises, they retreat to their mountain home and snuggle together to sleep.

How to say it: cluh-FAIR-ee

Height: 2' 00" **Weight:** 16.5 lbs.

Possible Moves: Pound, Growl, Encore, Sing, Double Slap, Defense Curl, Follow Me, Minimize, Wake-Up Slap, Bestow, Cosmic Power, Lucky Chant, Metronome, Gravity, Moonlight, Stored Power, Light Screen, Healing Wish, After You

CLEFFA
Star Shape Pokémon

REGION
JOHTO

TYPE: FAIRY

During a meteor shower, groups of Cleffa gather to dance in a circle. Their dance lasts until dawn and makes them very thirsty, so they sip dewdrops to rehydrate.

How to say it: CLEFF-uh

Height: 1' 00" **Weight:** 6.6 lbs.

Possible Moves: Pound, Charm, Encore, Sing, Sweet Kiss, Copycat, Magical Leaf

REGIONS
KALOS (COASTAL), KANTO

CLOYSTER

Bivalve Pokémon

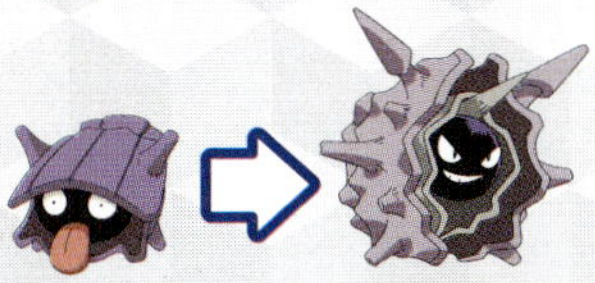

TYPE: WATER-ICE

By sucking in water and then shooting it out, Cloyster can propel itself through the sea. It also uses this method to fire its shell spikes in battle.

How to say it: CLOY-stur

Height: 4' 11"
Weight: 292.1 lbs.

Possible Moves: Hydro Pump, Shell Smash, Toxic Spikes, Withdraw, Supersonic, Protect, Aurora Beam, Spike Cannon, Spikes, Icicle Crash

LEGENDARY POKÉMON

REGION
UNOVA

COBALION

Iron Will Pokémon

TYPE: STEEL-FIGHTING

Like its body, Cobalion's heart is tough as steel. Legends say that in the past, it protected Pokémon from harmful people.

How to say it: koh-BAY-lee-un

Height: 6' 11" **Weight:** 551.2 lbs.

Possible Moves: Quick Attack, Leer, Double Kick, Metal Claw, Take Down, Helping Hand, Retaliate, Iron Head, Sacred Sword, Swords Dance, Quick Guard, Work Up, Metal Burst, Close Combat

Does not evolve

COFAGRIGUS

Coffin Pokémon

REGION
UNOVA

TYPE: GHOST

Cofagrigus resembles a coffin covered in solid gold. Stories say that when would-be thieves approach, it opens its lid and traps them inside.

How to say it: kof-uh-GREE-guss

Height: 5' 07"
Weight: 168.7 lbs.

Possible Moves: Astonish, Protect, Disable, Haze, Night Shade, Hex, Will-O-Wisp, Ominous Wind, Curse, Power Split, Guard Split, Scary Face, Shadow Ball, Grudge, Mean Look, Destiny Bond

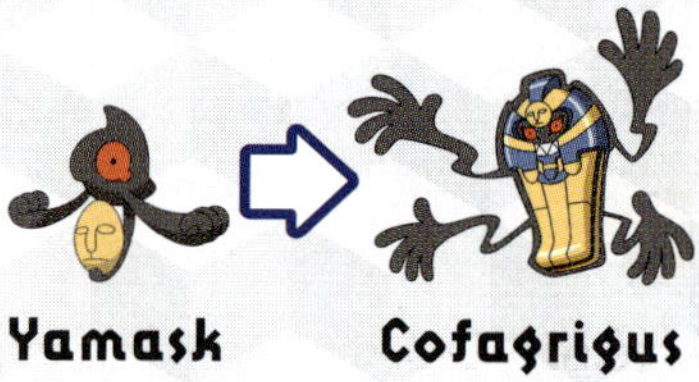

COMBEE

Tiny Bee Pokémon

REGIONS
KALOS (CENTRAL), SINNOH

TYPE: BUG-FLYING

Combee are always in search of honey, which they bring to their Vespiquen leader. They cluster together to sleep in a formation that resembles a hive.

How to say it: COMB-bee

Height: 1' 00" **Weight:** 12.1 lbs.

Possible Moves: Sweet Scent, Gust, Bug Bite, Bug Buzz

COMBUSKEN

REGION
HOENN

Young Fowl Pokémon

TYPE: FIRE-FIGHTING

Combusken runs through meadows and up mountains to strengthen its legs. It can deliver kicks at high speed and with crushing power.

How to say it: com-BUS-ken

Height: 2' 11"
Weight: 43.0 lbs.

Possible Moves: Scratch, Growl, Focus Energy, Ember, Double Kick, Peck, Sand Attack, Bulk Up, Quick Attack, Slash, Mirror Move, Sky Uppercut, Flare Blitz

Torchic Combusken Blaziken Mega Blaziken

CONKELDURR

REGIONS
KALOS (MOUNTAIN), UNOVA

Muscular Pokémon

TYPE: FIGHTING

Conkeldurr spin their concrete pillars to attack. It's said that long ago, people first learned about concrete from these Pokémon.

How to say it: kon-KELL-dur

Height: 4' 07" **Weight:** 191.8 lbs.

Possible Moves: Pound, Leer, Focus Energy, Bide, Low Kick, Rock Throw, Wake-Up Slap, Chip Away, Bulk Up, Rock Slide, Dynamic Punch, Scary Face, Hammer Arm, Stone Edge, Focus Punch, Superpower

Timburr Gurdurr Conkeldurr

CORPHISH

Ruffian Pokémon

REGIONS
HOENN, KALOS (COASTAL)

TYPE: WATER

Corphish aren't picky about what they eat or where they live. Because of this, their numbers have increased substantially.

How to say it: COR-fish

Height: 2' 00"
Weight: 25.4 lbs.

Possible Moves: Bubble, Harden, Vice Grip, Leer, Bubble Beam, Protect, Knock Off, Taunt, Night Slash, Crabhammer, Swords Dance, Crunch, Guillotine

CORSOLA

Coral Pokémon

REGIONS
JOHTO, KALOS (COASTAL)

TYPE: WATER-ROCK

Corsola prefer warm water and migrate south when it gets cold. When the sun hits their branches just right, they sparkle in many colors.

How to say it: COR-soh-la

Height: 2' 00"
Weight: 11.0 lbs.

Possible Moves: Tackle, Harden, Bubble, Recover, Refresh, Bubble Beam, Ancient Power, Lucky Chant, Spike Cannon, Iron Defense, Rock Blast, Endure, Aqua Ring, Power Gem, Mirror Coat, Earth Power, Flail

Does not evolve

REGION
UNOVA

COTTONEE

Cotton Puff Pokémon

TYPE: GRASS-FAIRY

When threatened, it releases cotton from its body to act as a decoy while it escapes. When several Cottonee stick together, they resemble a cloud drifting through the sky.

How to say it: KAHT-ton-ee

Height: 1' 00"
Weight: 1.3 lbs.

Possible Moves: Absorb, Growth, Leech Seed, Stun Spore, Mega Drain, Cotton Spore, Razor Leaf, Poison Powder, Giga Drain, Charm, Helping Hand, Energy Ball, Cotton Guard, Sunny Day, Endeavor, Solar Beam

Cottonee → Whimsicott

REGION
HOENN

CRADILY

Barnacle Pokémon

TYPE: ROCK-GRASS

After evolving, Cradily leaves its rock and wanders freely to find food along the bottom of the sea. It can also anchor its body to withstand rough seas.

How to say it: cray-DILLY

Height: 4' 11"
Weight: 133.2 lbs.

Possible Moves: Astonish, Constrict, Acid, Ingrain, Confuse Ray, Amnesia, Ancient Power, Gastro Acid, Energy Ball, Stockpile, Spit Up, Swallow, Wring Out

Lileep → Cradily

CRANIDOS

Head Butt Pokémon

REGION
SINNOH

TYPE: ROCK

Cranidos lived in the ancient jungle and cleared its path by headbutting trees to make them fall down. It was restored from a fossil.

How to say it: CRANE-ee-dose

Height: 2' 11"
Weight: 69.4 lbs.

Possible Moves: Headbutt, Leer, Focus Energy, Pursuit, Take Down, Scary Face, Assurance, Chip Away, Ancient Power, Zen Headbutt, Screech, Head Smash

Cranidos → Rampardos

CRAWDAUNT

Rogue Pokémon

REGIONS
HOENN, KALOS (CENTRAL)

TYPE: WATER-DARK

Crawdaunt doesn't tolerate company, and if another Pokémon enters its territory, it's in for a battle. The only time Crawdaunt isn't itching for a fight is just after it sheds its shell, when its soft body is vulnerable.

How to say it: CRAW-daunt

Height: 3' 07" **Weight:** 72.3 lbs.

Possible Moves: Guillotine, Bubble, Harden, Vice Grip, Leer, Bubble Beam, Protect, Knock Off, Swift, Taunt, Night Slash, Crabhammer, Swords Dance, Crunch

Corphish → Crawdaunt

TYPE: PSYCHIC

The glimmering particles that trail from Cresselia's wings resemble a veil. This Legendary Pokémon, which brings happy dreams, is said to be a symbol of the crescent moon.

How to say it: cres-SEL-ee-uh

Height: 4' 11"
Weight: 188.7 lbs.

Possible Moves: Confusion, Double Team, Safeguard, Mist, Aurora Beam, Future Sight, Slash, Moonlight, Psycho Cut, Psycho Shift, Psychic

REGION
SINNOH

CRESSELIA

Lunar Pokémon

LEGENDARY POKÉMON

Does not evolve

CROAGUNK

Toxic Mouth Pokémon

REGIONS
KALOS (CENTRAL), SINNOH

TYPE: POISON-FIGHTING

Croagunk produces its distinctive croaking sound by inflating the poison sacs in its cheeks. The sound often startles an opponent so it can get in a poisonous jab.

How to say it: CROW-gunk

Height: 2' 04" **Weight:** 50.7 lbs.

Possible Moves: Astonish, Mud-Slap, Poison Sting, Taunt, Pursuit, Feint Attack, Revenge, Swagger, Mud Bomb, Sucker Punch, Venoshock, Nasty Plot, Poison Jab, Sludge Bomb, Belch, Flatter

CROBAT

Bat Pokémon

REGIONS
JOHTO, KALOS (CENTRAL)

TYPE: POISON-FLYING

Crobat's four wings cut through the air with barely a sound. If it's been flying a long way, it starts alternating wings, flapping with one pair and letting the other pair rest.

How to say it: CROW-bat

Height: 5' 11" **Weight:** 165.3 lbs.

Possible Moves: Cross Poison, Screech, Leech Life, Supersonic, Astonish, Bite, Wing Attack, Confuse Ray, Swift, Air Cutter, Acrobatics, Mean Look, Poison Fang, Haze, Air Slash

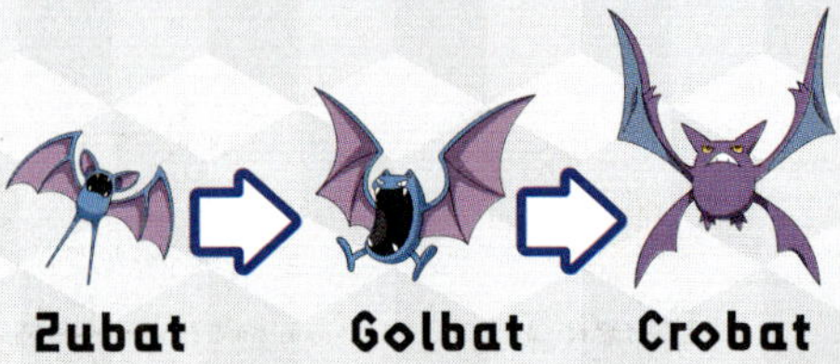

CROCONAW

REGION JOHTO

Big Jaw Pokémon

TYPE: WATER

Each of Croconaw's fangs ends in a barb that resembles a fishhook. When it grips a foe in its fearsome jaws, escape is nearly impossible.

How to say it: CROCK-oh-naw

Height: 3' 07" **Weight:** 55.1 lbs.

Possible Moves: Scratch, Leer, Water Gun, Rage, Bite, Scary Face, Ice Fang, Flail, Crunch, Chip Away, Slash, Screech, Thrash, Aqua Tail, Superpower, Hydro Pump

CRUSTLE

REGION KALOS (COASTAL), UNOVA

Stone Home Pokémon

TYPE: BUG-ROCK

Because Crustle carries a heavy slab of rock everywhere it goes, its legs are extremely strong. Battles between them are determined by whose rock breaks first.

How to say it: KRUS-tul

Height: 4' 07" **Weight:** 440.9 lbs.

Possible Moves: Shell Smash, Rock Blast, Withdraw, Sand Attack, Feint Attack, Smack Down, Rock Polish, Bug Bite, Stealth Rock, Rock Slide, Slash, X-Scissor, Flail, Rock Wrecker

CRYOGONAL

Crystallizing Pokémon

REGIONS
KALOS (MOUNTAIN), UNOVA

TYPE: ICE

Cryogonal's crystalline structure is made of ice formed in snow clouds. With its long chains of ice crystals, it unleashes a freezing attack.

How to say it: kry-AH-guh-nul

Height: 3' 07"
Weight: 326.3 lbs.

Possible Moves: Bind, Ice Shard, Sharpen, Rapid Spin, Icy Wind, Mist, Haze, Aurora Beam, Acid Armor, Ice Beam, Light Screen, Reflect, Slash, Confuse Ray, Recover, Solar Beam, Night Slash, Sheer Cold

Does not evolve

CUBCHOO

Chill Pokémon

REGIONS
KALOS (MOUNTAIN), UNOVA

TYPE: ICE

Even a healthy Cubchoo always has a runny nose. Its sniffles power its freezing attacks.

How to say it: cub-CHOO

Height: 1' 08"
Weight: 18.7 lbs.

Possible Moves: Growl, Powder Snow, Bide, Icy Wind, Play Nice, Fury Swipes, Brine, Endure, Charm, Slash, Flail, Rest, Blizzard, Hail, Thrash, Sheer Cold

Cubchoo → Beartic

REGIONS
KALOS (COASTAL), KANTO

CUBONE
Lonely Pokémon

TYPE: GROUND

When Cubone looks at the full moon, it often sees an image of its lost mother. Its tears leave stains on the skull it wears.

How to say it: CUE-bone

Height: 1' 04"
Weight: 14.3 lbs.

Possible Moves: Growl, Tail Whip, Bone Club, Headbutt, Leer, Focus Energy, Bonemerang, Rage, False Swipe, Thrash, Fling, Bone Rush, Endeavor, Double-Edge, Retaliate

Cubone Marowak

REGION
JOHTO

CYNDAQUIL
Fire Mouse Pokémon

TYPE: FIRE

The protective flames on Cyndaquil's back are an indicator of its mood. A sputtering fire means it's tired, while anger makes the flames burn high and hot.

How to say it: SIN-da-kwill

Height: 1' 08" **Weight:** 17.4 lbs.

Possible Moves: Tackle, Leer, Smokescreen, Ember, Quick Attack, Flame Wheel, Defense Curl, Flame Charge, Swift, Lava Plume, Flamethrower, Inferno, Rollout, Double-Edge

Cyndaquil Quilava Typhlosion

DARKRAI

Pitch-Black Pokémon

REGION
SINNOH

MYTHICAL POKÉMON

TYPE: DARK

Darkrai defends its territory by sending intruders into a deep sleep, where they are tormented by terrible nightmares.

How to say it: DARK-rye

Height: 4' 11" **Weight:** 111.3 lbs.

Possible Moves: Ominous Wind, Disable, Quick Attack, Hypnosis, Feint Attack, Nightmare, Double Team, Haze, Nasty Plot, Dream Eater, Dark Pulse

Does not evolve

REGION
UNOVA

DARMANITAN

Blazing Pokémon

TYPE: FIRE

Fueled by its internal fire, Darmanitan can throw a punch hard enough to destroy a dump truck. To recover from a serious battle, it turns to stone so it can meditate undisturbed.

How to say it: dar-MAN-ih-tan

Height: 4' 03"
Weight: 204.8 lbs.

Possible Moves: Tackle, Rollout, Incinerate, Rage, Fire Fang, Headbutt, Swagger, Facade, Fire Punch, Work Up, Thrash, Belly Drum, Flare Blitz, Hammer Arm, Taunt, Superpower, Overheat

Darumaka Darmanitan

REGION
UNOVA

DARUMAKA

Zen Charm Pokémon

TYPE: FIRE

Darumaka tucks its hands and feet into its body to sleep, but its internal fire still burns at searing temperatures. Long ago, people used its intense body heat to warm themselves.

How to say it: dah-roo-MAH-kuh

Height: 2' 00" **Weight:** 82.7 lbs.

Possible Moves: Tackle, Rollout, Incinerate, Rage, Fire Fang, Headbutt, Uproar, Facade, Fire Punch, Work Up, Thrash, Belly Drum, Flare Blitz, Taunt, Superpower, Overheat

Darumaka Darmanitan

DEDENNE

Antenna Pokémon

REGION
KALOS (COASTAL)

TYPE: ELECTRIC-FAIRY

Dedenne uses its whiskers like antennae to communicate over long distances using electrical waves. It can soak up electricity through its tail.

How to say it: deh-DEN-nay

Height: 0' 08"
Weight: 4.9 lbs.

Possible Moves: Tackle, Tail Whip, Thunder Shock, Charge, Charm, Parabolic Charge, Nuzzle, Thunder Wave, Volt Switch, Rest, Snore, Charge Beam, Entrainment, Play Rough, Thunder, Discharge

Does not evolve

DEERLING

Season Pokémon

REGION
UNOVA

Autumn Form

Summer Form

Winter Form

Spring Form

TYPE: NORMAL-GRASS

Deerling's fur changes with the seasons. Shifts in temperature and humidity affect the color and even the scent of its fur.

How to say it: DEER-ling

Height: 2' 00" **Weight:** 43.0 lbs.

Possible Moves: Tackle, Camouflage, Growl, Sand Attack, Double Kick, Leech Seed, Feint Attack, Take Down, Jump Kick, Aromatherapy, Energy Ball, Charm, Nature Power, Double-Edge, Solar Beam

Deerling Sawsbuck

DEINO

Irate Pokémon

REGIONS
KALOS (MOUNTAIN), UNOVA

TYPE: DARK-DRAGON

Deino can't see, so they explore their surroundings by biting and crashing into things. Because of this, they are often covered in cuts and scratches.

How to say it: DY-noh

Height: 2' 07"
Weight: 38.1 lbs.

Possible Moves: Tackle, Dragon Rage, Focus Energy, Bite, Headbutt, Dragon Breath, Roar, Crunch, Slam, Dragon Pulse, Work Up, Dragon Rush, Body Slam, Scary Face, Hyper Voice, Outrage

Deino Zweilous Hydreigon

DELCATTY

Prim Pokémon

REGIONS
HOENN, KALOS (CENTRAL)

TYPE: NORMAL

Delcatty lives according to its own whims, eating and sleeping as the mood strikes it. If awakened by another Pokémon, it moves elsewhere to continue its nap.

How to say it: dell-CAT-tee

Height: 3' 07"
Weight: 71.9 lbs.

Possible Moves: Fake Out, Attract, Sing, Double Slap

Skitty Delcatty

DELIBIRD

Delivery Pokémon

REGIONS
JOHTO, KALOS (MOUNTAIN)

TYPE: ICE-FLYING

With Delibird's help, a famous climber was able to summit the tallest mountain in the world! This Pokémon always stores extra food in its rolled-up tail and shares it with travelers.

How to say it: DELL-ee-bird

Height: 2' 11"
Weight: 35.3 lbs.

Possible Move: Present

Does not evolve

DELPHOX

Fox Pokémon

REGION
KALOS (CENTRAL)

TYPE: FIRE-PSYCHIC

The mystical Delphox uses a flaming branch as a focus for its psychic visions. When it gazes into the fire, it can see the future.

How to say it: DELL-fox

Height: 4' 11" **Weight:** 86.0 lbs.

Possible Moves: Future Sight, Role Play, Switcheroo, Shadow Ball, Scratch, Tail Whip, Ember, Howl, Flame Charge, Psybeam, Fire Spin, Lucky Chant, Light Screen, Psyshock, Mystical Fire, Flamethrower, Will-O-Wisp, Psychic, Sunny Day, Magic Room, Fire Blast

Fennekin Braixen Delphox

MYTHICAL POKÉMON

REGION
HOENN

DEOXYS

DNA Pokémon

TYPE: PSYCHIC

From the crystal on its chest, Deoxys can shoot out laser beams. This highly intelligent Pokémon came into being when a virus mutated during a fall from space.

How to say it: dee-OCKS-iss

Height: 5' 07" **Weight:** 134.0 lbs.

Possible Moves: Leer, Wrap, Night Shade, Teleport, Knock Off, Pursuit, Psychic, Snatch, Psycho Shift, Zen Headbutt, Cosmic Power, Recover, Hyper Beam

Does not evolve

DEWGONG
Sea Lion Pokémon

REGION
KANTO

TYPE: WATER-ICE

Long ago, a sailor saw Dewgong taking a nap on the ice and thought it was a mermaid. It sleeps best in the bitter cold.

How to say it: DOO-gong

Height: 5' 07"
Weight: 264.6 lbs.

Possible Moves: Headbutt, Growl, Signal Beam, Icy Wind, Encore, Ice Shard, Rest, Aqua Ring, Aurora Beam, Aqua Jet, Brine, Sheer Cold, Take Down, Dive, Aqua Tail, Ice Beam, Safeguard, Hail

DEWOTT
Discipline Pokémon

REGION
UNOVA

TYPE: WATER

Dewott must undergo disciplined training to master the flowing techniques it uses when wielding its two scalchops in battle.

How to say it: DOO-wot

Height: 2' 07" **Weight:** 54.0 lbs.

Possible Moves: Tackle, Tail Whip, Water Gun, Water Sport, Focus Energy, Razor Shell, Fury Cutter, Water Pulse, Revenge, Aqua Jet, Encore, Aqua Tail, Retaliate, Swords Dance, Hydro Pump

TYPE: STEEL-DRAGON

It is said Dialga can control time with its mighty roar. In ancient times, it was revered as a legend.

How to say it: dee-AL-guh

Height: 17' 09"
Weight: 1,505.8 lbs.

Possible Moves: Dragon Breath, Scary Face, Metal Claw, Ancient Power, Slash, Power Gem, Metal Burst, Dragon Claw, Earth Power, Aura Sphere, Iron Tail, Flash Cannon

REGION
SINNOH

DIALGA

Temporal Pokémon

LEGENDARY POKÉMON

Does not evolve

DIANCIE

Jewel Pokémon

REGION
KALOS (COASTAL)

MYTHICAL POKÉMON

TYPE: ROCK-FAIRY

According to myth, when Carbink suddenly transforms into Diancie, its dazzling appearance is the most beautiful sight in existence. It has the power to compress carbon from the atmosphere, forming diamonds between its hands.

How to say it: die-AHN-see

Height: 2' 04"
Weight: 19.4 lbs.

Possible Moves: Tackle, Harden, Rock Throw, Sharpen, Smack Down, Reflect, Stealth Rock, Guard Split, Ancient Power, Flail, Skill Swap, Trick Room, Stone Edge, Moonblast, Diamond Storm, Light Screen, Safeguard

MEGA DIANCIE

Jewel Pokémon

TYPE: ROCK-FAIRY

Height: 3' 07"
Weight: 61.3 lbs.

Does not evolve

DIGGERSBY
Digging Pokémon

REGION
KALOS (CENTRAL)

TYPE: NORMAL-GROUND

Diggersby can use their ears like excavators to move heavy boulders. Construction workers like having them around.

How to say it: DIH-gurz-bee

Height: 3' 03" **Weight:** 93.5 lbs.

Possible Moves: Hammer Arm, Rototiller, Bulldoze, Swords Dance, Tackle, Agility, Leer, Quick Attack, Mud-Slap, Take Down, Mud Shot, Double Kick, Odor Sleuth, Flail, Dig, Bounce, Super Fang, Facade, Earthquake

DIGLETT
Mole Pokémon

REGIONS
KALOS (MOUNTAIN), KANTO

TYPE: GROUND

Farmers love having Diglett around. As these Pokémon burrow through the ground, they leave the soil in perfect condition for planting.

How to say it: DIG-let

Height: 0' 08"
Weight: 1.8 lbs.

Possible Moves: Scratch, Sand Attack, Growl, Astonish, Mud-Slap, Magnitude, Bulldoze, Sucker Punch, Mud Bomb, Earth Power, Dig, Slash, Earthquake, Fissure

DITTO
Transform Pokémon

REGIONS
KALOS (MOUNTAIN), KANTO

TYPE: NORMAL

Ditto can alter the structure of its cells to change its shape. This works best if it has an example to copy—if it tries to copy another shape from memory, it sometimes gets things wrong.

How to say it: DIT-toe

Height: 1' 00"
Weight: 8.8 lbs.

Possible Move: Transform

Does not evolve

DODRIO
Triple Bird Pokémon

REGIONS
KALOS (CENTRAL), KANTO

TYPE: NORMAL-FLYING

Dodrio has three heads, three hearts, and three sets of lungs. It can keep watch in all directions and run a long way without getting tired.

How to say it: doe-DREE-oh

Height: 5' 11"
Weight: 187.8 lbs.

Possible Moves: Pluck, Peck, Growl, Quick Attack, Rage, Fury Attack, Pursuit, Uproar, Acupressure, Tri Attack, Agility, Drill Peck, Endeavor, Thrash

Doduo → Dodrio

REGIONS
KALOS (CENTRAL), KANTO

DODUO

Twin Bird Pokémon

TYPE: NORMAL-FLYING

While one of Doduo's heads sleeps, the other stays alert to watch for danger. Its brains are identical.

How to say it: doe-DOO-oh

Height: 4' 07" **Weight:** 86.4 lbs.

Possible Moves: Peck, Growl, Quick Attack, Rage, Fury Attack, Pursuit, Uproar, Acupressure, Double Hit, Agility, Drill Peck, Endeavor, Thrash

Doduo **Dodrio**

REGION
JOHTO

DONPHAN

Armor Pokémon

TYPE: NORMAL

Donphan curls up in a ball to attack with a high-speed rolling tackle. Such an attack can knock down a house!

How to say it: DON-fan

Height: 3' 07"
Weight: 264.6 lbs.

Possible Moves: Fire Fang, Thunder Fang, Horn Attack, Growl, Defense Curl, Bulldoze, Rapid Spin, Knock Off, Rollout, Magnitude, Slam, Fury Attack, Assurance, Scary Face, Earthquake, Giga Impact

Phanpy **Donphan**

DOUBLADE

Sword Pokémon

REGION
KALOS (CENTRAL)

TYPE: STEEL-GHOST

The two swords that make up Doublade's body fight together in intricate slashing patterns that bewilder even accomplished swordsmen.

How to say it: DUH-blade

Height: 2' 07"
Weight: 9.9 lbs.

Possible Moves: Tackle, Swords Dance, Fury Cutter, Metal Sound, Pursuit, Autotomize, Shadow Sneak, Aerial Ace, Retaliate, Slash, Iron Defense, Night Slash, Power Trick, Iron Head, Sacred Sword

Honedge Doublade Aegislash

DRAGALGE

Mock Kelp Pokémon

REGION
KALOS (COASTAL)

TYPE: POISON-DRAGON

Toxic and territorial, Dragalge defend their homes from anything that enters. Even large ships aren't safe from their poison.

How to say it: druh-GAL-jee

Height: 5' 11"
Weight: 179.7 lbs.

Possible Moves: Dragon Tail, Twister, Tackle, Smokescreen, Water Gun, Feint Attack, Tail Whip, Bubble, Acid, Camouflage, Poison Tail, Water Pulse, Double Team, Toxic, Aqua Tail, Sludge Bomb, Hydro Pump, Dragon Pulse

Skrelp Dragalge

REGIONS
KALOS (MOUNTAIN), KANTO

DRAGONAIR

Dragon Pokémon

TYPE: DRAGON

Dragonair's internal energy can be discharged from special crystals on its body. Apparently, when this happens, it can change the local weather.

How to say it: DRAG-gon-AIR

Height: 13' 01" **Weight:** 36.4 lbs.

Possible Moves: Wrap, Leer, Thunder Wave, Twister, Dragon Rage, Slam, Agility, Dragon Tail, Aqua Tail, Dragon Rush, Safeguard, Dragon Dance, Outrage, Hyper Beam

Dratini → Dragonair → Dragonite

DRAGONITE

Dragon Pokémon

REGIONS
KALOS (MOUNTAIN), KANTO

TYPE: DRAGON-FLYING

Dragonite can fly around the whole world in less than a day. It lives far out at sea and comes to the aid of wrecked ships.

How to say it: DRAG-gon-ite

Height: 7' 03"
Weight: 463.0 lbs.

Possible Moves: Hurricane, Fire Punch, Thunder Punch, Roost, Wrap, Leer, Thunder Wave, Twister, Dragon Rage, Slam, Agility, Dragon Tail, Aqua Tail, Dragon Rush, Safeguard, Wing Attack, Dragon Dance, Outrage, Hyper Beam

DRAPION

Ogre Scorpion Pokémon

REGIONS
KALOS (MOUNTAIN), SINNOH

TYPE: POISON-DARK

Drapion's strong arms could tear a car into scrap metal. The claws on its arms and tail are extremely toxic.

How to say it: DRAP-ee-on

Height: 4' 03"
Weight: 135.6 lbs.

Possible Moves: Thunder Fang, Ice Fang, Fire Fang, Bite, Poison Sting, Leer, Knock Off, Pin Missile, Acupressure, Pursuit, Bug Bite, Poison Fang, Venoshock, Hone Claws, Toxic Spikes, Night Slash, Scary Face, Crunch, Fell Stinger, Cross Poison

DRATINI

Dragon Pokémon

REGIONS
KALOS (MOUNTAIN), KANTO

TYPE: DRAGON

As Dratini grows, it is constantly in molt, shedding its skin to accommodate the life energy that builds up within it.

How to say it: dra-TEE-nee

Height: 5' 11"
Weight: 7.3 lbs.

Possible Moves: Wrap, Leer, Thunder Wave, Twister, Dragon Rage, Slam, Agility, Dragon Tail, Aqua Tail, Dragon Rush, Safeguard, Dragon Dance, Outrage, Hyper Beam

Dratini → Dragonair → Dragonite

DRIFBLIM

Blimp Pokémon

REGIONS
KALOS (COASTAL), SINNOH

TYPE: GHOST-FLYING

During the day, Drifblim tend to be sleepy. They take flight at dusk, but since they can't control their direction, they'll drift away wherever the wind blows them.

How to say it: DRIFF-blim

Height: 3' 11" **Weight:** 33.1 lbs.

Possible Moves: Phantom Force, Constrict, Minimize, Astonish, Gust, Focus Energy, Payback, Ominous Wind, Stockpile, Hex, Swallow, Spit Up, Shadow Ball, Amnesia, Baton Pass, Explosion

Drifloon → Drifblim

DRIFLOON

Balloon Pokémon

REGIONS
KALOS (COASTAL), SINNOH

TYPE: GHOST-FLYING

Known as "the Signpost for Wandering Spirits," Drifloon itself was formed by spirits. It prefers humid weather and is happiest when it's floating through damp air.

How to say it: DRIFF-loon

Height: 1' 04"
Weight: 2.6 lbs.

Possible Moves: Constrict, Minimize, Astonish, Gust, Focus Energy, Payback, Ominous Wind, Stockpile, Hex, Swallow, Spit Up, Shadow Ball, Amnesia, Baton Pass, Explosion

Drifloon Drifblim

DRILBUR

Mole Pokémon

REGION
UNOVA

TYPE: GROUND

Drilbur bores through the ground by bringing its claws together to form a sharp point and rotating its entire body. In this way, it can travel underground as fast as thirty MPH.

How to say it: DRIL-bur

Height: 1' 00" **Weight:** 18.7 lbs.

Possible Moves: Scratch, Mud Sport, Rapid Spin, Mud-Slap, Fury Swipes, Metal Claw, Dig, Hone Claws, Slash, Rock Slide, Earthquake, Swords Dance, Sandstorm, Drill Run, Fissure

Drilbur Excadrill

REGION
KANTO

DROWZEE

Hypnosis Pokémon

TYPE: PSYCHIC

Ever wake up with an itchy nose? It might be because a Drowzee was lurking nearby, trying to draw out your dreams.

How to say it: DROW-zee

Height: 3' 03"
Weight: 71.4 lbs.

Possible Moves: Pound, Hypnosis, Disable, Confusion, Headbutt, Poison Gas, Meditate, Psybeam, Psych Up, Synchronoise, Zen Headbutt, Swagger, Psychic, Nasty Plot, Psyshock, Future Sight

Drowzee Hypno

REGIONS
KALOS (MOUNTAIN), UNOVA

DRUDDIGON

Cave Pokémon

TYPE: DRAGON

Druddigon can't move if it gets too cold, so it soaks up the sun with its wings. It can navigate tight caves at a brisk pace.

How to say it: DRUD-dih-gahn

Height: 5' 03"
Weight: 306.4 lbs.

Possible Moves: Leer, Scratch, Hone Claws, Bite, Scary Face, Dragon Rage, Slash, Crunch, Dragon Claw, Chip Away, Revenge, Night Slash, Dragon Tail, Rock Climb, Superpower, Outrage

Does not evolve

DUCKLETT
Water Bird Pokémon

REGIONS
KALOS (CENTRAL), UNOVA

TYPE: WATER-FLYING

Skilled swimmers, Ducklett dive underwater in search of delicious peat moss. When enemies approach, they kick up water with their wings to cover their retreat.

How to say it: DUK-lit

Height: 1' 08"
Weight: 12.1 lbs.

Possible Moves: Water Gun, Water Sport, Defog, Wing Attack, Water Pulse, Aerial Ace, Bubble Beam, Feather Dance, Aqua Ring, Air Slash, Roost, Rain Dance, Tailwind, Brave Bird, Hurricane

Ducklett → Swanna

DUGTRIO
Mole Pokémon

REGIONS
KALOS (MOUNTAIN), KANTO

TYPE: GROUND

When it comes to digging, Dugtrio knows that three heads are better than one. The triplets think alike and work together.

How to say it: dug-TREE-oh

Height: 2' 04" **Weight:** 73.4 lbs.

Possible Moves: Rototiller, Night Slash, Tri Attack, Scratch, Sand Attack, Growl, Astonish, Mud-Slap, Magnitude, Bulldoze, Sucker Punch, Sand Tomb, Mud Bomb, Earth Power, Dig, Slash, Earthquake, Fissure

Diglett → Dugtrio

DUNSPARCE

Land Snake Pokémon

REGIONS
JOHTO, KALOS (CENTRAL)

TYPE: NORMAL

Dunsparce uses its tail like a drill to dig a burrow, scooting backward into the tunnel. Its underground nest is like a maze.

How to say it: DUN-sparce

Height: 4' 11"
Weight: 30.9 lbs.

Possible Moves: Rage, Defense Curl, Rollout, Spite, Pursuit, Screech, Yawn, Ancient Power, Take Down, Roost, Glare, Dig, Double-Edge, Coil, Endure, Drill Run, Endeavor, Flail

Does not evolve

DUOSION

Mitosis Pokémon

REGIONS
KALOS (COASTAL), UNOVA

TYPE: PSYCHIC

Duosion's brain is divided into two, so sometimes it tries to do two different things at the same time. When the brains are thinking together, Duosion's psychic power is at its strongest.

How to say it: doo-OH-zhun

Height: 2' 00" **Weight:** 17.6 lbs.

Possible Moves: Psywave, Reflect, Rollout, Snatch, Hidden Power, Light Screen, Charm, Recover, Psyshock, Endeavor, Future Sight, Pain Split, Psychic, Skill Swap, Heal Block, Wonder Room

Solosis Duosion Reuniclus

DURANT
Iron Ant Pokémon

REGIONS
KALOS (MOUNTAIN), UNOVA

TYPE: BUG-STEEL

The heavily armored Durant work together to keep attackers away from their colony. Durant and Heatmor are natural enemies.

How to say it: dur-ANT

Height: 1' 00"
Weight: 72.8 lbs.

Possible Moves:
Guillotine, Iron Defense, Metal Sound, Vice Grip, Sand Attack, Fury Cutter, Bite, Agility, Metal Claw, Bug Bite, Crunch, Iron Head, Dig, Entrainment, X-Scissor

Does not evolve

DUSCLOPS
Beckon Pokémon

REGION
HOENN

TYPE: GHOST

There is no escape for anything absorbed into the hollow body of Dusclops. When it waves its hands and focuses its single eye, it can entrance a foe to do its will.

How to say it: DUS-klops

Height: 5' 03" **Weight:** 67.5 lbs.

Possible Moves: Fire Punch, Ice Punch, Thunder Punch, Gravity, Bind, Leer, Night Shade, Disable, Foresight, Astonish, Confuse Ray, Shadow Sneak, Pursuit, Curse, Will-O-Wisp, Shadow Punch, Hex, Mean Look, Payback, Future Sight

Duskull Dusclops Dusknoir

REGION
HOENN

DUSKNOIR

Gripper Pokémon

TYPE: GHOST

Dusknoir senses signals from the spirit world with the antenna on its head. The signals tell it to guide lost spirits . . . and sometimes people.

How to say it: DUSK-nwar

Height: 7' 03" **Weight:** 235.0 lbs.

Possible Moves: Fire Punch, Ice Punch, Thunder Punch, Gravity, Bind, Leer, Night Shade, Disable, Foresight, Astonish, Confuse Ray, Shadow Sneak, Pursuit, Curse, Will-O-Wisp, Shadow Punch, Hex, Mean Look, Payback, Future Sight

Duskull Dusclops Dusknoir

REGION
HOENN

DUSKULL

Requiem Pokémon

TYPE: GHOST

Parents sometimes threaten misbehaving children with a visit from Duskull. It can pass through walls in pursuit of its target, but gives up the chase at sunrise.

How to say it: DUS-kull

Height: 2' 07" **Weight:** 33.1 lbs.

Possible Moves: Leer, Night Shade, Disable, Foresight, Astonish, Confuse Ray, Shadow Sneak, Pursuit, Curse, Will-O-Wisp, Hex, Mean Look, Payback, Future Sight

Duskull Dusclops Dusknoir

DUSTOX

Poison Moth Pokémon

REGION
HOENN

TYPE: BUG-POISON

City lights attract Dustox in swarms. This is unfortunate, because their wings scatter poisonous dust, and their feeding habits quickly strip trees bare.

How to say it: DUS-tocks

Height: 3' 11"
Weight: 69.7 lbs.

Possible Moves: Confusion, Gust, Protect, Moonlight, Psybeam, Whirlwind, Light Screen, Silver Wind, Toxic, Bug Buzz, Quiver Dance

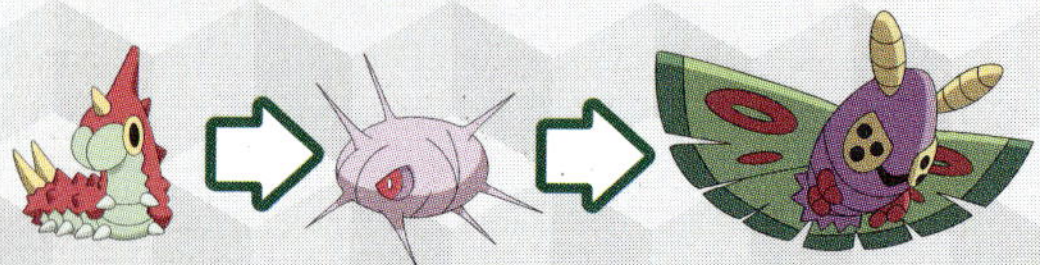

Wurmple Cascoon Dustox

DWEBBLE

Rock Inn Pokémon

REGIONS
KALOS (COASTAL), UNOVA

TYPE: BUG-ROCK

Using a special liquid from its mouth, Dwebble hollows out a rock to use as its shell. It becomes very anxious without a proper rock.

How to say it: DWEHB-bul

Height: 1' 00"
Weight: 32.0 lbs.

Possible Moves: Fury Cutter, Rock Blast, Withdraw, Sand Attack, Feint Attack, Smack Down, Rock Polish, Bug Bite, Stealth Rock, Rock Slide, Slash, X-Scissor, Shell Smash, Flail, Rock Wrecker

Dwebble Crustle

TYPE: ELECTRIC

Eelektrik wraps its long body around its opponent and gives off a paralyzing electric shock from the round markings on its sides. Its appetite is quite large.

How to say it: ee-LEK-trik

Height: 3' 11"
Weight: 48.5 lbs.

Possible Moves: Headbutt, Thunder Wave, Spark, Charge Beam, Bind, Acid, Discharge, Crunch, Thunderbolt, Acid Spray, Coil, Wild Charge, Gastro Acid, Zap Cannon, Thrash

REGION
UNOVA

EELEKTRIK

Elefish Pokémon

REGION
UNOVA

EELEKTROSS

Elefish Pokémon

TYPE: ELECTRIC

With their gaping sucker mouths, electrically charged fangs, and long arms that allow them to crawl up on land, Eelektross are dangerous opponents.

How to say it: ee-LEK-trahs

Height: 6' 11"
Weight: 177.5 lbs.

Possible Moves: Crush Claw, Headbutt, Acid, Discharge, Crunch

EEVEE
Evolution Pokémon

REGIONS
KALOS (COASTAL), KANTO

TYPE: NORMAL

The amazingly adaptive Eevee can evolve into many different Pokémon, depending on its environment. This allows it to withstand harsh conditions.

How to say it: EE-vee

Height: 1' 00"
Weight: 14.3 lbs.

Possible Moves: Helping Hand, Growl, Tackle, Tail Whip, Sand Attack, Baby-Doll Eyes, Swift, Quick Attack, Bite, Refresh, Covet, Take Down, Charm, Baton Pass, Double-Edge, Last Resort, Trump Card

EKANS

Snake Pokémon

REGIONS
KALOS (MOUNTAIN), KANTO

TYPE: POISON

When Ekans rests, it coils its long body up into a spiral. In this position, it can quickly raise its head to challenge a foe.

How to say it: ECK-kins

Height: 6' 07"
Weight: 15.2 lbs.

Possible Moves: Wrap, Leer, Poison Sting, Bite, Glare, Screech, Acid, Stockpile, Swallow, Spit Up, Acid Spray, Mud Bomb, Gastro Acid, Belch, Haze, Coil, Gunk Shot

Ekans Arbok

ELECTABUZZ

Electric Pokémon

REGION
KANTO

TYPE: ELECTRIC

During thunderstorms, Electabuzz climb to high places, hoping to be struck by lightning. Because they can absorb the bolts safely, they sometimes act as lightning rods.

How to say it: ee-LECK-tuh-buzz

Height: 3' 07" **Weight:** 66.1 lbs.

Possible Moves: Quick Attack, Leer, Thunder Shock, Low Kick, Swift, Shock Wave, Light Screen, Electro Ball, Thunder Punch, Discharge, Thunderbolt, Screech, Thunder

Elekid Electabuzz Electivire

ELECTIVIRE

Thunderbolt Pokémon

REGION
SINNOH

TYPE: ELECTRIC

Electricity crackles between Electivire's horns and the tips of its tails. When it forms a circuit with its tails, its opponent receives a powerful shock.

How to say it: e-LECT-uh-vire

Height: 5' 11"
Weight: 305.6 lbs.

Possible Moves: Fire Punch, Quick Attack, Leer, Thunder Shock, Low Kick, Swift, Shock Wave, Light Screen, Electro Ball, Thunder Punch, Discharge, Thunderbolt, Screech, Thunder, Giga Impact

ELECTRIKE

Lightning Pokémon

REGIONS
HOENN, KALOS (COASTAL)

TYPE: ELECTRIC

Electrike's long fur stores up static electricity when it runs at blinding speed. It can use this electricity to charge up its leg muscles and run even faster.

How to say it: eh-LEK-trike

Height: 2' 00"
Weight: 33.5 lbs.

Possible Moves: Tackle, Thunder Wave, Leer, Howl, Quick Attack, Spark, Odor Sleuth, Bite, Thunder Fang, Roar, Discharge, Charge, Wild Charge, Thunder

ELECTRODE

Ball Pokémon

REGIONS
KALOS (MOUNTAIN), KANTO

TYPE: ELECTRIC

Electrode feeds by absorbing electricity, often from power plants or lightning storms. If it eats too much at once, it explodes.

How to say it: ee-LECK-trode

Height: 3' 11"
Weight: 146.8 lbs.

Possible Moves: Magnetic Flux, Charge, Tackle, Sonic Boom, Spark, Eerie Impulse, Rollout, Screech, Charge Beam, Light Screen, Electro Ball, Self-Destruct, Swift, Magnet Rise, Gyro Ball, Explosion, Mirror Coat

ELEKID

Electric Pokémon

REGION
JOHTO

TYPE: ELECTRIC

Elekid tries to avoid touching metal, because doing so discharges the electricity it stores inside its body. If that happens, it spins its arms to charge up again.

How to say it: el-EH-kid

Height: 2' 00" **Weight:** 51.8 lbs.

Possible Moves: Quick Attack, Leer, Thunder Shock, Low Kick, Swift, Shock Wave, Light Screen, Electro Ball, Thunder Punch, Discharge, Thunderbolt, Screech, Thunder

ELGYEM
Cerebral Pokémon

REGION
UNOVA

TYPE: PSYCHIC

It's said Elgyem were first discovered in the desert after a UFO crashed there fifty years ago. Their psychic power can compress an opponent's brain and cause terrible headaches.

How to say it: ELL-jee-ehm

Height: 1' 08"
Weight: 19.8 lbs.

Possible Moves: Confusion, Growl, Heal Block, Miracle Eye, Psybeam, Headbutt, Hidden Power, Imprison, Simple Beam, Zen Headbutt, Psych Up, Psychic, Calm Mind, Recover, Guard Split, Power Split, Synchronoise, Wonder Room

EMBOAR
Mega Fire Pig Pokémon

REGION
UNOVA

TYPE: FIRE-FIGHTING

With the fiery beard that covers its chin, Emboar can set its fists ablaze and throw flaming punches. Its battle moves are speedy and powerful.

How to say it: EHM-bohr

Height: 5' 03" **Weight:** 330.7 lbs.

Possible Moves: Hammer Arm, Tackle, Tail Whip, Ember, Odor Sleuth, Defense Curl, Flame Charge, Arm Thrust, Smog, Rollout, Take Down, Heat Crash, Assurance, Flamethrower, Head Smash, Roar, Flare Blitz

EMOLGA
Sky Squirrel Pokémon

REGIONS
KALOS (COASTAL), UNOVA

TYPE: ELECTRIC-FLYING

When Emolga stretches out its limbs, the membrane connecting them spreads like a cape and allows it to glide through the air. It makes its abode high in the trees.

How to say it: ee-MAHL-guh

Height: 1' 04"
Weight: 11.0 lbs.

Possible Moves: Thunder Shock, Quick Attack, Tail Whip, Charge, Spark, Nuzzle, Pursuit, Double Team, Shock Wave, Electro Ball, Acrobatics, Light Screen, Encore, Volt Switch, Agility, Discharge

Does not evolve

EMPOLEON
Emperor Pokémon

REGION
SINNOH

TYPE: WATER-STEEL

With the sharp edges of its wings, Empoleon can slash through drifting ice as it swims faster than a speedboat. The length of its trident-like horns indicates its power.

How to say it: em-PO-lee-on

Height: 5' 07" **Weight:** 186.3 lbs.

Possible Moves: Tackle, Growl, Bubble, Swords Dance, Peck, Metal Claw, Bubble Beam, Swagger, Fury Attack, Brine, Aqua Jet, Whirlpool, Mist, Drill Peck, Hydro Pump

Piplup Prinplup Empoleon

ENTEI
Volcano Pokémon

REGION
JOHTO

LEGENDARY POKÉMON

TYPE: FIRE

People say that Entei came into being when a volcano erupted. This Legendary Pokémon carries the heat of magma in its fiery heart.

How to say it: EN-tay

Height: 6' 11" **Weight:** 436.5 lbs.

Possible Moves: Bite, Leer, Ember, Roar, Fire Spin, Stomp, Flamethrower, Swagger, Fire Fang, Lava Plume, Extrasensory, Fire Blast, Calm Mind, Eruption

Does not evolve

ESCAVALIER

Cavalry Pokémon

REGIONS
KALOS (MOUNTAIN), UNOVA

TYPE: BUG-STEEL

The stolen Shelmet shell protects Escavalier's body like armor. It uses its double lances to attack.

How to say it: ess-KAH-vuh-LEER

Height: 3' 03"
Weight: 72.8 lbs.

Possible Moves: Double-Edge, Fell Stinger, Peck, Leer, Quick Guard, Twineedle, Fury Attack, Headbutt, False Swipe, Bug Buzz, Slash, Iron Head, Iron Defense, X-Scissor, Reversal, Swords Dance, Giga Impact

Karrablast → Escavalier

ESPEON

Sun Pokémon

REGIONS
JOHTO, KALOS (COASTAL)

TYPE: PSYCHIC

When Espeon finds its Trainer worthy, its loyalty knows no bounds. It apparently learned to predict danger so it could keep its Trainer safe.

How to say it: ESS-pee-on

Height: 2' 11"
Weight: 58.4 lbs.

Possible Moves: Helping Hand, Tackle, Tail Whip, Sand Attack, Confusion, Quick Attack, Swift, Psybeam, Future Sight, Psych Up, Morning Sun, Psychic, Last Resort, Power Swap

Eevee → Espeon

ESPURR

Restraint Pokémon

REGION
KALOS (CENTRAL)

TYPE: PSYCHIC

Espurr emits powerful psychic energy from organs in its ears. It has to fold its ears down to keep the power contained.

How to say it: ESS-purr

Height: 1' 00" **Weight:** 7.7 lbs.

Possible Moves: Scratch, Leer, Covet, Confusion, Light Screen, Psybeam, Fake Out, Disarming Voice, Psyshock

EXCADRILL

Subterrene Pokémon

REGION
UNOVA

TYPE: GROUND-STEEL

Excadrill live several hundred feet underground, where they use their strong steel claws to dig out nests and tunnels. Sometimes that causes big trouble for subway systems.

How to say it: EKS-kuh-dril

Height: 2' 04" **Weight:** 89.1 lbs.

Possible Moves: Scratch, Mud Sport, Rapid Spin, Mud-Slap, Fury Swipes, Metal Claw, Dig, Hone Claws, Slash, Rock Slide, Horn Drill, Earthquake, Swords Dance, Sandstorm, Drill Run, Fissure

EXEGGCUTE

Egg Pokémon

REGIONS
KALOS (COASTAL), KANTO

TYPE: GRASS-PSYCHIC

The six eggs that make up Exeggcute's body spin around a common center. When the eggs begin to crack, this Pokémon is ready to evolve.

How to say it: ECKS-egg-cute

Height: 1' 04" **Weight:** 5.5 lbs.

Possible Moves: Barrage, Uproar, Hypnosis, Reflect, Leech Seed, Bullet Seed, Stun Spore, Poison Powder, Sleep Powder, Confusion, Worry Seed, Natural Gift, Solar Beam, Extrasensory, Bestow

Exeggcute Exeggutor

EXEGGUTOR

Coconut Pokémon

REGIONS
KALOS (COASTAL), KANTO

TYPE: GRASS-PSYCHIC

A tropical Pokémon, Exeggutor has three heads that keep growing when they get enough sun. Exeggcute are thought to form from the fallen heads of Exeggutor.

How to say it: ecks-EGG-u-tore

Height: 6' 07"
Weight: 264.6 lbs.

Possible Moves: Seed Bomb, Barrage, Hypnosis, Confusion, Stomp, Psyshock, Egg Bomb, Wood Hammer, Leaf Storm

Exeggcute Exeggutor

EXPLOUD

Loud Noise Pokémon

REGIONS
HOENN, KALOS (CENTRAL)

TYPE: NORMAL

When Exploud takes a deep breath through the tubes that cover its body, watch out! It's about to unleash a thunderous bellow that will shake the ground around it.

How to say it: ecks-PLOWD

Height: 4' 11" **Weight:** 185.2 lbs.

Possible Moves: Boomburst, Ice Fang, Fire Fang, Thunder Fang, Pound, Uproar, Astonish, Howl, Bite, Supersonic, Stomp, Screech, Crunch, Roar, Synchronoise, Rest, Sleep Talk, Hyper Voice, Hyper Beam

Whismur Loudred Exploud

FARFETCH'D

REGIONS
KALOS (CENTRAL), KANTO

Wild Duck Pokémon

TYPE: NORMAL-FLYING

Farfetch'd always carries its trusty plant stalk. Sometimes, two of them will fight over a superior stalk.

How to say it: FAR-fetched

Height: 2' 07"
Weight: 33.1 lbs.

Possible Moves: Brave Bird, Poison Jab, Peck, Sand Attack, Leer, Fury Cutter, Fury Attack, Aerial Ace, Knock Off, Slash, Air Cutter, Swords Dance, Agility, Night Slash, Acrobatics, Feint, False Swipe, Air Slash

Does not evolve

FEAROW

REGIONS
KALOS (MOUNTAIN), KANTO

Beak Pokémon

TYPE: NORMAL-FLYING

Fearow's long, thin beak is the perfect tool for digging up food from the dirt or catching it in the water.

How to say it: FEER-oh

Height: 3' 11"
Weight: 83.8 lbs.

Possible Moves: Drill Run, Pluck, Peck, Growl, Leer, Fury Attack, Pursuit, Aerial Ace, Mirror Move, Agility, Assurance, Roost, Drill Peck

Spearow → Fearow

FEEBAS

Fish Pokémon

REGION
HOENN

TYPE: WATER

Feebas isn't much to look at, but its hardy nature and persistent survival instinct let it live in any aquatic environment.

How to say it: FEE-bass

Height: 2' 00"
Weight: 16.3 lbs.

Possible Moves: Splash, Tackle, Flail

FENNEKIN

Fox Pokémon

REGION
KALOS
(CENTRAL)

TYPE: FIRE

Searing heat radiates from Fennekin's large ears to keep opponents at a distance. It often snacks on twigs to gain energy.

How to say it: FEN-ik-in

Height: 1' 04"   **Weight:** 20.7 lbs.

Possible Moves: Scratch, Tail Whip, Ember, Howl, Flame Charge, Psybeam, Fire Spin, Lucky Chant, Light Screen, Psyshock, Flamethrower, Will-O-Wisp, Psychic, Sunny Day, Magic Room, Fire Blast

FERALIGATR

REGION
JOHTO

Big Jaw Pokémon

TYPE: WATER

Feraligatr uses its gaping maw as an intimidation tactic. Its powerful legs propel it into a high-speed charge.

How to say it: fer-AL-ee-gay-tur

Height: 7' 07"
Weight: 195.8 lbs.

Possible Moves: Scratch, Leer, Water Gun, Rage, Bite, Scary Face, Ice Fang, Flail, Agility, Crunch, Chip Away, Slash, Screech, Thrash, Aqua Tail, Superpower, Hydro Pump

Totodile Croconaw Feraligatr

FERROSEED

REGIONS
KALOS (COASTAL), UNOVA

Thorn Seed Pokémon

TYPE: GRASS-STEEL

Ferroseed use their spikes to cling to cave ceilings and absorb iron. They can also shoot those spikes to cover their escape when enemies approach.

How to say it: fer-AH-seed

Height: 2' 00"
Weight: 41.4 lbs.

Possible Moves: Tackle, Harden, Rollout, Curse, Metal Claw, Pin Missile, Gyro Ball, Iron Defense, Mirror Shot, Ingrain, Self-Destruct, Iron Head, Payback, Flash Cannon, Explosion

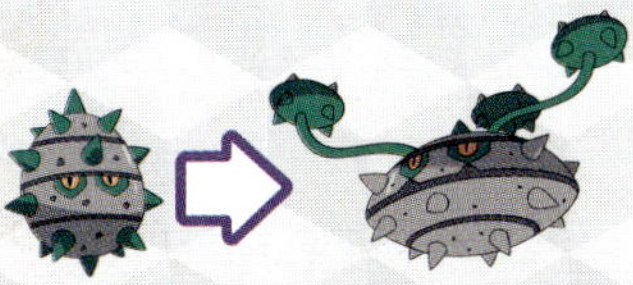

Ferroseed Ferrothorn

FERROTHORN

Thorn Pod Pokémon

REGIONS
KALOS (COASTAL), UNOVA

TYPE: GRASS-STEEL

Ferrothorn swings its spiked feelers to attack. It likes to hang from the ceiling of a cave and shower spikes on anyone passing below.

How to say it: fer-AH-thorn

Height: 3' 03" **Weight:** 242.5 lbs.

Possible Moves: Rock Climb, Tackle, Harden, Rollout, Curse, Metal Claw, Pin Missile, Gyro Ball, Iron Defense, Mirror Shot, Ingrain, Self-Destruct, Power Whip, Iron Head, Payback, Flash Cannon, Explosion

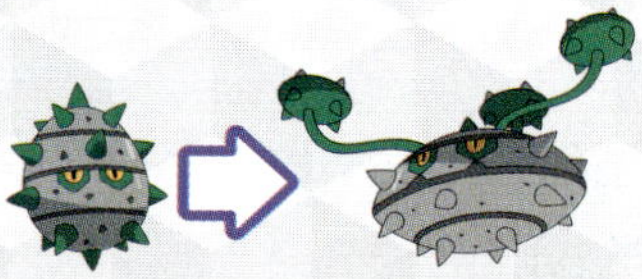

Ferroseed Ferrothorn

FINNEON

Wing Fish Pokémon

REGION
SINNOH

TYPE: WATER

If Finneon soaks up enough sunlight during the day, the patterns on its body give off light when night falls on the sea where it lives.

How to say it: FINN-ee-onn

Height: 1' 04"
Weight: 15.4 lbs.

Possible Moves: Pound, Water Gun, Attract, Rain Dance, Gust, Water Pulse, Captivate, Safeguard, Aqua Ring, Whirlpool, U-turn, Bounce, Silver Wind, Soak

Finneon Lumineon

FLAAFFY

Wool Pokémon

REGIONS
JOHTO, KALOS (COASTAL)

TYPE: ELECTRIC

Parts of Flaaffy's body are covered in wool that generates static electricity and builds up a charge. Its skin is resistant to electricity, so it doesn't shock itself by accident.

How to say it: FLAH-fee

Height: 2' 07"
Weight: 29.3 lbs.

Possible Moves: Tackle, Growl, Thunder Wave, Thunder Shock, Cotton Spore, Charge, Take Down, Electro Ball, Confuse Ray, Power Gem, Discharge, Cotton Guard, Signal Beam, Light Screen, Thunder

FLABÉBÉ

Single Bloom Pokémon

REGION
KALOS (CENTRAL)

TYPE: FAIRY

Each Flabébé has a special connection with the flower it holds. They take care of their flowers and use them as an energy source.

How to say it: flah-BAY-BAY

Height: 0' 04" **Weight:** 0.2 lbs.

Possible Moves: Tackle, Vine Whip, Fairy Wind, Lucky Chant, Razor Leaf, Wish, Magical Leaf, Grassy Terrain, Petal Blizzard, Aromatherapy, Misty Terrain, Moonblast, Petal Dance, Solar Beam

FLAREON

Flame Pokémon

REGIONS
KALOS (COASTAL), KANTO

TYPE: FIRE

Flareon's body can become very hot, so it fluffs out its soft fur to release excess heat into its surroundings. Even so, it can reach more than 1,600 degrees Fahrenheit.

How to say it: FLAIR-ee-on

Height: 2' 11"
Weight: 55.1 lbs.

Possible Moves: Helping Hand, Tackle, Tail Whip, Sand Attack, Ember, Quick Attack, Bite, Fire Fang, Fire Spin, Scary Face, Smog, Lava Plume, Last Resort, Flare Blitz

Eevee → Flareon

FLETCHINDER

Ember Pokémon

REGION
KALOS (CENTRAL)

TYPE: FIRE-FLYING

As the flame sac on Fletchinder's belly slowly heats up, it flies faster and faster. It produces embers from its beak.

How to say it: FLETCH-in-der

Height: 2' 04"
Weight: 35.3 lbs.

Possible Moves: Tackle, Growl, Quick Attack, Peck, Agility, Flail, Ember, Roost, Razor Wind, Natural Gift, Flame Charge, Acrobatics, Me First, Tailwind, Steel Wing

Fletchling → Fletchinder → Talonflame

REGION
KALOS (CENTRAL)

FLETCHLING

Tiny Robin Pokémon

TYPE: NORMAL-FLYING

Flocks of Fletchling sing to one another in beautiful voices to communicate. If an intruder threatens their territory, they will defend it fiercely.

How to say it: FLETCH-ling

Height: 1' 00"
Weight: 3.7 lbs.

Possible Moves: Tackle, Growl, Quick Attack, Peck, Agility, Flail, Roost, Razor Wind, Natural Gift, Flame Charge, Acrobatics, Me First, Tailwind, Steel Wing

Fletchling Fletchinder Talonflame

REGION
KALOS (MOUNTAIN), SINNOH

FLOATZEL

Sea Weasel Pokémon

TYPE: WATER

The flotation sac that surrounds its entire body makes Floatzel very good at rescuing people in the water. It can float them to safety like an inflatable raft.

How to say it: FLOAT-zul

Height: 3' 07" **Weight:** 73.9 lbs.

Possible Moves: Ice Fang, Crunch, Sonic Boom, Growl, Water Sport, Quick Attack, Water Gun, Pursuit, Swift, Aqua Jet, Double Hit, Whirlpool, Razor Wind, Aqua Tail, Agility, Hydro Pump

Buizel Floatzel

FLOETTE

Single Bloom Pokémon

REGION
KALOS (CENTRAL)

TYPE: FAIRY

Floette keeps watch over flower beds and will rescue a flower if it starts to droop. It dances to celebrate the spring bloom.

How to say it: floh-ET

Height: 0' 08"
Weight: 2.0 lbs.

Possible Moves: Tackle, Vine Whip, Fairy Wind, Lucky Chant, Razor Leaf, Wish, Magical Leaf, Grassy Terrain, Petal Blizzard, Aromatherapy, Misty Terrain, Moonblast, Petal Dance, Solar Beam

FLORGES

Garden Pokémon

REGION
KALOS (CENTRAL)

TYPE: FAIRY

Long ago, Florges were a welcome sight on castle grounds, where they would create elaborate flower gardens.

How to say it: FLORE-jess

Height: 3' 07"
Weight: 22.0 lbs.

Possible Moves: Disarming Voice, Lucky Chant, Wish, Magical Leaf, Flower Shield, Grass Knot, Grassy Terrain, Petal Blizzard, Misty Terrain, Moonblast, Petal Dance, Aromatherapy

FLYGON

Mystic Pokémon

REGIONS
HOENN, KALOS (MOUNTAIN)

TYPE: GROUND-DRAGON

When Flygon flaps its wings, it stirs up the sand to create a concealing sandstorm. The vibration of the wings also produces musical tones, making it sound like the Pokémon is singing through the sandstorm.

How to say it: FLY-gon

Height: 6' 07" **Weight:** 180.8 lbs.

Possible Moves: Sonic Boom, Sand Attack, Feint Attack, Sand Tomb, Mud-Slap, Bide, Bulldoze, Rock Slide, Supersonic, Screech, Dragon Breath, Earth Power, Sandstorm, Dragon Tail, Hyper Beam, Dragon Claw

Trapinch Vibrava Flygon

FOONGUS

Mushroom Pokémon

REGIONS
KALOS (MOUNTAIN), UNOVA

TYPE: GRASS-POISON

Foongus uses its deceptive Poké Ball pattern to lure people or Pokémon close. Then it attacks with poison spores.

How to say it: FOON-gus

Height: 0' 08"
Weight: 2.2 lbs.

Possible Moves: Absorb, Growth, Astonish, Bide, Mega Drain, Ingrain, Feint Attack, Sweet Scent, Giga Drain, Toxic, Synthesis, Clear Smog, Solar Beam, Rage Powder, Spore

Foongus Amoonguss

FORRETRESS
Bagworm Pokémon

REGION
JOHTO

TYPE: BUG-STEEL

Forretress is protected by a shell of solid steel. It opens the shell to catch food, but slams it shut again so quickly that no one can see inside.

How to say it: FOR-it-TRESS

Height: 3' 11"
Weight: 277.3 lbs.

Possible Moves: Toxic Spikes, Tackle, Protect, Self-Destruct, Bug Bite, Take Down, Rapid Spin, Bide, Natural Gift, Spikes, Mirror Shot, Autotomize, Payback, Explosion, Iron Defense, Gyro Ball, Double-Edge, Magnet Rise, Zap Cannon, Heavy Slam

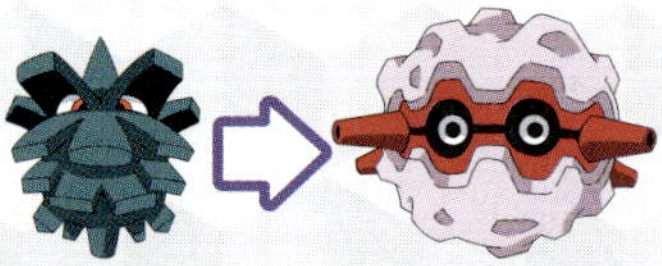

Pineco → Forretress

FRAXURE
Axe Jaw Pokémon

REGIONS
KALOS (CENTRAL), UNOVA

TYPE: DRAGON

Fraxure clash in intense battles over territory. After a battle is over, they always remember to sharpen their tusks on smooth stones so they'll be ready for the next battle.

How to say it: FRAK-shur

Height: 3' 03" **Weight:** 79.4 lbs.

Possible Moves: Scratch, Leer, Assurance, Dragon Rage, Dual Chop, Scary Face, Slash, False Swipe, Dragon Claw, Dragon Dance, Taunt, Dragon Pulse, Swords Dance, Guillotine, Outrage, Giga Impact

Axew → Fraxure → Haxorus

FRILLISH

REGION
UNOVA

Floating Pokémon

TYPE: WATER-GHOST

When battling underwater, Frillish uses poison to stun its opponent, then wraps the foe in its veil-like arms and drags it down into the depths.

How to say it: FRIL-lish

Height: 3' 11"
Weight: 72.8 lbs.

Possible Moves: Bubble, Water Sport, Absorb, Night Shade, Bubble Beam, Recover, Water Pulse, Ominous Wind, Brine, Rain Dance, Hex, Hydro Pump, Wring Out, Water Spout

Male Form

Female Form

Frillish Jellicent

FROAKIE

REGION
KALOS
(CENTRAL)

Bubble Frog Pokémon

TYPE: WATER

The foamy bubbles that cover Froakie's body protect its sensitive skin from damage. It's always alert to any changes in its environment.

How to say it: FRO-kee

Height: 1' 00"
Weight: 15.4 lbs.

Possible Moves: Pound, Growl, Bubble, Quick Attack, Lick, Water Pulse, Smokescreen, Round, Fling, Smack Down, Substitute, Bounce, Double Team, Hydro Pump

Froakie Frogadier Greninja

FROGADIER

Bubble Frog Pokémon

REGION
KALOS (CENTRAL)

TYPE: WATER

Swift and sure, Frogadier coats pebbles in a bubbly foam and then flings them with pinpoint accuracy. It has spectacular jumping and climbing skills.

How to say it: FROG-uh-deer

Height: 2' 00"
Weight: 24.0 lbs.

Possible Moves: Pound, Growl, Bubble, Quick Attack, Lick, Water Pulse, Smokescreen, Round, Fling, Smack Down, Substitute, Bounce, Double Team, Hydro Pump

FROSLASS

Snow Land Pokémon

REGION
SINNOH

TYPE: ICE-GHOST

With its icy breath, Froslass can freeze its opponents solid. Some believe the first Froslass was created when a woman became lost in the snowy mountains.

How to say it: FROS-lass

Height: 4' 03"
Weight: 58.6 lbs.

Possible Moves: Powder Snow, Leer, Double Team, Astonish, Icy Wind, Confuse Ray, Ominous Wind, Wake-Up Slap, Captivate, Ice Shard, Hail, Blizzard, Destiny Bond

FURFROU
Poodle Pokémon

REGION
KALOS (CENTRAL)

TYPE: NORMAL

An experienced groomer can trim Furfrou's fluffy coat into many different styles. Being groomed in this way makes the Pokémon both fancier and faster.

How to say it: FUR-froo

Height: 3' 11"
Weight: 61.7 lbs.

Possible Moves: Tackle, Growl, Sand Attack, Baby-Doll Eyes, Headbutt, Tail Whip, Bite, Odor Sleuth, Retaliate, Take Down, Charm, Sucker Punch, Cotton Guard

Does not evolve

FURRET
Long Body Pokémon

REGIONS
JOHTO, KALOS (CENTRAL)

TYPE: NORMAL

With its long, thin body and impressive speed, Furret has an evasive edge in battle. It can often wriggle right out of an opponent's grasp.

How to say it: FUR-ret

Height: 5' 11"
Weight: 71.6 lbs.

Possible Moves: Scratch, Foresight, Defense Curl, Quick Attack, Fury Swipes, Helping Hand, Follow Me, Slam, Rest, Sucker Punch, Amnesia, Baton Pass, Me First, Hyper Voice

Sentret → Furret

GABITE
Cave Pokémon

REGIONS
KALOS (MOUNTAIN), SINNOH

TYPE: DRAGON-GROUND

While digging to expand its nest, Gabite sometimes finds sparkly gems that then become part of its hoard.

How to say it: gab-BITE

Height: 4' 07" **Weight:** 123.5 lbs.

Possible Moves: Tackle, Sand Attack, Dragon Rage, Sandstorm, Take Down, Sand Tomb, Dual Chop, Slash, Dragon Claw, Dig, Dragon Rush

Gible → Gabite → Garchomp → Mega Garchomp

REGIONS
KALOS (CENTRAL), SINNOH

GALLADE

Blade Pokémon

TYPE: PSYCHIC-FIGHTING

A master of the blade, Gallade battles using the swordlike appendages that extend from its elbows.

How to say it: GAL-laid

Height: 5' 03"
Weight: 114.6 lbs.

Possible Moves: Stored Power, Close Combat, Leaf Blade, Night Slash, Leer, Confusion, Double Team, Teleport, Fury Cutter, Slash, Heal Pulse, Swords Dance, Psycho Cut, Helping Hand, Feint, False Swipe, Protect

MEGA GALLADE

Blade Pokémon

TYPE: PSYCHIC-FIGHTING

Height: 5' 03"
Weight: 124.3 lbs.

Ralts → Kirlia → Gallade → Mega Gallade

GALVANTULA
Elespider Pokémon

REGION
UNOVA

TYPE: BUG-ELECTRIC

Galvantula's webs crackle with electricity, which shocks anything that blunders into them. It can also spin an electric barrier in battle.

How to say it: gal-VAN-choo-luh

Height: 2' 07"
Weight: 31.5 lbs.

Possible Moves: String Shot, Leech Life, Spider Web, Thunder Wave, Screech, Fury Cutter, Electroweb, Bug Bite, Gastro Acid, Slash, Electro Ball, Signal Beam, Agility, Sucker Punch, Discharge, Bug Buzz

Joltik → Galvantula

GARBODOR
Trash Heap Pokémon

REGIONS
KALOS (MOUNTAIN), UNOVA

TYPE: POISON

Garbodor wraps its long left arm around an opponent to bring it within range of its poisonous breath. It creates new kinds of poison by eating garbage.

How to say it: gar-BOH-dur

Height: 6' 03" **Weight:** 236.6 lbs.

Possible Moves: Pound, Poison Gas, Recycle, Toxic Spikes, Acid Spray, Double Slap, Sludge, Stockpile, Swallow, Body Slam, Sludge Bomb, Clear Smog, Toxic, Amnesia, Belch, Gunk Shot, Explosion

Trubbish → Garbodor

REGIONS
KALOS (MOUNTAIN), SINNOH

GARCHOMP

Mach Pokémon

TYPE: DRAGON-GROUND

Garchomp can fly faster than the speed of sound. When it assumes a streamlined position for flight, it looks like a fighter jet.

How to say it: gar-CHOMP

Height: 6' 03"
Weight: 209.4 lbs.

Possible Moves: Fire Fang, Tackle, Sand Attack, Dragon Rage, Sandstorm, Take Down, Sand Tomb, Dual Chop, Slash, Dragon Claw, Dig, Crunch, Dragon Rush

MEGA GARCHOMP

Mach Pokémon

TYPE: DRAGON-GROUND

Height: 6' 03"
Weight: 209.4 lbs.

GARDEVOIR

Embrace Pokémon

REGIONS
HOENN, KALOS (CENTRAL)

TYPE: PSYCHIC-FAIRY

Fiercely protective of its Trainer, Gardevoir can see into the future to detect a threat to that Trainer. It responds by unleashing the full strength of its psychic powers.

How to say it: GAR-dee-VWAR

Height: 5' 03"
Weight: 106.7 lbs.

Possible Moves: Moonblast, Stored Power, Misty Terrain, Healing Wish, Growl, Confusion, Double Team, Teleport, Wish, Magical Leaf, Heal Pulse, Calm Mind, Psychic, Imprison, Future Sight, Captivate, Hypnosis, Dream Eater

MEGA GARDEVOIR

Embrace Pokémon

TYPE: PSYCHIC-FAIRY

Height: 5' 03"
Weight: 106.7 lbs.

GASTLY
Gas Pokémon

REGIONS
KALOS (MOUNTAIN), KANTO

TYPE: GHOST-POISON

Gastly's body is made of gas clouds that can be disrupted by strong winds. Groups of them sometimes huddle close to a house for protection.

How to say it: GAST-lee

Height: 4' 03"
Weight: 0.2 lbs.

Possible Moves: Hypnosis, Lick, Spite, Mean Look, Curse, Night Shade, Confuse Ray, Sucker Punch, Payback, Shadow Ball, Dream Eater, Dark Pulse, Destiny Bond, Hex, Nightmare

Gastly → Haunter → Gengar → Mega Gengar

GASTRODON EAST SEA
Sea Slug Pokémon

REGION
SINNOH

TYPE: WATER-GROUND

It's said that Gastrodon were once covered by protective shells, but over the ages, those shells have vanished. When threatened, they release purple fluid to cover their escape.

How to say it: GAS-tro-donn

Height: 2' 11" **Weight:** 65.9 lbs.

Possible Moves: Mud-Slap, Mud Sport, Harden, Water Pulse, Mud Bomb, Hidden Power, Rain Dance, Body Slam, Muddy Water, Recover

Shellos (East Sea) → Gastrodon (East Sea)

GASTRODON WEST SEA

Sea Slug Pokémon

REGION
SINNOH

TYPE: WATER-GROUND

Gastrodon lives in shallow waters. It can grow back any body part that is ripped off.

How to say it: GAS-tro-donn

Height: 2' 11"
Weight: 65.9 lbs.

Possible Moves: Mud-Slap, Mud Sport, Harden, Water Pulse, Mud Bomb, Hidden Power, Rain Dance, Body Slam, Muddy Water, Recover

Shellos (West Sea) → Gastrodon (West Sea)

GENESECT

Paleozoic Pokémon

REGION
UNOVA

TYPE: BUG-STEEL

The powerful cannon on Genesect's back is the result of Team Plasma's meddling. This Mythical Pokémon is 300 million years old.

How to say it: JEN-uh-sekt

Height: 4' 11"
Weight: 181.9 lbs.

Possible Moves: Fell Stinger, Techno Blast, Quick Attack, Magnet Rise, Metal Claw, Screech, Fury Cutter, Lock-On, Flame Charge, Magnet Bomb, Slash, Metal Sound, Signal Beam, Tri Attack, X-Scissor, Bug Buzz, Simple Beam, Zap Cannon, Hyper Beam, Self-Destruct

Does not evolve

MYTHICAL POKÉMON

GENGAR
Shadow Pokémon

REGIONS
KALOS (MOUNTAIN), KANTO

TYPE: GHOST-POISON

If your shadow suddenly runs away, it might be a Gengar stalking you through the darkness.

How to say it: GHEN-gar

Height: 4' 11"
Weight: 89.3 lbs.

Possible Moves:
Hypnosis, Lick, Spite, Mean Look, Curse, Night Shade, Confuse Ray, Sucker Punch, Shadow Punch, Payback, Shadow Ball, Dream Eater, Dark Pulse, Destiny Bond, Hex, Nightmare

MEGA GENGAR
Shadow Pokémon

TYPE: GHOST-POISON

Height: 4' 07"
Weight: 89.3 lbs.

GEODUDE

Rock Pokémon

REGIONS
KALOS (MOUNTAIN), KANTO

TYPE: ROCK-GROUND

As a Geodude grows older, its rough edges are smoothed away. When it sleeps, it digs into the ground, where it resembles a rock.

How to say it: JEE-oh-dude

Height: 1' 04"
Weight: 44.1 lbs.

Possible Moves: Tackle, Defense Curl, Mud Sport, Rock Polish, Rollout, Magnitude, Rock Throw, Rock Blast, Smack Down, Self-Destruct, Bulldoze, Stealth Rock, Earthquake, Explosion, Double-Edge, Stone Edge

GIBLE

Land Shark Pokémon

REGIONS
KALOS (MOUNTAIN), SINNOH

TYPE: DRAGON-GROUND

Gible dig holes in the walls of warm caves to make their nests. Don't get too close, or they might pounce!

How to say it: GIB-bull

Height: 2' 04" **Weight:** 45.2 lbs.

Possible Moves: Tackle, Sand Attack, Dragon Rage, Sandstorm, Take Down, Sand Tomb, Slash, Dragon Claw, Dig, Dragon Rush

REGIONS
KALOS (COASTAL), UNOVA

GIGALITH

Compressed Pokémon

TYPE: ROCK

After Gigalith soaks up the sun's rays, it uses its energy core to process that energy into a weapon. A blast of its compressed energy can destroy a mountain.

How to say it: GIH-gah-lith

Height: 5' 07"
Weight: 573.2 lbs.

Possible Moves: Tackle, Harden, Sand Attack, Headbutt, Rock Blast, Mud-Slap, Iron Defense, Smack Down, Power Gem, Rock Slide, Stealth Rock, Sandstorm, Stone Edge, Explosion

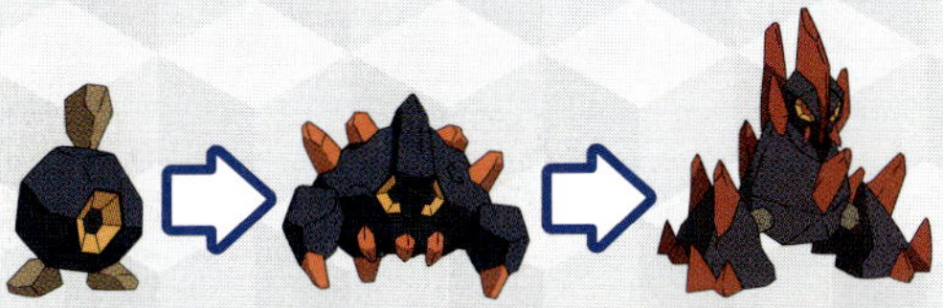

Roggenrola Boldore Gigalith

REGION
JOHTO

GIRAFARIG

Long Neck Pokémon

TYPE: NORMAL-PSYCHIC

The brain that controls Girafarig's secondary head is too small to think and just reacts to its surroundings. It tends to attack anyone who approaches from behind.

How to say it: jir-RAF-uh-rig

Height: 4' 11"
Weight: 91.5 lbs.

Possible Moves: Power Swap, Guard Swap, Astonish, Tackle, Growl, Confusion, Odor Sleuth, Stomp, Agility, Psybeam, Baton Pass, Assurance, Double Hit, Psychic, Zen Headbutt, Crunch

Does not evolve

GIRATINA ORIGIN FORME

Renegade Pokémon

REGION
SINNOH

LEGENDARY POKÉMON

TYPE: GHOST-DRAGON

As punishment, the Legendary Pokémon Giratina was banished to another dimension, where everything is distorted and reversed.

How to say it: gear-uh-TEE-na

Height: 22' 08" **Weight:** 1,433.0 lbs.

Possible Moves: Dragon Breath, Scary Face, Ominous Wind, Ancient Power, Slash, Shadow Sneak, Destiny Bond, Dragon Claw, Earth Power, Aura Sphere, Shadow Claw, Shadow Force, Hex

Does not evolve

REGION
SINNOH

GIRATINA ALTERED FORME

Renegade Pokémon

LEGENDARY POKÉMON

Does not evolve

GLACEON

Fresh Snow Pokémon

REGIONS
KALOS (COASTAL), SINNOH

TYPE: ICE

The icy Glaceon has amazing control over its body temperature. It can freeze its own fur and then fire the frozen hairs like needles at an opponent.

How to say it: GLACE-ee-on

Height: 2' 07" **Weight:** 57.1 lbs.

Possible Moves: Helping Hand, Tackle, Tail Whip, Sand Attack, Icy Wind, Quick Attack, Bite, Ice Fang, Ice Shard, Barrier, Mirror Coat, Hail, Last Resort, Blizzard

REGION
HOENN

GLALIE

Face Pokémon

TYPE: ICE

Glalie's rocky body is surrounded by a sturdy shell of ice, which it creates by freezing water vapor in the air around it. It can also create amazing ice sculptures with this power.

How to say it: GLAY-lee

Height: 4' 11"
Weight: 565.5 lbs.

Possible Moves: Powder Snow, Leer, Double Team, Bite, Icy Wind, Headbutt, Protect, Ice Fang, Crunch, Ice Beam, Hail, Blizzard, Sheer Cold

MEGA GLALIE

Face Pokémon

TYPE: ICE

Height: 6' 11"
Weight: 772.1 lbs.

GLAMEOW

Catty Pokémon

REGION
SINNOH

TYPE: NORMAL

When it's feeling happy and friendly, Glameow purrs winningly and performs a lovely dance with its spiraling tail. When it's in a bad mood, however, the claws come out.

How to say it: GLAM-meow

Height: 1' 08"
Weight: 8.6 lbs.

Possible Moves: Fake Out, Scratch, Growl, Hypnosis, Feint Attack, Fury Swipes, Charm, Assist, Captivate, Slash, Sucker Punch, Attract, Hone Claws

GLIGAR

Fly Scorpion Pokémon

REGIONS
JOHTO, KALOS (MOUNTAIN)

TYPE: GROUND-FLYING

Gliding silently through the air, Gligar can strike from above to grab onto an opponent's face with all four of its claws. The barb on its tail is poisonous.

How to say it: GLY-gar

Height: 3' 07" **Weight:** 142.9 lbs.

Possible Moves: Poison Sting, Sand Attack, Harden, Knock Off, Quick Attack, Fury Cutter, Feint Attack, Acrobatics, Slash, U-turn, Screech, X-Scissor, Sky Uppercut, Swords Dance, Guillotine

REGIONS
KALOS (MOUNTAIN), SINNOH

GLISCOR

Fang Scorpion Pokémon

TYPE: GROUND-FLYING

Gliscor hangs upside down from trees, watching for its chance to attack. At the right moment, it silently swoops, with its long tail ready to seize its opponent.

How to say it: GLY-score

Height: 6' 07"
Weight: 93.7 lbs.

Possible Moves: Guillotine, Thunder Fang, Ice Fang, Fire Fang, Poison Jab, Sand Attack, Harden, Knock Off, Quick Attack, Fury Cutter, Feint Attack, Acrobatics, Night Slash, U-turn, Screech, X-Scissor, Sky Uppercut, Swords Dance

REGIONS
KALOS (CENTRAL), KANTO

GLOOM

Weed Pokémon

TYPE: GRASS-POISON

Gloom doesn't always smell terrible—when it feels safe and relaxed, its aroma fades. However, its nectar usually carries an awful stench.

How to say it: GLOOM

Height: 2' 07" **Weight:** 19.0 lbs.

Possible Moves: Absorb, Sweet Scent, Acid, Poison Powder, Stun Spore, Sleep Powder, Mega Drain, Lucky Chant, Natural Gift, Moonlight, Giga Drain, Petal Blizzard, Petal Dance, Grassy Terrain

GOGOAT
Mount Pokémon

REGION
KALOS (CENTRAL)

TYPE: GRASS

This perceptive Pokémon can read its riders' feelings by paying attention to their grip on its horns. Gogoat also use their horns in battles for leadership.

How to say it: GO-goat

Height: 5' 07"
Weight: 200.6 lbs.

Possible Moves: Aerial Ace, Tackle, Growth, Vine Whip, Tail Whip, Leech Seed, Razor Leaf, Worry Seed, Synthesis, Take Down, Bulldoze, Seed Bomb, Bulk Up, Double-Edge, Horn Leech, Leaf Blade, Milk Drink, Earthquake

GOLBAT
Bat Pokémon

REGIONS
KALOS (CENTRAL), KANTO

TYPE: POISON-FLYING

With its four sharp fangs, Golbat feeds on living beings. Darkness gives it an advantage in battle, and it prefers to attack on pitch-black nights.

How to say it: GOL-bat

Height: 5' 03" **Weight:** 121.3 lbs.

Possible Moves: Screech, Leech Life, Supersonic, Astonish, Bite, Wing Attack, Confuse Ray, Swift, Air Cutter, Acrobatics, Mean Look, Poison Fang, Haze, Air Slash

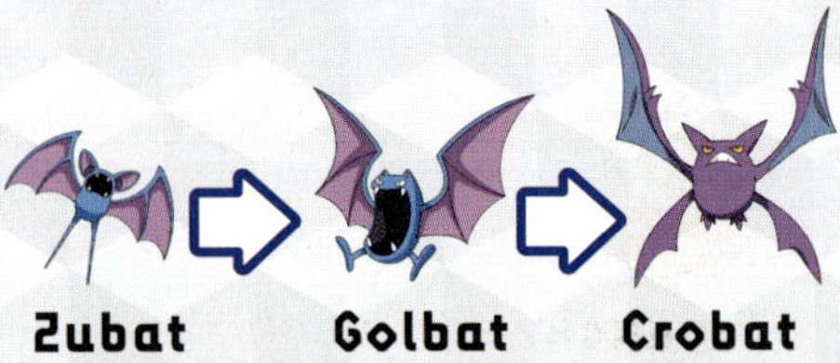

REGIONS
KALOS (CENTRAL), KANTO

GOLDEEN

Goldfish Pokémon

TYPE: WATER

Goldeen's long, elegant fins wave gracefully in the water. It's hard to keep this lovely Pokémon in an aquarium, because its horn can break through thick glass.

How to say it: GOL-deen

Height: 2' 00"
Weight: 33.1 lbs.

Possible Moves: Peck, Tail Whip, Water Sport, Supersonic, Horn Attack, Water Pulse, Flail, Aqua Ring, Fury Attack, Waterfall, Horn Drill, Agility, Soak, Megahorn

Goldeen   Seaking

REGIONS
KALOS (CENTRAL), KANTO

GOLDUCK

Duck Pokémon

TYPE: WATER

The webbing on its legs makes Golduck an excellent swimmer. Even when facing strong currents and towering waves, it can cut through the water to rescue shipwreck victims.

How to say it: GOL-duck

Height: 5' 07"   **Weight:** 168.9 lbs.

Possible Moves: Aqua Jet, Water Sport, Scratch, Tail Whip, Water Gun, Disable, Confusion, Water Pulse, Fury Swipes, Screech, Zen Headbutt, Aqua Tail, Soak, Psych Up, Amnesia, Hydro Pump, Wonder Room

Psyduck   Golduck

GOLEM

Megaton Pokémon

REGIONS
KALOS (MOUNTAIN), KANTO

TYPE: ROCK-GROUND

People who live on mountainsides sometimes dig grooves to keep Golem from rolling right into their houses.

How to say it: GO-lum

Height: 4' 07"
Weight: 661.4 lbs.

Possible Moves: Heavy Slam, Tackle, Defense Curl, Mud Sport, Rock Polish, Steamroller, Magnitude, Rock Throw, Rock Blast, Smack Down, Self-Destruct, Bulldoze, Stealth Rock, Earthquake, Explosion, Double-Edge, Stone Edge

Geodude Graveler Golem

GOLETT

Automaton Pokémon

REGIONS
KALOS (COASTAL), UNOVA

TYPE: GROUND-GHOST

Sculpted from clay and animated by a mysterious internal energy, Golett are the product of ancient science.

How to say it: GO-let

Height: 3' 03"
Weight: 202.8 lbs.

Possible Moves: Pound, Astonish, Defense Curl, Mud-Slap, Rollout, Shadow Punch, Iron Defense, Mega Punch, Magnitude, Dynamic Punch, Night Shade, Curse, Earthquake, Hammer Arm, Focus Punch

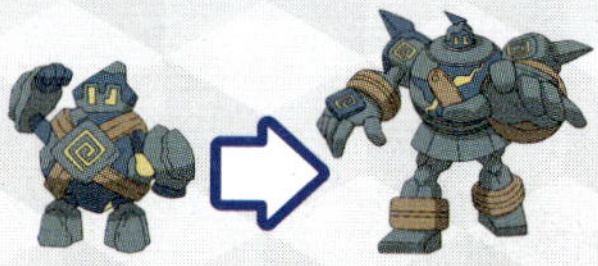

Golett Golurk

GOLURK
Automaton Pokémon

REGIONS
KALOS (COASTAL), UNOVA

TYPE: GROUND-GHOST

The seal on Golurk's chest keeps its energy contained and stops it from going wild. Long ago, these Pokémon were created as protectors.

How to say it: GO-lurk

Height: 9' 02"
Weight: 727.5 lbs.

Possible Moves: Phantom Force, Focus Punch, Pound, Astonish, Defense Curl, Mud-Slap, Rollout, Shadow Punch, Iron Defense, Mega Punch, Magnitude, Dynamic Punch, Night Shade, Curse, Heavy Slam, Earthquake, Hammer Arm

GOODRA
Dragon Pokémon

REGION
KALOS (MOUNTAIN)

TYPE: DRAGON

The affectionate Goodra just loves to give its Trainer a big hug! Unfortunately, its hugs leave the recipient covered in goo.

How to say it: GOO-druh

Height: 6' 07" **Weight:** 331.8 lbs.

Possible Moves: Outrage, Feint, Tackle, Bubble, Absorb, Protect, Bide, Dragon Breath, Rain Dance, Flail, Body Slam, Muddy Water, Dragon Pulse, Aqua Tail, Power Whip

GOOMY

Soft Tissue Pokémon

REGION
KALOS (MOUNTAIN)

TYPE: DRAGON

The slippery membrane that covers Goomy's body deflects the fists and feet of its attackers. To keep itself from drying out, it stays away from the sun.

How to say it: GOO-mee

Height: 1' 00"
Weight: 6.2 lbs.

Possible Moves: Tackle, Bubble, Absorb, Protect, Bide, Dragon Breath, Rain Dance, Flail, Body Slam, Muddy Water, Dragon Pulse

GOREBYSS

South Sea Pokémon

REGIONS
HOENN, KALOS (COASTAL)

TYPE: WATER

Gorebyss is tougher than it looks. Its long, slender body is built to withstand the crushing pressure at the bottom of the ocean. Regular attacks just won't do much.

How to say it: GORE-a-biss

Height: 5' 11"
Weight: 49.8 lbs.

Possible Moves: Whirlpool, Confusion, Agility, Water Pulse, Amnesia, Aqua Ring, Captivate, Baton Pass, Dive, Psychic, Aqua Tail, Hydro Pump

GOTHITA
Fixation Pokémon

REGIONS
KALOS (MOUNTAIN), UNOVA

TYPE: PSYCHIC

Gothita's wide eyes are always fixed on something. It seems when they stare like that, they're seeing what others cannot.

How to say it: GAH-THEE-tah

Height: 1' 04"
Weight: 12.8 lbs.

Possible Moves: Pound, Confusion, Tickle, Play Nice, Fake Tears, Double Slap, Psybeam, Embargo, Feint Attack, Psyshock, Flatter, Future Sight, Heal Block, Psychic, Telekinesis, Charm, Magic Room

GOTHITELLE
Astral Body Pokémon

REGIONS
KALOS (MOUNTAIN), UNOVA

TYPE: PSYCHIC

Gothitelle observes the stars to predict the future. It sometimes distorts the air around itself to reveal faraway constellations.

How to say it: GAH-thih-tell

Height: 4' 11"
Weight: 97.0 lbs.

Possible Moves: Pound, Confusion, Tickle, Play Nice, Fake Tears, Double Slap, Psybeam, Embargo, Feint Attack, Psyshock, Flatter, Future Sight, Heal Block, Psychic, Telekinesis, Charm, Magic Room

GOTHORITA

Manipulate Pokémon

REGIONS
KALOS (MOUNTAIN), UNOVA

TYPE: PSYCHIC

Gothorita draw their power from starlight. On starry nights, they can make stones float and control people's movements with their enhanced psychic power.

How to say it: GAH-thoh-REE-tah

Height: 2' 04" **Weight:** 39.7 lbs.

Possible Moves: Pound, Confusion, Tickle, Play Nice, Fake Tears, Double Slap, Psybeam, Embargo, Feint Attack, Psyshock, Flatter, Future Sight, Heal Block, Psychic, Telekinesis, Charm, Magic Room

GOURGEIST

Pumpkin Pokémon

REGION
KALOS (MOUNTAIN)

TYPE: GHOST-GRASS

During the new moon, the eerie song of the Gourgeist echoes through town, bringing woe to anyone who hears it.

How to say it: GORE-guyst

Height: 2' 11" **Weight:** 27.6 lbs.

Possible Moves: Explosion, Phantom Force, Trick, Astonish, Confuse Ray, Scary Face, Trick-or-Treat, Worry Seed, Razor Leaf, Leech Seed, Bullet Seed, Shadow Sneak, Shadow Ball, Pain Split, Seed Bomb

GRANBULL

Fairy Pokémon

REGIONS
JOHTO, KALOS (COASTAL)

TYPE: FAIRY

The weight of the huge fangs in Granbull's lower jaw throw the Pokémon off balance, so it has to walk with its head tilted back. It generally doesn't bite unless startled.

How to say it: GRAN-bull

Height: 4' 07"
Weight: 107.4 lbs.

Possible Moves: Outrage, Ice Fang, Fire Fang, Thunder Fang, Tackle, Scary Face, Tail Whip, Charm, Bite, Lick, Headbutt, Roar, Rage, Play Rough, Payback, Crunch

GRAVELER

Rock Pokémon

REGIONS
KALOS (MOUNTAIN), KANTO

TYPE: ROCK-GROUND

Graveler loves to eat rocks, and moss-covered rocks are a favorite snack. It will munch its way up the side of a mountain if it's hungry.

How to say it: GRAV-el-ler

Height: 3' 03"
Weight: 231.5 lbs.

Possible Moves: Tackle, Defense Curl, Mud Sport, Rock Polish, Rollout, Magnitude, Rock Throw, Rock Blast, Smack Down, Self-Destruct, Bulldoze, Stealth Rock, Earthquake, Explosion, Double-Edge, Stone Edge

GRENINJA

Ninja Pokémon

REGION
KALOS
(CENTRAL)

TYPE: WATER-DARK

Greninja can compress water into sharp-edged throwing stars. With the grace of a ninja, it slips in and out of sight to attack from the shadows.

How to say it: greh-NIN-jah

Height: 4' 11" **Weight:** 88.2 lbs.

Possible Moves: Night Slash, Role Play, Mat Block, Pound, Growl, Bubble, Quick Attack, Lick, Water Pulse, Smokescreen, Shadow Sneak, Spikes, Feint Attack, Water Shuriken, Substitute, Extrasensory, Double Team, Haze, Hydro Pump

REGION
KANTO

GRIMER
Sludge Pokémon

TYPE: POISON

Because its body is like sludge, Grimer can squeeze itself into small openings like sewer pipes. The fluid it gives off is full of germs.

How to say it: GRIME-er

Height: 2' 11"
Weight: 66.1 lbs.

Possible Moves: Poison Gas, Pound, Harden, Mud-Slap, Disable, Minimize, Sludge, Mud Bomb, Fling, Screech, Sludge Bomb, Acid Armor, Sludge Wave, Gunk Shot, Memento

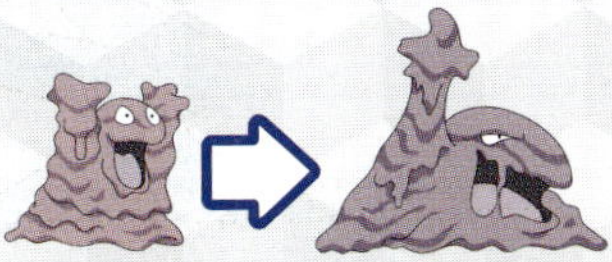

Grimer → Muk

REGION
SINNOH

GROTLE
Grove Pokémon

TYPE: GRASS

Grotle leaves the shade of its forest home to soak up sunlight with its shell. It's good at finding clear water, and smaller Pokémon often ride on its back when they're thirsty.

How to say it: GRAHT-ull

Height: 3' 07" **Weight:** 213.8 lbs.

Possible Moves: Tackle, Withdraw, Absorb, Razor Leaf, Curse, Bite, Mega Drain, Leech Seed, Synthesis, Crunch, Giga Drain, Leaf Storm

Turtwig → Grotle → Torterra

GROUDON

Continent Pokémon

REGION
HOENN

LEGENDARY POKÉMON

TYPE: GROUND

Legends say that Groudon is the land personified. When it channels the full power of nature, it can expand the landmass with eruptions of magma. This Pokémon often clashes with Kyogre.

How to say it: GRAU-don

Height: 11' 06"
Weight: 2,094.4 lbs.

Possible Moves: Mud Shot, Scary Face, Lava Plume, Hammer Arm, Rest, Earthquake, Ancient Power, Eruption, Bulk Up, Earth Power, Fissure, Solar Beam, Fire Blast

PRIMAL GROUDON

Continent Pokémon

TYPE: GROUND-FIRE

Height: 16' 05"
Weight: 2,204.0 lbs.

REGION
HOENN

GROVYLE

Wood Gecko Pokémon

TYPE: GRASS

Grovyle can travel so swiftly from branch to branch that it looks like it's flying through the forest. The leaves on its body are excellent camouflage.

How to say it: GROW-vile

Height: 2' 11" **Weight:** 47.6 lbs.

Possible Moves: Pound, Leer, Absorb, Quick Attack, Fury Cutter, Pursuit, Screech, Leaf Blade, Agility, Slam, Detect, False Swipe, Leaf Storm

Treecko → Grovyle → Sceptile → Mega Sceptile

TYPE: FIRE

Growlithe has an excellent nose and a good memory for scents. It can even sniff out people's emotions.

How to say it: GROWL-ith

Height: 2' 04" **Weight:** 41.9 lbs.

Possible Moves: Bite, Roar, Ember, Leer, Odor Sleuth, Helping Hand, Flame Wheel, Reversal, Fire Fang, Flame Burst, Take Down, Flamethrower, Agility, Crunch, Retaliate, Heat Wave, Flare Blitz

REGION
KANTO

GROWLITHE

Puppy Pokémon

Growlithe → Arcanine

GRUMPIG
Manipulate Pokémon

REGIONS
HOENN,
KALOS
(COASTAL)

TYPE: PSYCHIC

Grumpig breaks into a strange dance when it's using its black pearls to focus its psychic power. Many collectors consider the pearls to be priceless artwork.

How to say it: GRUM-pig

Height: 2' 11"
Weight: 157.6 lbs.

Possible Moves: Splash, Psywave, Odor Sleuth, Psybeam, Psych Up, Confuse Ray, Magic Coat, Zen Headbutt, Rest, Snore, Power Gem, Psyshock, Payback, Psychic, Bounce

GULPIN
Stomach Pokémon

REGIONS
HOENN,
KALOS
(CENTRAL)

TYPE: POISON

Gulpin's stomach takes up most of its body, so there's not much room for its other organs. Its powerful digestive enzymes make short work of anything it swallows.

How to say it: GULL-pin

Height: 1' 04"
Weight: 22.7 lbs.

Possible Moves: Pound, Yawn, Poison Gas, Sludge, Amnesia, Encore, Toxic, Acid Spray, Stockpile, Spit Up, Swallow, Belch, Sludge Bomb, Gastro Acid, Wring Out, Gunk Shot

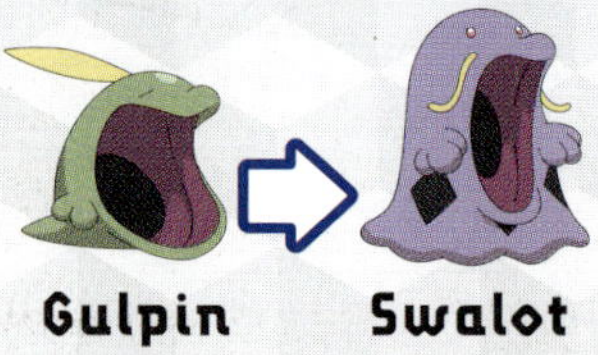

REGIONS
KALOS (MOUNTAIN), UNOVA

GURDURR

Muscular Pokémon

TYPE: FIGHTING

With its strong muscles, Gurdurr can wield its steel beam with ease in battle. It's so sturdy that a whole team of wrestlers couldn't knock it down.

How to say it: GUR-dur

Height: 3' 11" **Weight:** 88.2 lbs.

Possible Moves: Pound, Leer, Focus Energy, Bide, Low Kick, Rock Throw, Wake-Up Slap, Chip Away, Bulk Up, Rock Slide, Dynamic Punch, Scary Face, Hammer Arm, Stone Edge, Focus Punch, Superpower

Timburr Gurdurr Conkeldurr

GYARADOS

Atrocious Pokémon

REGIONS
KALOS (CENTRAL), KANTO

TYPE: WATER-FLYING

After evolving, Gyarados experiences a shift in the cellular structure of its brain. This may explain why it is so violent, sometimes going on month-long rampages.

How to say it: GARE-uh-dos

Height: 21' 04"
Weight: 518.1 lbs.

Possible Moves: Thrash, Bite, Dragon Rage, Leer, Twister, Ice Fang, Aqua Tail, Rain Dance, Hydro Pump, Dragon Dance, Hyper Beam

MEGA GYARADOS

Atrocious Pokémon

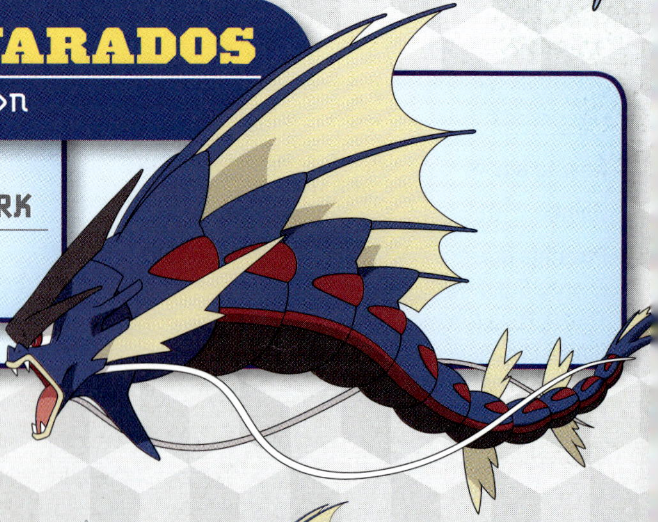

TYPE: WATER-DARK

Height: 21' 04"
Weight: 672.4 lbs.

REGION
SINNOH

HAPPINY

Playhouse Pokémon

TYPE: NORMAL

In the pouch on its belly, Happiny carefully stores a round, white stone that resembles an egg. It sometimes offers this stone to those it likes.

How to say it: hap-PEE-nee

Height: 2' 00"
Weight: 53.8 lbs.

Possible Moves: Pound, Charm, Copycat, Refresh, Sweet Kiss

REGIONS
HOENN,
KALOS
(COASTAL)

HARIYAMA

Arm Thrust Pokémon

TYPE: FIGHTING

Don't let Hariyama's bulk fool you—it's made of pure muscle. A single strike from its open palm can snap a thick tree in half.

How to say it: HAR-ee-YAH-mah

Height: 7' 07" **Weight:** 559.5 lbs.

Possible Moves: Brine, Tackle, Focus Energy, Sand Attack, Arm Thrust, Vital Throw, Fake Out, Whirlwind, Knock Off, Smelling Salts, Belly Drum, Force Palm, Seismic Toss, Wake-Up Slap, Endure, Close Combat, Reversal, Heavy Slam

HAUNTER

Gas Pokémon

REGIONS
KALOS (MOUNTAIN), KANTO

TYPE: GHOST-POISON

Don't ever let a Haunter lick you! Its ghostly tongue can steal your life energy.

How to say it: HAUNT-ur

Height: 5' 03" **Weight:** 0.2 lbs.

Possible Moves: Hypnosis, Lick, Spite, Mean Look, Curse, Night Shade, Confuse Ray, Sucker Punch, Shadow Punch, Payback, Shadow Ball, Dream Eater, Dark Pulse, Destiny Bond, Hex, Nightmare

HAWLUCHA

Wrestling Pokémon

REGION
KALOS (COASTAL)

TYPE: FIGHTING-FLYING

Hawlucha prefers to fight by diving at its foes from above. This aerial advantage makes up for its small size.

How to say it: haw-LOO-cha

Height: 2' 07" **Weight:** 47.4 lbs.

Possible Moves: Detect, Tackle, Hone Claws, Karate Chop, Wing Attack, Roost, Aerial Ace, Encore, Fling, Flying Press, Bounce, Endeavor, Feather Dance, High Jump Kick, Sky Attack, Sky Drop, Swords Dance

Does not evolve

HAXORUS

Axe Jaw Pokémon

REGIONS
KALOS (CENTRAL), UNOVA

TYPE: DRAGON

Haxorus can cut through steel with its mighty tusks, which stay sharp no matter what. Its body is heavily armored.

How to say it: HAK-soar-us

Height: 5' 11"
Weight: 232.6 lbs.

Possible Moves: Outrage, Scratch, Leer, Assurance, Dragon Rage, Dual Chop, Scary Face, Slash, False Swipe, Dragon Claw, Dragon Dance, Taunt, Dragon Pulse, Swords Dance, Guillotine, Giga Impact

Axew → Fraxure → Haxorus

HEATMOR

Anteater Pokémon

REGIONS
KALOS (MOUNTAIN), UNOVA

TYPE: FIRE

Heatmor can control the flame from its mouth like a tongue, and the fire is so hot that it can melt through steel. Heatmor and Durant are natural enemies.

How to say it: HEET-mohr

Height: 4' 07"
Weight: 127.9 lbs.

Possible Moves: Inferno, Hone Claws, Tackle, Incinerate, Lick, Odor Sleuth, Bind, Fire Spin, Fury Swipes, Snatch, Flame Burst, Bug Bite, Slash, Amnesia, Flamethrower, Stockpile, Spit Up, Swallow

Does not evolve

HEATRAN
Lava Dome Pokémon

REGION
SINNOH

LEGENDARY POKÉMON

TYPE: FIRE-STEEL

Heatran makes its home in caves carved out by volcanic eruptions. This Legendary Pokémon's feet can dig into rock, allowing it to walk on walls and ceilings.

How to say it: HEE-tran

Height: 5' 07" **Weight:** 948.0 lbs.

Possible Moves: Ancient Power, Leer, Fire Fang, Metal Sound, Crunch, Scary Face, Lava Plume, Fire Spin, Iron Head, Earth Power, Heat Wave, Stone Edge, Magma Storm

Does not evolve

HELIOLISK

Generator Pokémon

REGION
KALOS (COASTAL)

TYPE: ELECTRIC-NORMAL

Heliolisk generates electricity by spreading its frill out wide to soak up the sun. It uses this energy to boost its speed.

How to say it: HEE-lee-oh-lisk

Height: 3' 03"
Weight: 46.3 lbs.

Possible Moves: Eerie Impulse, Electrify, Razor Wind, Quick Attack, Thunder, Charge, Parabolic Charge

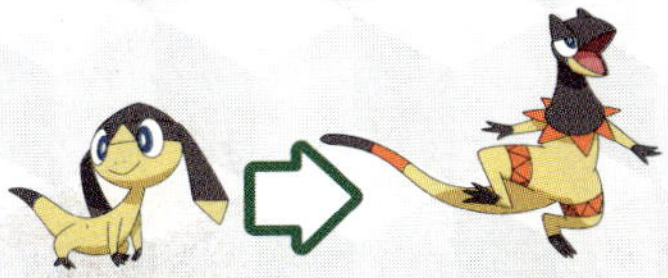

Helioptile Heliolisk

HELIOPTILE

Generator Pokémon

REGION
KALOS (COASTAL)

TYPE: ELECTRIC-NORMAL

The frills on Helioptile's head soak up sunlight and create electricity. In this way, they can generate enough energy to keep them going without food.

How to say it: hee-lee-AHP-tile

Height: 1' 08" **Weight:** 13.2 lbs.

Possible Moves: Pound, Tail Whip, Thunder Shock, Charge, Mud-Slap, Quick Attack, Razor Wind, Parabolic Charge, Thunder Wave, Bulldoze, Volt Switch, Electrify, Thunderbolt

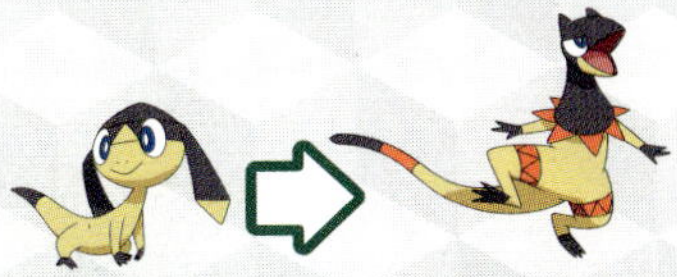

Helioptile Heliolisk

HERACROSS

Single Horn Pokémon

REGIONS
JOHTO, KALOS (COASTAL)

TYPE: BUG-FIGHTING

Though its feet end in sharp claws, Heracross doesn't use them as a weapon. Instead, it digs them into the ground to brace itself while it uses its giant horn to scoop up an enemy.

How to say it: HAIR-uh-cross

Height: 4' 11"
Weight: 119.0 lbs.

Possible Moves: Arm Thrust, Bullet Seed, Night Slash, Tackle, Leer, Horn Attack, Endure, Fury Attack, Aerial Ace, Chip Away, Counter, Brick Break, Take Down, Pin Missile, Close Combat, Feint, Reversal, Megahorn

MEGA HERACROSS

Single Horn Pokémon

TYPE: BUG-FIGHTING

Height: 5' 07"
Weight: 137.8 lbs.

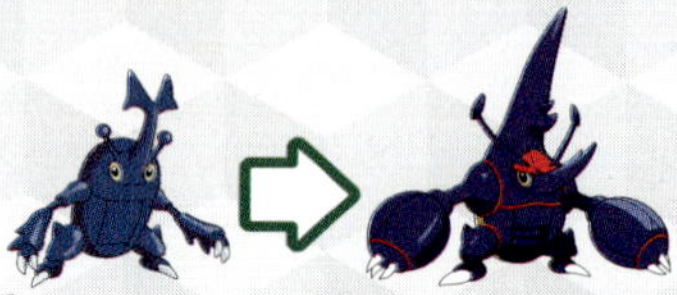

Heracross → Mega Heracross

REGION
UNOVA

HERDIER

Loyal Dog Pokémon

TYPE: NORMAL

Herdier is known for its unwavering loyalty, even helping its Trainer take care of other Pokémon. The black fur on its back protects it like a cape.

How to say it: HERD-ee-er

Height: 2' 11"
Weight: 32.4 lbs.

Possible Moves: Leer, Tackle, Odor Sleuth, Bite, Helping Hand, Take Down, Work Up, Crunch, Roar, Retaliate, Reversal, Last Resort, Giga Impact

REGIONS
KALOS (COASTAL), SINNOH

HIPPOPOTAS

Hippo Pokémon

TYPE: GROUND

Hippopotas lives in a dry environment. Its body gives off sand instead of sweat, and this sandy shield keeps it protected from water and germs.

How to say it: HIP-poh-puh-TOSS

Height: 2' 07"
Weight: 109.1 lbs.

Possible Moves: Tackle, Sand Attack, Bite, Yawn, Take Down, Dig, Sand Tomb, Crunch, Earthquake, Double-Edge, Fissure

HIPPOWDON

Heavyweight Pokémon

REGIONS
KALOS (COASTAL), SINNOH

TYPE: GROUND

Hippowdon stores sand inside its body and expels it through the ports on its sides to create a twisting sandstorm in battle.

How to say it: hip-POW-don

Height: 6' 07"
Weight: 661.4 lbs.

Possible Moves: Ice Fang, Fire Fang, Thunder Fang, Tackle, Sand Attack, Bite, Yawn, Take Down, Dig, Sand Tomb, Crunch, Earthquake, Double-Edge, Fissure

HITMONCHAN

Punching Pokémon

REGION
KANTO

TYPE: FIGHTING

Hitmonchan has the fighting spirit of a world-class boxer. It's extremely driven and never gives up.

How to say it: HIT-mon-chan

Height: 4' 07"
Weight: 110.7 lbs.

Possible Moves: Revenge, Comet Punch, Agility, Pursuit, Mach Punch, Bullet Punch, Feint, Vacuum Wave, Quick Guard, Thunder Punch, Ice Punch, Fire Punch, Sky Uppercut, Mega Punch, Detect, Focus Punch, Counter, Close Combat

REGION
KANTO

HITMONLEE

Kicking Pokémon

TYPE: FIGHTING

Hitmonlee can extend its legs like springs to deliver kicks with tremendous force. It's always careful to stretch and loosen up after battle.

How to say it: HIT-mon-lee

Height: 4' 11"
Weight: 109.8 lbs.

Possible Moves: Revenge, Double Kick, Meditate, Rolling Kick, Jump Kick, Brick Break, Focus Energy, Feint, High Jump Kick, Mind Reader, Foresight, Wide Guard, Blaze Kick, Endure, Mega Kick, Close Combat, Reversal

REGION
JOHTO

HITMONTOP

Handstand Pokémon

TYPE: FIGHTING

Hitmontop's spinning kicks balance offense and defense. Walking is a less efficient mode of travel for it than spinning.

How to say it: HIT-mon-TOP

Height: 4' 07" **Weight:** 105.8 lbs.

Possible Moves: Revenge, Rolling Kick, Focus Energy, Pursuit, Quick Attack, Triple Kick, Rapid Spin, Counter, Feint, Agility, Gyro Ball, Wide Guard, Quick Guard, Detect, Close Combat, Endeavor

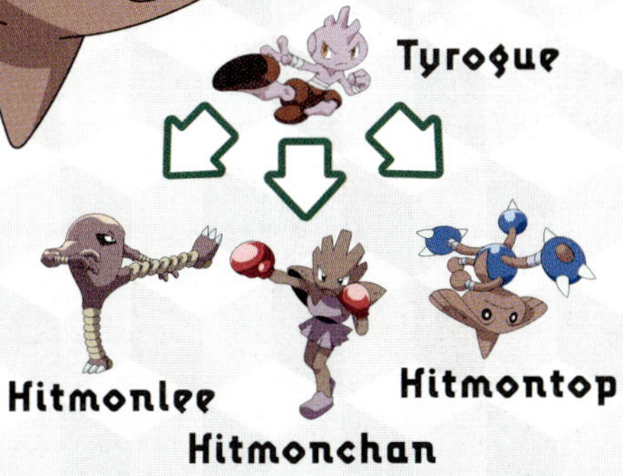

HO-OH

Rainbow Pokémon

REGION
JOHTO

LEGENDARY POKÉMON

TYPE: FIRE-FLYING

When Ho-Oh's feathers catch the light at different angles, they glow in a rainbow of colors. Legend says these feathers bring joy to whoever holds one.

How to say it: HOE-OH

Height: 12' 06"
Weight: 438.7 lbs.

Possible Moves: Whirlwind, Weather Ball, Gust, Brave Bird, Extrasensory, Sunny Day, Fire Blast, Sacred Fire, Punishment, Ancient Power, Safeguard, Recover, Future Sight, Natural Gift, Calm Mind, Sky Attack

Does not evolve

HONCHKROW

Big Boss Pokémon

REGIONS
KALOS (MOUNTAIN), SINNOH

TYPE: DARK-FLYING

When Honchkrow cries out in its deep voice, several Murkrow will appear to answer the call. Honchkrow is most active after dark.

How to say it: HONCH-krow

Height: 2' 11"
Weight: 60.2 lbs.

Possible Moves: Night Slash, Sucker Punch, Astonish, Pursuit, Haze, Wing Attack, Swagger, Nasty Plot, Foul Play, Quash, Dark Pulse

Murkrow → Honchkrow

HONEDGE

Sword Pokémon

REGION
KALOS (CENTRAL)

TYPE: STEEL-GHOST

Beware when approaching a Honedge! Those foolish enough to wield it like a sword will quickly find themselves wrapped in its blue cloth and drained of energy.

How to say it: HONE-ej

Height: 2' 07"
Weight: 4.4 lbs.

Possible Moves: Tackle, Swords Dance, Fury Cutter, Metal Sound, Pursuit, Autotomize, Shadow Sneak, Aerial Ace, Retaliate, Slash, Iron Defense, Night Slash, Power Trick, Iron Head, Sacred Sword

HOOTHOOT

Owl Pokémon

REGIONS
JOHTO, KALOS (MOUNTAIN)

TYPE: NORMAL-FLYING

Hoothoot has a special sense organ that allows it to track the rotation of the planet. It always starts to hoot at the same time of day, and this timing is so exact you could set your watch by it.

How to say it: HOOT-HOOT

Height: 2' 04" **Weight:** 46.7 lbs.

Possible Moves: Tackle, Growl, Foresight, Hypnosis, Peck, Uproar, Reflect, Confusion, Echoed Voice, Take Down, Air Slash, Zen Headbutt, Synchronoise, Extrasensory, Psycho Shift, Roost, Dream Eater

HOPPIP

Cottonweed Pokémon

REGIONS
JOHTO, KALOS (CENTRAL)

TYPE: GRASS-FLYING

Since Hoppip floats on the wind, it must cluster together with others to withstand strong gusts. Otherwise, it might be blown away!

How to say it: HOP-pip

Height: 1' 04"
Weight: 1.1 lbs.

Possible Moves: Splash, Synthesis, Tail Whip, Tackle, Fairy Wind, Poison Powder, Stun Spore, Sleep Powder, Bullet Seed, Leech Seed, Mega Drain, Acrobatics, Rage Powder, Cotton Spore, U-turn, Worry Seed, Giga Drain, Bounce, Memento

Hoppip → Skiploom → Jumpluff

HORSEA

Dragon Pokémon

REGIONS
KALOS (COASTAL), KANTO

TYPE: WATER

Horsea wraps its tail around solid objects on the seafloor to avoid being swept away in a strong current. When threatened, it spits a cloud of ink to cover its escape.

How to say it: HOR-see

Height: 1' 04" **Weight:** 17.6 lbs.

Possible Moves: Water Gun, Smokescreen, Leer, Bubble, Focus Energy, Bubble Beam, Agility, Twister, Brine, Hydro Pump, Dragon Dance, Dragon Pulse

Horsea → Seadra → Kingdra

HOUNDOOM

Dark Pokémon

REGIONS
JOHTO, KALOS (COASTAL)

TYPE: DARK-FIRE

Houndoom choose who will lead their pack by engaging in fierce battles. You can often identify a pack leader by its sharply angled horns.

How to say it: HOWN-doom

Height: 4' 07"
Weight: 77.2 lbs.

Possible Moves: Inferno, Nasty Plot, Thunder Fang, Leer, Ember, Howl, Smog, Roar, Bite, Odor Sleuth, Beat Up, Fire Fang, Feint Attack, Embargo, Foul Play, Flamethrower, Crunch

MEGA HOUNDOOM

Dark Pokémon

TYPE: DARK-FIRE

Height: 6' 03"
Weight: 109.1 lbs.

Houndour → Houndoom → Mega Houndoom

HOUNDOUR

Dark Pokémon

REGIONS
JOHTO, KALOS (COASTAL)

TYPE: DARK-FIRE

Houndour are known for their teamwork. They hunt in packs and use different kinds of cries to coordinate their group attacks.

How to say it: HOWN-dowr

Height: 2' 00"
Weight: 23.8 lbs.

Possible Moves: Leer, Ember, Howl, Smog, Roar, Bite, Odor Sleuth, Beat Up, Fire Fang, Feint Attack, Embargo, Foul Play, Flamethrower, Crunch, Nasty Plot, Inferno

Houndour Houndoom Mega Houndoom

HUNTAIL

Deep Sea Pokémon

REGIONS
HOENN, KALOS (COASTAL)

TYPE: WATER

Huntail lives in the darkest depths of the sea, so people didn't know about it for a long time. Its tail, which resembles a small creature, sometimes tricks others into attacking.

How to say it: HUN-tail

Height: 5' 07"
Weight: 59.5 lbs.

Possible Moves: Whirlpool, Bite, Screech, Water Pulse, Scary Face, Ice Fang, Brine, Baton Pass, Dive, Crunch, Aqua Tail, Hydro Pump

Clamperl Huntail

HYDREIGON

Brutal Pokémon

REGIONS
KALOS (MOUNTAIN), UNOVA

TYPE: DARK-DRAGON

The smaller heads on Hydreigon's arms don't have brains, but they can still eat. Any movement within its line of sight will be greeted with a frightening attack.

How to say it: hy-DRY-gahn

Height: 5' 11" **Weight:** 352.7 lbs.

Possible Moves: Outrage, Hyper Voice, Tri Attack, Dragon Rage, Focus Energy, Bite, Headbutt, Dragon Breath, Roar, Crunch, Slam, Dragon Pulse, Work Up, Dragon Rush, Body Slam, Scary Face

Deino Zweilous Hydreigon

HYPNO

Hypnosis Pokémon

REGION
KANTO

TYPE: PSYCHIC

As Hypno's pendulum swings and shines, anyone watching falls into a hypnotic trance. To enhance the effect, it always keeps the pendulum polished.

How to say it: HIP-no

Height: 5' 03" **Weight:** 166.7 lbs.

Possible Moves: Nightmare, Switcheroo, Pound, Hypnosis, Disable, Confusion, Headbutt, Poison Gas, Meditate, Psybeam, Psych Up, Synchronoise, Zen Headbutt, Swagger, Psychic, Nasty Plot, Psyshock, Future Sight

Drowzee Hypno

IGGLYBUFF

Balloon Pokémon

REGIONS
JOHTO, KALOS (MOUNTAIN)

TYPE: NORMAL-FAIRY

Before it evolves, Igglybuff's vocal cords are underdeveloped, and singing hurts its throat. Its soft, squishy body gives off a sweet, calming aroma.

How to say it: IG-lee-buff

Height: 1' 00"
Weight: 2.2 lbs.

Possible Moves: Sing, Charm, Defense Curl, Pound, Sweet Kiss, Copycat

Igglybuff Jigglypuff Wigglytuff

ILLUMISE

Firefly Pokémon

REGIONS
HOENN, KALOS (CENTRAL)

TYPE: BUG

Illumise gives off a sweet scent that attracts Volbeat by the dozen. Then, it directs the swarm in drawing patterns of light across the night sky.

How to say it: EE-loom-MEE-zay

Height: 2' 00"
Weight: 39.0 lbs.

Possible Moves: Tackle, Play Nice, Sweet Scent, Charm, Moonlight, Quick Attack, Wish, Encore, Flatter, Helping Hand, Zen Headbutt, Bug Buzz, Covet

Does not evolve

REGION
SINNOH

INFERNAPE

Flame Pokémon

TYPE: FIRE-FIGHTING

Swift and agile, Infernape puts all four of its limbs to use in its distinctive fighting style. The fire on its head mirrors the fire in its spirit.

How to say it: in-FER-nape

Height: 3' 11" **Weight:** 121.3 lbs.

Possible Moves: Scratch, Leer, Ember, Taunt, Mach Punch, Fury Swipes, Flame Wheel, Feint, Punishment, Close Combat, Fire Spin, Acrobatics, Calm Mind, Flare Blitz

Chimchar Monferno Infernape

INKAY

Revolving Pokémon

REGION
KALOS (COASTAL)

TYPE: DARK-PSYCHIC

The spots on Inkay's body emit a flashing light. This light confuses its opponents, giving it a chance to escape.

How to say it: in-kay

Height: 1' 04"
Weight: 7.7 lbs.

Possible Moves: Tackle, Peck, Constrict, Reflect, Foul Play, Swagger, Psywave, Topsy-Turvy, Hypnosis, Psybeam, Switcheroo, Payback, Light Screen, Pluck, Psycho Cut, Slash, Night Slash, Superpower

IVYSAUR

Seed Pokémon

REGIONS
KALOS (CENTRAL), KANTO

TYPE: GRASS-POISON

Carrying the weight of the bud on its back makes Ivysaur's legs stronger. When the bud is close to blooming, the Pokémon spends more time sleeping in the sun.

How to say it: EYE-vee-sore

Height: 3' 03" **Weight:** 28.7 lbs.

Possible Moves: Tackle, Growl, Leech Seed, Vine Whip, Poison Powder, Sleep Powder, Take Down, Razor Leaf, Sweet Scent, Growth, Double-Edge, Worry Seed, Synthesis, Solar Beam

JELLICENT

Floating Pokémon

TYPE: WATER-GHOST

Though most of its body is made of seawater, Jellicent should not be underestimated. Stories tell of a whole fleet of shipwrecks on the floor of its ocean home.

How to say it: JEL-ih-sent

Height: 7' 03"
Weight: 297.6 lbs.

Possible Moves: Bubble, Water Sport, Absorb, Night Shade, Bubble Beam, Recover, Water Pulse, Ominous Wind, Brine, Rain Dance, Hex, Hydro Pump, Wring Out, Water Spout

Male Form

Female Form

JIGGLYPUFF

Balloon Pokémon

TYPE: NORMAL-FAIRY

Jigglypuff's primary weapon is its song, which lulls opponents to sleep. Because it never stops to breathe while singing, long battles can put it in danger.

How to say it: JIG-lee-puff

Height: 1' 08" **Weight:** 12.1 lbs.

Possible Moves: Sing, Defense Curl, Pound, Play Nice, Disable, Round, Rollout, Double Slap, Rest, Body Slam, Gyro Ball, Wake-Up Slap, Mimic, Hyper Voice, Disarming Voice, Double-Edge

JIRACHI

Wish Pokémon

REGION
HOENN

MYTHICAL POKÉMON

TYPE: STEEL-PSYCHIC

According to myth, if you write your wish on one of the notes attached to Jirachi's head and then sing to it in a pure voice, the Pokémon will awaken from its thousand-year slumber and grant your wish.

How to say it: jer-AH-chi

Height: 1' 00" **Weight:** 2.4 lbs.

Possible Moves: Wish, Confusion, Rest, Swift, Helping Hand, Psychic, Refresh, Rest, Zen Headbutt, Double-Edge, Gravity, Healing Wish, Future Sight, Cosmic Power, Last Resort, Doom Desire

Does not evolve

JOLTEON

Lightning Pokémon

REGIONS
KALOS (COASTAL), KANTO

TYPE: ELECTRIC

Jolteon's fur carries a static charge, and its body generates electricity. It can channel this electricity during battle to call down a thunderbolt!

How to say it: JOL-tee-on

Height: 2' 07" **Weight:** 54.0 lbs.

Possible Moves: Helping Hand, Tackle, Tail Whip, Sand Attack, Thunder Shock, Quick Attack, Double Kick, Thunder Fang, Pin Missile, Agility, Thunder Wave, Discharge, Last Resort, Thunder

Eevee Jolteon

JOLTIK

Attaching Pokémon

REGION
UNOVA

TYPE: BUG-ELECTRIC

Joltik can't produce their own electricity, so they attach to larger Pokémon and suck up the static electricity given off. They store this energy in a special pouch.

How to say it: JOHL-tik

Height: 0' 04" **Weight:** 1.3 lbs.

Possible Moves: String Shot, Leech Life, Spider Web, Thunder Wave, Screech, Fury Cutter, Electroweb, Bug Bite, Gastro Acid, Slash, Electro Ball, Signal Beam, Agility, Sucker Punch, Discharge, Bug Buzz

Joltik Galvantula

JUMPLUFF
Cottonweed Pokémon

REGIONS
JOHTO, KALOS (CENTRAL)

TYPE: GRASS-FLYING

If Jumpluff hits a patch of cold air while it's drifting on the wind, it will return to the ground to await a warm breeze. The winds carry its fluffy body across the sea and around the world.

How to say it: JUM-pluff

Height: 2' 07"
Weight: 6.6 lbs.

Possible Moves: Splash, Synthesis, Tail Whip, Tackle, Fairy Wind, Poison Powder, Stun Spore, Sleep Powder, Bullet Seed, Leech Seed, Mega Drain, Acrobatics, Rage Powder, Cotton Spore, U-turn, Worry Seed, Giga Drain, Bounce, Memento

Hoppip → Skiploom → Jumpluff

JYNX
Human Shape Pokémon

REGIONS
KALOS (MOUNTAIN), KANTO

TYPE: ICE-PSYCHIC

Jynx has a hypnotic, rhythmic walk that makes it look like it's dancing. People who watch it move often find themselves dancing along.

How to say it: JINX

Height: 4' 07" **Weight:** 89.5 lbs.

Possible Moves: Draining Kiss, Perish Song, Pound, Lick, Lovely Kiss, Powder Snow, Double Slap, Ice Punch, Heart Stamp, Mean Look, Fake Tears, Wake-Up Slap, Avalanche, Body Slam, Wring Out, Blizzard

Smoochum → Jynx

REGION KANTO

KABUTO

Shellfish Pokémon

TYPE: ROCK-WATER

Kabuto has remained unchanged for three hundred million years. It was restored from a fossil, but every once in a while, a living specimen is discovered in the wild.

How to say it: kuh-BOO-toe

Height: 1' 08"
Weight: 25.4 lbs.

Possible Moves: Scratch, Harden, Absorb, Leer, Mud Shot, Sand Attack, Endure, Aqua Jet, Mega Drain, Metal Sound, Ancient Power, Wring Out

REGION KANTO

KABUTOPS

Shellfish Pokémon

TYPE: ROCK-WATER

Long ago, Kabutops swam through ancient seas in search of food. Its legs and gills are just beginning to adapt to a life on land.

How to say it: KA-boo-tops

Height: 4' 03"
Weight: 89.3 lbs.

Possible Moves: Feint, Scratch, Harden, Absorb, Leer, Mud Shot, Sand Attack, Endure, Aqua Jet, Mega Drain, Slash, Metal Sound, Ancient Power, Wring Out, Night Slash

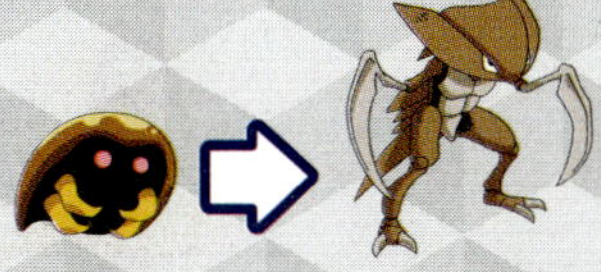

KADABRA

Psi Pokémon

REGIONS
KALOS (CENTRAL), KANTO

TYPE: PSYCHIC

The silver spoon Kadabra carries intensifies its brain waves. Only those with strong minds should attempt to train this Pokémon.

How to say it: kuh-DAH-bra

Height: 4' 03"   **Weight:** 124.6 lbs.

Possible Moves: Teleport, Kinesis, Confusion, Disable, Miracle Eye, Ally Switch, Psybeam, Reflect, Telekinesis, Recover, Psycho Cut, Role Play, Psychic, Future Sight, Trick

KAKUNA

Cocoon Pokémon

REGIONS
KALOS (CENTRAL), KANTO

TYPE: BUG-POISON

Kakuna appears motionless from the outside, but inside its shell, it's busily preparing to evolve. Sometimes the shell heats up from this activity.

How to say it: kah-KOO-na

Height: 2' 00"
Weight: 22.0 lbs.

Possible Move: Harden

REGIONS
KALOS (COASTAL), KANTO

KANGASKHAN

Parent Pokémon

TYPE: NORMAL

A little Kangaskhan playing on its own should be left alone. The Parent Pokémon always keeps careful watch and will attack any aggressor.

How to say it: KANG-gas-con

Height: 7' 03"
Weight: 176.4 lbs.

Possible Moves: Comet Punch, Leer, Fake Out, Tail Whip, Bite, Double Hit, Rage, Mega Punch, Chip Away, Dizzy Punch, Crunch, Endure, Outrage, Sucker Punch, Reversal

MEGA KANGASKHAN

Parent Pokémon

TYPE: NORMAL

Height: 7' 03"
Weight: 220.5 lbs.

Kangaskhan Mega Kangaskhan

KARRABLAST

Clamping Pokémon

REGIONS
KALOS (MOUNTAIN), UNOVA

TYPE: BUG

Karrablast often attack Shelmet, trying to steal their shells. When electrical energy envelops them at the same time, they both evolve.

How to say it: KAIR-ruh-blast

Height: 1' 08"
Weight: 13.0 lbs.

Possible Moves: Peck, Leer, Endure, Fury Cutter, Fury Attack, Headbutt, False Swipe, Bug Buzz, Slash, Take Down, Scary Face, X-Scissor, Flail, Swords Dance, Double-Edge

Karrablast → Escavalier

KECLEON

Color Swap Pokémon

REGIONS
HOENN, KALOS (CENTRAL)

TYPE: NORMAL

Kecleon is a master of camouflage and can change the color of its skin to hide in any environment. However, its zigzag pattern is always the same.

How to say it: KEH-clee-on

Height: 3' 03" **Weight:** 48.5 lbs.

Possible Moves: Synchronoise, Ancient Power, Thief, Tail Whip, Astonish, Lick, Scratch, Bind, Feint Attack, Fury Swipes, Feint, Psybeam, Shadow Sneak, Slash, Screech, Substitute, Sucker Punch, Shadow Claw

Does not evolve

MYTHICAL POKÉMON

REGION
UNOVA

KELDEO

Colt Pokémon

Ordinary Forme

Resolute Forme

TYPE: WATER-FIGHTING

Keldeo travels the world visiting beaches and riverbanks, where it can race across the water. When this Mythical Pokémon is filled with resolve, it gains a blinding speed.

How to say it: KELL-dee-oh

Height: 4' 07" **Weight:** 106.9 lbs.

Possible Moves: Aqua Jet, Leer, Double Kick, Bubble Beam, Take Down, Helping Hand, Retaliate, Aqua Tail, Sacred Sword, Swords Dance, Quick Guard, Work Up, Hydro Pump, Close Combat

Does not evolve

KINGDRA

Dragon Pokémon

REGIONS
JOHTO, KALOS (COASTAL)

TYPE: WATER-DRAGON

Kingdra makes its home so deep in the ocean that nothing else lives there. Some people think its yawn influences the currents.

How to say it: KING-dra

Height: 5' 11"
Weight: 335.1 lbs.

Possible Moves: Dragon Pulse, Yawn, Water Gun, Smokescreen, Leer, Bubble, Focus Energy, Bubble Beam, Agility, Twister, Brine, Hydro Pump, Dragon Dance

KINGLER

Pincer Pokémon

REGION
KANTO

TYPE: WATER

When one Kingler waves to another with its giant claw, it's sending a message. They can't hold long conversations this way, though, because waving those heavy claws is tiring.

How to say it: KING-ler

Height: 4' 03" **Weight:** 132.3 lbs.

Possible Moves: Wide Guard, Mud Sport, Bubble, Vice Grip, Leer, Harden, Bubble Beam, Mud Shot, Metal Claw, Stomp, Protect, Guillotine, Slam, Brine, Crabhammer, Flail

KIRLIA

Emotion Pokémon

REGIONS
HOENN, KALOS (CENTRAL)

TYPE: PSYCHIC-FAIRY

A Kirlia whose Trainer has a positive attitude develops a shining beauty. When this Pokémon uses its psychic powers, strange mirages surround it.

How to say it: KERL-lee-ah

Height: 2' 07" **Weight:** 44.5 lbs.

Possible Moves: Growl, Confusion, Double Team, Teleport, Lucky Chant, Magical Leaf, Heal Pulse, Calm Mind, Psychic, Imprison, Future Sight, Charm, Hypnosis, Dream Eater, Stored Power

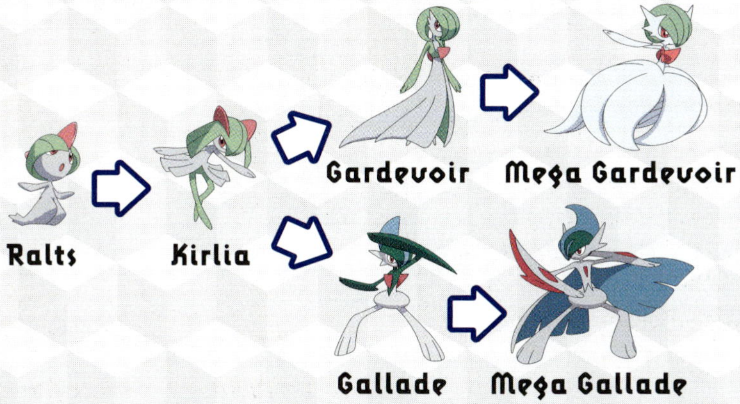

KLANG
Gear Pokémon

REGION
UNOVA

TYPE: STEEL

Klang's body is made up of one mini-gear and one bigger gear, which change their rotation to communicate with other Klang. It can shoot the mini-gear at an opponent in battle.

How to say it: KLANG

Height: 2' 00"
Weight: 112.4 lbs.

Possible Moves: Vice Grip, Charge, Thunder Shock, Gear Grind, Bind, Charge Beam, Autotomize, Mirror Shot, Screech, Discharge, Metal Sound, Shift Gear, Lock-On, Zap Cannon, Hyper Beam

Klink → Klang → Klinklang

KLEFKI
Key Ring Pokémon

REGION
KALOS (MOUNTAIN)

TYPE: STEEL-FAIRY

To keep valuables locked up tight, give the key to a Klefki. This Pokémon loves to collect keys, and it will guard its collection with all its might.

How to say it: KLEF-key

Height: 0' 08" **Weight:** 6.6 lbs.

Possible Moves: Fairy Lock, Tackle, Fairy Wind, Astonish, Metal Sound, Spikes, Draining Kiss, Crafty Shield, Foul Play, Torment, Mirror Shot, Imprison, Recycle, Play Rough, Magic Room, Heal Block

Does not evolve

TYPE: STEEL

The two mini-gears that make up Klink's body are meant for each other. If they get separated, they won't mesh with any other mini-gear until they find each other again.

How to say it: KLEENK

Height: 1' 00"
Weight: 46.3 lbs.

Possible Moves: Vice Grip, Charge, Thunder Shock, Gear Grind, Bind, Charge Beam, Autotomize, Mirror Shot, Screech, Discharge, Metal Sound, Shift Gear, Lock-On, Zap Cannon, Hyper Beam

REGION UNOVA

KLINK

Gear Pokémon

TYPE: STEEL

Klinklang stores energy in its red core and charges itself up by spinning that gear rapidly. It can shoot the energy from the spikes on its outer ring.

How to say it: KLEENK-klang

Height: 2' 00"
Weight: 178.6 lbs.

Possible Moves: Vice Grip, Charge, Thunder Shock, Gear Grind, Bind, Charge Beam, Autotomize, Mirror Shot, Screech, Discharge, Metal Sound, Shift Gear, Lock-On, Zap Cannon, Hyper Beam

REGION UNOVA

KLINKLANG

Gear Pokémon

KOFFING

Poison Gas Pokémon

REGION
KANTO

TYPE: POISON

The gases that fill Koffing's body are extremely toxic. When it's under attack, it releases this poisonous gas from jets on its surface.

How to say it: CAWF-ing

Height: 2' 00"
Weight: 2.2 lbs.

Possible Moves: Poison Gas, Tackle, Smog, Smokescreen, Assurance, Clear Smog, Self-Destruct, Sludge, Haze, Gyro Ball, Explosion, Sludge Bomb, Destiny Bond, Memento

Koffing → Weezing

KRABBY

River Crab Pokémon

REGION
KANTO

TYPE: WATER

Krabby dig holes in sandy beaches to make their homes. When the food supply is limited, they sometimes fight over territory.

How to say it: CRA-bee

Height: 1' 04"
Weight: 614.3 lbs.

Possible Moves: Mud Sport, Bubble, Vice Grip, Leer, Harden, Bubble Beam, Mud Shot, Metal Claw, Stomp, Protect, Guillotine, Slam, Brine, Crabhammer, Flail

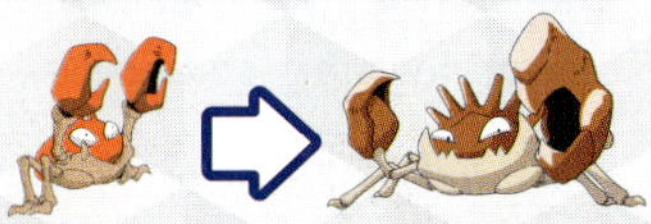

Krabby → Kingler

REGION
SINNOH

KRICKETOT

Cricket Pokémon

TYPE: BUG

The sound of Kricketot's antennae knocking together resembles the sound of a xylophone. They use these sounds to communicate.

How to say it: KRICK-eh-tot

Height: 1' 00" **Weight:** 4.9 lbs.

Possible Moves: Growl, Bide, Struggle Bug, Bug Bite

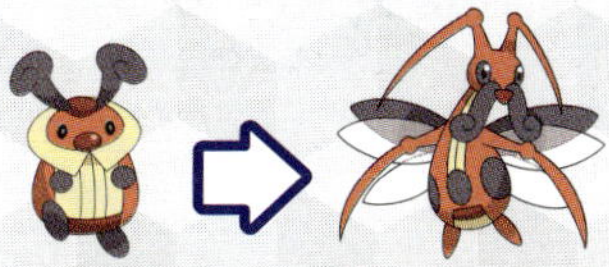

Kricketot Kricketune

REGION
SINNOH

KRICKETUNE

Cricket Pokémon

TYPE: BUG

Kricketune composes many different melodies that reflect its emotional state. Researchers are trying to determine whether the patterns of its music have a deeper meaning.

How to say it: KRICK-eh-toon

Height: 3' 03" **Weight:** 56.2 lbs.

Possible Moves: Growl, Bide, Fury Cutter, Leech Life, Sing, Focus Energy, Slash, X-Scissor, Screech, Taunt, Night Slash, Bug Buzz, Perish Song

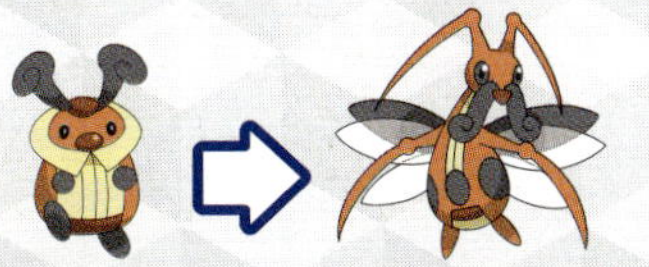

Kricketot Kricketune

KROKOROK

Desert Croc Pokémon

REGIONS
KALOS (COASTAL), UNOVA

TYPE: GROUND-DARK

The membranes that cover Krokorok's eyes not only protect them during sandstorms, but also act like heat sensors, enabling it to navigate in total darkness.

How to say it: KRAHK-oh-rahk

Height: 3' 03" **Weight:** 73.6 lbs.

Possible Moves: Leer, Rage, Bite, Sand Attack, Torment, Sand Tomb, Assurance, Mud-Slap, Embargo, Swagger, Crunch, Dig, Scary Face, Foul Play, Sandstorm, Earthquake, Thrash

KROOKODILE

Intimidation Pokémon

REGIONS
KALOS (COASTAL), UNOVA

TYPE: GROUND-DARK

Krookodile's formidable jaws are capable of crunching up cars. Triggered into violence by nearby movement, Krookodile will clamp onto its prey with all the might of those jaws.

How to say it: KROOK-oh-dyle

Height: 4' 11" **Weight:** 212.3 lbs.

Possible Moves: Outrage, Leer, Rage, Bite, Sand Attack, Torment, Sand Tomb, Assurance, Mud-Slap, Embargo, Swagger, Crunch, Dig, Scary Face, Foul Play, Sandstorm, Earthquake

LEGENDARY POKÉMON

REGION
HOENN

KYOGRE

Sea Basin Pokémon

TYPE: WATER

Legends say that Kyogre is the sea personified. When it channels the full power of nature, it can raise sea levels with mighty storms. This Pokémon often clashes with Groudon.

How to say it: kai-OH-gurr

Height: 14' 09"
Weight: 776.0 lbs.

Possible Moves: Water Pulse, Scary Face, Body Slam, Muddy Water, Aqua Ring, Ice Beam, Ancient Power, Water Spout, Calm Mind, Aqua Tail, Sheer Cold, Double-Edge, Hydro Pump

PRIMAL KYOGRE

Sea Basin Pokémon

TYPE: WATER

Height: 32' 02"
Weight: 948.0 lbs.

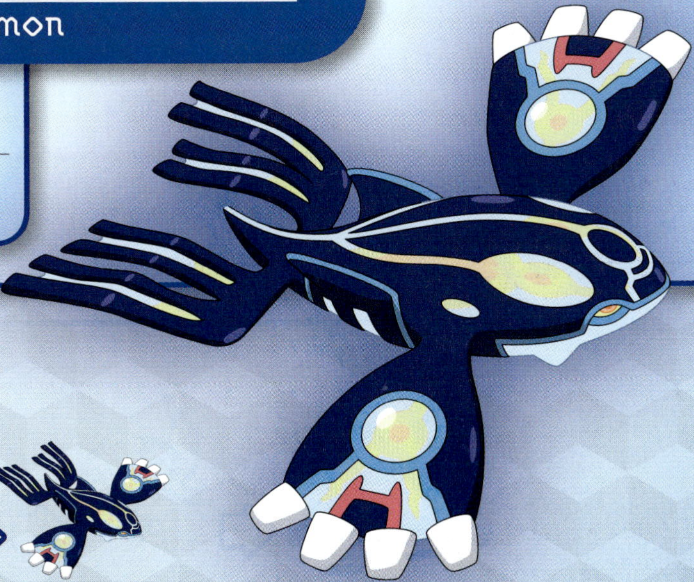

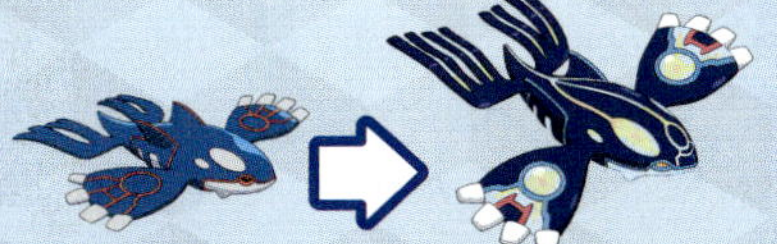

Kyogre   Primal Kyogre

KYUREM

Boundary Pokémon

REGION
UNOVA

LEGENDARY POKÉMON

Black Kyurem

White Kyurem

TYPE: DRAGON-ICE

When the freezing energy inside Kyurem leaked out, its entire body froze. Legends say it will become whole with the help of a hero who will bring truth or ideals.

How to say it: KYOO-rem

Height: 9' 10" **Weight:** 716.5 lbs.

Possible Moves: Icy Wind, Dragon Rage, Imprison, Ancient Power, Ice Beam, Dragon Breath, Slash, Scary Face, Glaciate, Dragon Pulse, Imprison, Endeavor, Blizzard, Outrage, Hyper Voice

Does not evolve

REGIONS
HOENN, KALOS (MOUNTAIN)

LAIRON

Iron Armor Pokémon

TYPE: STEEL-ROCK

Lairon lives near tasty, mineral-rich springs, where it tempers its body with iron from the water and rocks. It sometimes comes into conflict with miners going after the same iron ore it uses as a food source.

How to say it: LAIR-ron

Height: 2' 11"
Weight: 264.6 lbs.

Possible Moves: Tackle, Harden, Mud-Slap, Headbutt, Metal Claw, Iron Defense, Roar, Take Down, Iron Head, Protect, Metal Sound, Iron Tail, Autotomize, Heavy Slam, Double-Edge, Metal Burst

Aron → Lairon → Aggron → Mega Aggron

REGIONS
KALOS (MOUNTAIN), UNOVA

LAMPENT

Lamp Pokémon

TYPE: GHOST-FIRE

Lampent tends to lurk grimly around hospitals, waiting for someone to take a bad turn so it can absorb the departing spirit. The stolen spirits keep its fire burning.

How to say it: LAM-pent

Height: 2' 00" **Weight:** 28.7 lbs.

Possible Moves: Ember, Astonish, Minimize, Smog, Fire Spin, Confuse Ray, Night Shade, Will-O-Wisp, Flame Burst, Imprison, Hex, Memento, Inferno, Curse, Shadow Ball, Pain Split, Overheat

Litwick → Lampent → Chandelure

LANDORUS

Abundance Pokémon

REGION
UNOVA

LEGENDARY POKÉMON

TYPE: GROUND-FLYING

Because its arrival helps crops grow, Landorus is welcomed as "the Guardian of the Fields." This Legendary Pokémon uses the energy of wind and lightning to enrich the soil.

How to say it: LAN-duh-rus

Height: 4' 11" **Weight:** 149.9 lbs.

Possible Moves: Block, Mud Shot, Rock Tomb, Imprison, Punishment, Bulldoze, Rock Throw, Extrasensory, Swords Dance, Earth Power, Rock Slide, Earthquake, Sandstorm, Fissure, Stone Edge, Hammer Arm, Outrage

Does not evolve

REGIONS
JOHTO, KALOS (COASTAL)

LANTURN

Light Pokémon

TYPE: WATER-ELECTRIC

Lanturn's antenna produces a light bright enough to be seen from the surface when it's swimming deep in the ocean. Its nickname is "the Deep-sea Star."

How to say it: LAN-turn

Height: 3' 11" **Weight:** 49.6 lbs.

Possible Moves: Eerie Impulse, Water Gun, Supersonic, Thunder Wave, Flail, Bubble, Confuse Ray, Spark, Take Down, Stockpile, Swallow, Spit Up, Electro Ball, Bubble Beam, Signal Beam, Discharge, Aqua Ring, Hydro Pump, Ion Deluge, Charge

Chinchou → Lanturn

REGIONS
KALOS (COASTAL), KANTO

LAPRAS

Transport Pokémon

TYPE: WATER-ICE

When a Lapras sings a sad song at twilight, it's said to be looking for other Lapras. Because of human activity, these Pokémon are growing more rare.

How to say it: LAP-rus

Height: 8' 02" **Weight:** 485.0 lbs.

Possible Moves: Sing, Growl, Water Gun, Mist, Confuse Ray, Ice Shard, Water Pulse, Body Slam, Rain Dance, Perish Song, Ice Beam, Brine, Safeguard, Hydro Pump, Sheer Cold

Does not evolve

LARVESTA

Torch Pokémon

REGION
UNOVA

TYPE: BUG-FIRE

From its five horns, Larvesta sends out flames to keep attackers at bay. When it's ready to evolve, it spins a fiery cocoon.

How to say it: lar-VESS-tuh

Height: 3' 07"
Weight: 63.5 lbs.

Possible Moves: Ember, String Shot, Leech Life, Take Down, Flame Charge, Bug Bite, Double-Edge, Flame Wheel, Bug Buzz, Amnesia, Thrash, Flare Blitz

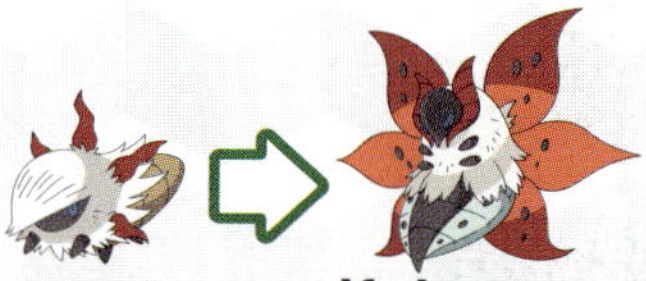

Larvesta → Volcarona

LARVITAR

Rock Skin Pokémon

REGIONS
JOHTO, KALOS (MOUNTAIN)

TYPE: ROCK-GROUND

Larvitar hatches from an egg buried deep underground. It has to eat its way to the surface by devouring the soil above it.

How to say it: LAR-vuh-tar

Height: 2' 00" **Weight:** 158.7 lbs.

Possible Moves: Bite, Leer, Sandstorm, Screech, Chip Away, Rock Slide, Scary Face, Thrash, Dark Pulse, Payback, Crunch, Earthquake, Stone Edge, Hyper Beam

Larvitar → Pupitar → Tyranitar → Mega Tyranitar

LEGENDARY POKÉMON

REGION
HOENN

LATIAS
Eon Pokémon

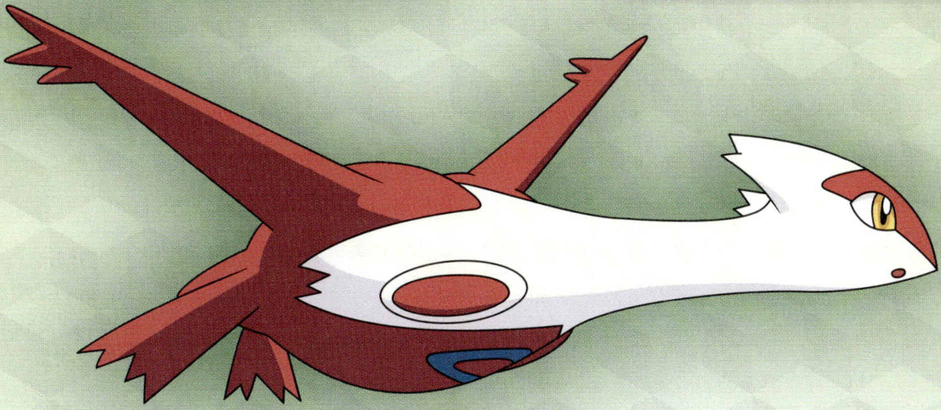

TYPE: DRAGON-PSYCHIC

Sensitive and intelligent, Latias can pick up on people's emotions and understand what they're saying. The down that covers its body can refract light to change its appearance.

How to say it: LAT-ee-ahs

Height: 4' 07" **Weight:** 88.2 lbs.

Possible Moves: Psywave, Wish, Helping Hand, Safeguard, Dragon Breath, Water Sport, Refresh, Mist Ball, Zen Headbutt, Recover, Psycho Shift, Charm, Psychic, Heal Pulse, Reflect Type, Guard Split, Dragon Pulse, Healing Wish

MEGA LATIAS
Eon Pokémon

TYPE: DRAGON-PSYCHIC

Height: 5' 11"
Weight: 114.6 lbs.

LATIOS

Eon Pokémon

REGION
HOENN

LEGENDARY POKÉMON

TYPE: DRAGON-PSYCHIC

Latios can project images into someone else's mind to share information. When it folds its forelegs back against its body, it could beat a jet plane in a race through the sky.

How to say it: LAT-ee-ose

Height: 6' 07" **Weight:** 132.3 lbs.

Possible Moves: Psywave, Heal Block, Helping Hand, Safeguard, Dragon Breath, Protect, Refresh, Luster Purge, Zen Headbutt, Recover, Psycho Shift, Dragon Dance, Psychic, Heal Pulse, Telekinesis, Power Split, Dragon Pulse, Memento

MEGA LATIOS

Eon Pokémon

TYPE: DRAGON-PSYCHIC

Height: 7' 07"
Weight: 154.3 lbs.

Latios Mega Latios

LEAFEON

Verdant Pokémon

REGIONS
KALOS (COASTAL), SINNOH

TYPE: GRASS

When Leafeon soaks up the sun for use in photosynthesis, it gives off clean, fresh air. It often takes naps in a sunny area to gather energy.

How to say it: LEAF-ee-on

Height: 3' 03"
Weight: 56.2 lbs.

Possible Moves: Tail Whip, Tackle, Helping Hand, Sand Attack, Razor Leaf, Quick Attack, Grass Whistle, Magical Leaf, Giga Drain, Swords Dance, Synthesis, Sunny Day, Last Resort, Leaf Blade

Eevee → Leafeon

LEAVANNY

Nurturing Pokémon

REGION
UNOVA

TYPE: BUG-GRASS

Leavanny loves to make warm clothes for smaller Pokémon, cutting up leaves with its arms and sewing them together with sticky silk from its mouth.

How to say it: lee-VAN-nee

Height: 3' 11" **Weight:** 45.2 lbs.

Possible Moves: False Swipe, Tackle, String Shot, Bug Bite, Razor Leaf, Struggle Bug, Slash, Helping Hand, Leaf Blade, X-Scissor, Entrainment, Swords Dance, Leaf Storm

Sewaddle → Swadloon → Leavanny

LEDIAN

Five Star Pokémon

REGIONS
JOHTO, KALOS (CENTRAL)

TYPE: BUG-FLYING

Ledian channels starlight for use as an energy source. Where the sky is clear and the stars shine bright, these Pokémon gather in large numbers.

How to say it: LEH-dee-an

Height: 4' 07"
Weight: 78.5 lbs.

Possible Moves: Tackle, Supersonic, Comet Punch, Light Screen, Reflect, Safeguard, Mach Punch, Baton Pass, Silver Wind, Agility, Swift, Double-Edge, Bug Buzz

LEDYBA

Five Star Pokémon

REGIONS
JOHTO, KALOS (CENTRAL)

TYPE: BUG-FLYING

Ledyba gives off a fragrant fluid that it uses to communicate with others. It changes the scent to indicate its emotions.

How to say it: LEH-dee-bah

Height: 3' 03" **Weight:** 23.8 lbs.

Possible Moves: Tackle, Supersonic, Comet Punch, Light Screen, Reflect, Safeguard, Mach Punch, Baton Pass, Silver Wind, Agility, Swift, Double-Edge, Bug Buzz

REGIONS
KALOS (MOUNTAIN), SINNOH

LICKILICKY

Licking Pokémon

TYPE: NORMAL

Lickilicky can make its long tongue even longer, stretching it out to wrap around food or foe. Its drool causes a lasting numbness.

How to say it: LICK-ee-LICK-ee

Height: 5' 07"
Weight: 308.6 lbs.

Possible Moves: Wring Out, Power Whip, Lick, Supersonic, Defense Curl, Knock Off, Wrap, Stomp, Disable, Slam, Rollout, Chip Away, Me First, Refresh, Screech, Gyro Ball

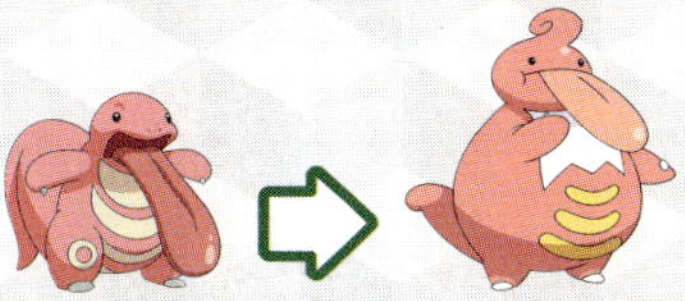

Lickitung → Lickilicky

TYPE: NORMAL

Lickitung learns about new things by licking them to discover their taste and texture. Sour tastes are not its favorite.

How to say it: LICK-it-tung

Height: 3' 11"
Weight: 144.4 lbs.

Possible Moves: Lick, Supersonic, Defense Curl, Knock Off, Wrap, Stomp, Disable, Slam, Rollout, Chip Away, Me First, Refresh, Screech, Power Whip, Wring Out

REGIONS
KALOS (MOUNTAIN), KANTO

LICKITUNG

Licking Pokémon

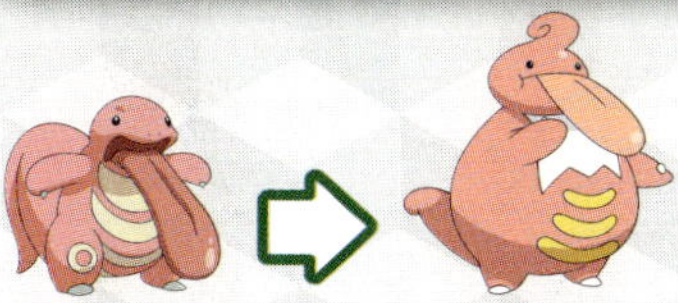

Lickitung → Lickilicky

LIEPARD

Cruel Pokémon

REGIONS
KALOS (MOUNTAIN), UNOVA

TYPE: DARK

Elegant and swift, Liepard can move through the night without a sound. It uses this stealth to execute sneak attacks.

How to say it: LY-purd

Height: 3' 07"
Weight: 82.7 lbs.

Possible Moves: Scratch, Growl, Assist, Sand Attack, Fury Swipes, Pursuit, Torment, Fake Out, Hone Claws, Assurance, Slash, Taunt, Night Slash, Snatch, Nasty Plot, Sucker Punch, Play Rough

Purrloin → Liepard

LILEEP

Sea Lily Pokémon

REGION
HOENN

TYPE: ROCK-GRASS

Lileep clings to a rock at the bottom of the sea and uses its tentacles to catch food. It was restored from a fossil.

How to say it: lil-LEEP

Height: 3' 03" **Weight:** 52.5 lbs.

Possible Moves: Astonish, Constrict, Acid, Ingrain, Confuse Ray, Amnesia, Gastro Acid, Ancient Power, Energy Ball, Stockpile, Spit Up, Swallow, Wring Out

Lileep → Cradily

REGION
UNOVA

LILLIGANT

Flowering Pokémon

TYPE: GRASS

Unless Lilligant gets just the right kind of care, it will wither and refuse to bloom. The blossom is so beautiful and fragrant that many Trainers decide they're up for the challenge.

How to say it: LIL-lih-gunt

Height: 3' 07"
Weight: 35.9 lbs.

Possible Moves: Growth, Leech Seed, Mega Drain, Synthesis, Teeter Dance, Quiver Dance, Petal Dance

Petilil Lilligant

REGION
UNOVA

LILLIPUP

Puppy Pokémon

TYPE: NORMAL

Lillipup doesn't let its courage override its intelligence when it comes to battling stronger opponents. With the sensitive hair around its face, it can pick up on slight movements nearby.

How to say it: LIL-ee-pup

Height: 1' 04"
Weight: 9.0 lbs.

Possible Moves: Leer, Tackle, Odor Sleuth, Bite, Helping Hand, Take Down, Work Up, Crunch, Roar, Retaliate, Reversal, Last Resort, Giga Impact

Lillipup Herdier Stoutland

LINOONE

Rushing Pokémon

REGIONS
HOENN, KALOS (CENTRAL)

TYPE: NORMAL

Because Linoone can only run in straight lines, curving roads pose quite a navigation problem. It charges ahead at top speed when hunting.

How to say it: line-NOON

Height: 1' 08"
Weight: 71.6 lbs.

Possible Moves:
Play Rough, Rototiller, Switcheroo, Tackle, Growl, Tail Whip, Headbutt, Sand Attack, Odor Sleuth, Mud Sport, Fury Swipes, Covet, Bestow, Slash, Rest, Belly Drum, Fling

LITLEO

Lion Cub Pokémon

REGION
KALOS (CENTRAL)

TYPE: FIRE-NORMAL

When Litleo is ready to get stronger, it leaves its pride to live alone. During a battle, its mane radiates intense heat.

How to say it: LIT-lee-oh

Height: 2' 00"
Weight: 29.8 lbs.

Possible Moves: Tackle, Leer, Ember, Work Up, Headbutt, Noble Roar, Take Down, Fire Fang, Endeavor, Echoed Voice, Flamethrower, Crunch, Hyper Voice, Incinerate, Overheat

LITWICK
Candle Pokémon

REGIONS
KALOS (MOUNTAIN), UNOVA

TYPE: GHOST-FIRE

Litwick pretends to guide people and Pokémon with its light, but following it is a bad idea. The ghostly flame absorbs life energy for use as fuel.

How to say it: LIT-wik

Height: 1' 00" **Weight:** 6.8 lbs.

Possible Moves: Ember, Astonish, Minimize, Smog, Fire Spin, Confuse Ray, Night Shade, Will-O-Wisp, Flame Burst, Imprison, Hex, Memento, Inferno, Curse, Shadow Ball, Pain Split, Overheat

Litwick Lampent Chandelure

LOMBRE
Jolly Pokémon

REGIONS
HOENN, KALOS (MOUNTAIN)

TYPE: WATER-GRASS

When the mischievous Lombre spots someone fishing, it swims up to tug on the line. The film that covers its body is unpleasantly slimy to the touch.

How to say it: LOM-brey

Height: 3' 11" **Weight:** 71.6 lbs.

Possible Moves: Astonish, Growl, Absorb, Nature Power, Fake Out, Fury Swipes, Water Sport, Bubble Beam, Zen Headbutt, Uproar, Hydro Pump

Lotad Lombre Ludicolo

LOPUNNY
Rabbit Pokémon

REGION
SINNOH

TYPE: NORMAL

Because its ears are quite fragile, Lopunny reacts to any rough touch with a kick. If it detects a threat, it leaps away.

How to say it: LAH-puh-nee

Height: 3' 11"
Weight: 73.4 lbs.

Possible Moves: Mirror Coat, Magic Coat, Splash, Pound, Defense Curl, Foresight, Endure, Return, Quick Attack, Jump Kick, Baton Pass, Agility, Dizzy Punch, After You, Charm, Entrainment, Bounce, Healing Wish

MEGA LOPUNNY
Caring Pokémon

TYPE: NORMAL

Height: 4' 03"
Weight: 62.4 lbs.

REGIONS
HOENN,
KALOS
(MOUNTAIN)

LOTAD
Water Weed Pokémon

TYPE: WATER-GRASS

The leaf on Lotad's head is too big and heavy for it to carry on land, so it floats on the surface of the water.

How to say it: LOW-tad

Height: 1' 08"
Weight: 5.7 lbs.

Possible Moves: Astonish, Growl, Absorb, Nature Power, Mist, Natural Gift, Mega Drain, Bubble Beam, Zen Headbutt, Rain Dance, Energy Ball

REGIONS
HOENN,
KALOS
(CENTRAL)

LOUDRED
Big Voice Pokémon

TYPE: NORMAL

Loudred shouts at such volume that it temporarily deafens itself. The sound waves it produces can knock down a wooden house.

How to say it: LOUD-red

Height: 3' 03" **Weight:** 89.3 lbs.

Possible Moves: Pound, Uproar, Astonish, Howl, Bite, Supersonic, Stomp, Screech, Roar, Synchronoise, Rest, Sleep Talk, Hyper Voice

LUCARIO

Aura Pokémon

REGIONS
KALOS (CENTRAL), SINNOH

TYPE: FIGHTING-STEEL

Sensing the auras that all beings emanate allows Lucario to read minds and predict movements. Lucario is also very sensitive to others' emotions.

How to say it: loo-CAR-ee-oh

Height: 3' 11"
Weight: 119.0 lbs.

Possible Moves: Extreme Speed, Dragon Pulse, Close Combat, Aura Sphere, Foresight, Quick Attack, Detect, Metal Claw, Counter, Feint, Power-Up Punch, Swords Dance, Metal Sound, Bone Rush, Quick Guard, Me First, Calm Mind, Heal Pulse

MEGA LUCARIO

Aura Pokémon

TYPE: FIGHTING-STEEL

Height: 4' 03"
Weight: 126.8 lbs.

Riolu → Lucario → Mega Lucario

LUDICOLO

Carefree Pokémon

TYPE: WATER-GRASS

Ludicolo just can't help leaping into a joyful dance when it hears a festive tune. Children who sing while hiking often attract its attention.

How to say it: LOO-dee-KO-low

Height: 4' 11" **Weight:** 121.3 lbs.

Possible Moves: Astonish, Growl, Mega Drain, Nature Power

LUGIA
Diving Pokémon

REGION
JOHTO

LEGENDARY POKÉMON

TYPE: PSYCHIC-FLYING

Lugia can knock down a house with one flutter of its enormously powerful wings. For the safety of others, this Legendary Pokémon lives at the bottom of the sea.

How to say it: LOO-gee-uh

Height: 17' 01" **Weight:** 476.2 lbs.

Possible Moves: Whirlwind, Weather Ball, Gust, Dragon Rush, Extrasensory, Rain Dance, Hydro Pump, Aeroblast, Punishment, Ancient Power, Safeguard, Recover, Future Sight, Natural Gift, Calm Mind, Sky Attack

Does not evolve

LUMINEON

Neon Pokémon

REGION
SINNOH

TYPE: WATER

Lumineon lives at the bottom of the deep blue sea. The patterns on its tail give off light, and it can use its front fins to crawl along the sand unnoticed.

How to say it: loo-MIN-ee-onn

Height: 3' 11"
Weight: 52.9 lbs.

Possible Moves: Pound, Water Gun, Attract, Rain Dance, Gust, Water Pulse, Captivate, Safeguard, Aqua Ring, Whirlpool, U-turn, Bounce, Silver Wind, Soak

Finneon Lumineon

LUNATONE

Meteorite Pokémon

REGIONS
HOENN, KALOS (COASTAL)

TYPE: ROCK-PSYCHIC

People think Lunatone came from space because it was first discovered near a meteorite. It floats to get around instead of walking, and its red eyes can freeze a foe with fear.

How to say it: LOO-nuh-tone

Height: 3' 03"
Weight: 370.4 lbs.

Possible Moves: Magic Room, Rock Throw, Tackle, Harden, Confusion, Hypnosis, Rock Polish, Psywave, Embargo, Rock Slide, Cosmic Power, Psychic, Heal Block, Stone Edge, Future Sight, Explosion, Moonblast

Does not evolve

LUVDISC

Rendezvous Pokémon

REGIONS
HOENN, KALOS (COASTAL)

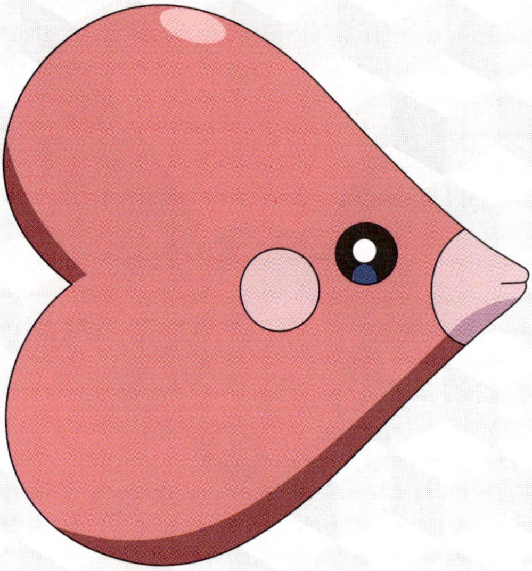

TYPE: WATER

Because of its pink, heart-shaped body and its habit of swimming around affectionate couples in shallow tropical seas, Luvdisc is considered a symbol of romance.

How to say it: LOVE-disk

Height: 2' 00"
Weight: 19.2 lbs.

Possible Moves: Tackle, Charm, Water Gun, Agility, Take Down, Lucky Chant, Water Pulse, Attract, Flail, Sweet Kiss, Hydro Pump, Aqua Ring, Captivate, Safeguard

Does not evolve

LUXIO

Spark Pokémon

REGION
SINNOH

TYPE: ELECTRIC

A powerful electric current arcs between Luxio's claws, making it a dangerous opponent in battle. They form small groups and live together.

How to say it: LUCKS-ee-oh

Height: 2' 11"
Weight: 67.2 lbs.

Possible Moves: Tackle, Leer, Charge, Spark, Bite, Roar, Swagger, Thunder Fang, Crunch, Scary Face, Discharge

REGION
SINNOH

LUXRAY

Gleam Eyes Pokémon

TYPE: ELECTRIC

Luxray's gleaming golden eyes can see right through solid objects. This is very useful when it's keeping watch for approaching threats or looking for food.

How to say it: LUCKS-ray

Height: 4' 07" **Weight:** 92.6 lbs.

Possible Moves: Tackle, Leer, Charge, Spark, Bite, Roar, Swagger, Thunder Fang, Crunch, Scary Face, Discharge, Wild Charge

MACHAMP

Superpower Pokémon

REGIONS
KALOS (COASTAL), KANTO

TYPE: FIGHTING

Though it is a master of martial arts, Machamp sometimes gets its four arms tangled up when trying to do more intricate tasks.

How to say it: muh-CHAMP

Height: 5' 03"
Weight: 286.6 lbs.

Possible Moves: Wide Guard, Low Kick, Leer, Focus Energy, Karate Chop, Low Sweep, Foresight, Seismic Toss, Revenge, Vital Throw, Submission, Wake-Up Slap, Cross Chop, Scary Face, Dynamic Punch

Machop Machoke Machamp

MACHOKE

Superpower Pokémon

REGIONS
KALOS (COASTAL), KANTO

TYPE: FIGHTING

Machoke never stop training. Even when they have jobs helping people with heavy labor, they spend their free time building up their muscles.

How to say it: muh-CHOKE

Height: 4' 11"
Weight: 155.4 lbs.

Possible Moves: Low Kick, Leer, Focus Energy, Karate Chop, Low Sweep, Foresight, Seismic Toss, Revenge, Vital Throw, Submission, Wake-Up Slap, Cross Chop, Scary Face, Dynamic Punch

Machop Machoke Machamp

MACHOP
Superpower Pokémon

REGIONS
KALOS (COASTAL), KANTO

TYPE: FIGHTING

Machop lifts a Graveler like a weight to make its muscles stronger. No matter how much it exercises, it never gets sore.

How to say it: muh-CHOP

Height: 2' 07"
Weight: 43.0 lbs.

Possible Moves: Low Kick, Leer, Focus Energy, Karate Chop, Low Sweep, Foresight, Seismic Toss, Revenge, Vital Throw, Submission, Wake-Up Slap, Cross Chop, Scary Face, Dynamic Punch

Machop Machoke Machamp

MAGBY
Live Coal Pokémon

REGION
JOHTO

TYPE: FIRE

A Magby that's breathing yellow flames is a healthy Magby. If the flames are smoking and sputtering, it probably needs to get some rest.

How to say it: MAG-bee

Height: 2' 04"
Weight: 47.2 lbs.

Possible Moves: Smog, Leer, Ember, Smokescreen, Feint Attack, Fire Spin, Confuse Ray, Flame Burst, Fire Punch, Lava Plume, Flamethrower, Sunny Day, Fire Blast

Magby Magmar Magmortar

MAGCARGO

Lava Pokémon

REGIONS
JOHTO, KALOS (MOUNTAIN)

TYPE: FIRE-ROCK

Magcargo's body is so hot that it vaporizes any nearby water. When the weather turns rainy, Magcargo is surrounded by a thick cloud of steam.

How to say it: mag-CAR-go

Height: 2' 07"
Weight: 121.3 lbs.

Possible Moves: Earth Power, Yawn, Smog, Ember, Rock Throw, Harden, Recover, Flame Burst, Ancient Power, Amnesia, Lava Plume, Shell Smash, Rock Slide, Body Slam, Flamethrower

MAGIKARP

Fish Pokémon

REGIONS
KALOS (CENTRAL), KANTO

TYPE: WATER

Though Magikarp is an exceptionally weak Pokémon when it comes to battle skills, it has an extremely strong constitution. It can live in the most polluted of water.

How to say it: MADGE-eh-karp

Height: 2' 11"
Weight: 22.0 lbs.

Possible Moves: Splash, Tackle, Flail

MAGMAR

Spitfire Pokémon

REGION
KANTO

TYPE: FIRE

When Magmar releases bursts of flame during a battle, any nearby plant life is in danger of catching fire.

How to say it: MAG-mar

Height: 4' 03"
Weight: 98.1 lbs.

Possible Moves: Smog, Leer, Ember, Smokescreen, Feint Attack, Fire Spin, Confuse Ray, Flame Burst, Fire Punch, Lava Plume, Flamethrower, Sunny Day, Fire Blast

Magby Magmar Magmortar

MAGMORTAR

Blast Pokémon

REGION
SINNOH

TYPE: FIRE

Magmortar makes its home inside a volcano's crater. Its breath is searingly hot, as are the fireballs it blasts out of its arms.

How to say it: mag-MOR-tur

Height: 5' 03"
Weight: 149.9 lbs.

Possible Moves: Thunder Punch, Smog, Leer, Ember, Smokescreen, Feint Attack, Fire Spin, Confuse Ray, Flame Burst, Fire Punch, Lava Plume, Flamethrower, Sunny Day, Fire Blast, Hyper Beam

Magby Magmar Magmortar

MAGNEMITE

Magnet Pokémon

REGIONS
KALOS (MOUNTAIN), KANTO

TYPE: ELECTRIC-STEEL

A sudden power failure can sometimes be traced to many Magnemite draining energy from the power lines that feed a building.

How to say it: MAG-nuh-mite

Height: 1' 00"
Weight: 13.2 lbs.

Possible Moves: Tackle, Supersonic, Thunder Shock, Sonic Boom, Thunder Wave, Magnet Bomb, Spark, Mirror Shot, Metal Sound, Electro Ball, Flash Cannon, Screech, Discharge, Lock-On, Magnet Rise, Gyro Ball, Zap Cannon

Magnemite → Magneton → Magnezone

MAGNETON

Magnet Pokémon

REGIONS
KALOS (MOUNTAIN), KANTO

TYPE: ELECTRIC-STEEL

The magnetic field that surrounds Magneton can wreak havoc on electronics and other machines. Having this Pokémon around can be very bad for business.

How to say it: MAG-nuh-ton

Height: 3' 03" **Weight:** 132.3 lbs.

Possible Moves: Zap Cannon, Tri Attack, Tackle, Supersonic, Thunder Shock, Sonic Boom, Electric Terrain, Thunder Wave, Magnet Bomb, Spark, Mirror Shot, Metal Sound, Electro Ball, Flash Cannon, Screech, Discharge, Lock-On, Magnet Rise, Gyro Ball

Magnemite → Magneton → Magnezone

MAGNEZONE

Magnet Area Pokémon

REGIONS
KALOS (MOUNTAIN), SINNOH

TYPE: ELECTRIC-STEEL

Magnezone give off a strong magnetic field that they can't always control. Sometimes they attract one another by accident and stick so tightly that they have trouble separating.

How to say it: MAG-nuh-zone

Height: 3' 11"
Weight: 396.8 lbs.

Possible Moves: Zap Cannon, Magnetic Flux, Mirror Coat, Barrier, Tackle, Supersonic, Sonic Boom, Thunder Shock, Electric Terrain, Thunder Wave, Magnet Bomb, Spark, Mirror Shot, Metal Sound, Electro Ball, Flash Cannon, Screech, Discharge, Lock-On, Magnet Rise, Gyro Ball

MAKUHITA

Guts Pokémon

REGIONS
HOENN, KALOS (COASTAL)

TYPE: FIGHTING

If the tireless Makuhita gets knocked down in battle, it always gets up again. Every time it does so, it builds up energy for Evolution.

How to say it: MAK-oo-HEE-ta

Height: 3' 03"
Weight: 190.5 lbs.

Possible Moves: Tackle, Focus Energy, Sand Attack, Arm Thrust, Vital Throw, Fake Out, Whirlwind, Knock Off, Smelling Salts, Belly Drum, Force Palm, Seismic Toss, Wake-Up Slap, Endure, Close Combat, Reversal, Heavy Slam

MALAMAR

Overturning Pokémon

REGION
KALOS (COASTAL)

TYPE: DARK-PSYCHIC

With hypnotic compulsion, Malamar can control the actions of others, forcing them to do its will. The movement of its tentacles can put anyone watching into a trance.

How to say it: MAL-uh-MAR

Height: 4' 11"
Weight: 103.6 lbs.

Possible Moves: Superpower, Reversal, Tackle, Peck, Constrict, Reflect, Foul Play, Swagger, Psywave, Topsy-Turvy, Hypnosis, Psybeam, Switcheroo, Payback, Light Screen, Pluck, Psycho Cut, Slash, Night Slash

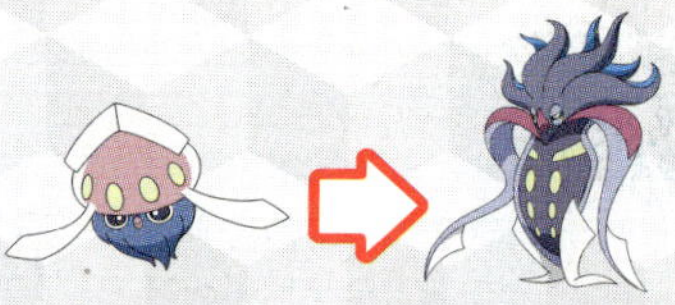

MAMOSWINE

Twin Tusk Pokémon

REGIONS
KALOS (MOUNTAIN), SINNOH

TYPE: ICE-GROUND

Mamoswine have been around since the last ice age, but the warmer climate reduced their population. Their huge twin tusks are formed of ice.

How to say it: MAM-oh-swine

Height: 8' 02"
Weight: 641.5 lbs.

Possible Moves: Scary Face, Ancient Power, Peck, Odor Sleuth, Mud Sport, Powder Snow, Mud-Slap, Endure, Mud Bomb, Hail, Ice Fang, Take Down, Double Hit, Mist, Thrash, Earthquake, Blizzard

MYTHICAL POKÉMON

REGION
SINNOH

MANAPHY

Seafaring Pokémon

TYPE: WATER

From its earliest days, Manaphy has possessed the power to form close bonds with any Pokémon, no matter what kind.

How to say it: man-UH-fee

Height: 1' 00" **Weight:** 3.1 lbs.

Possible Moves: Tail Glow, Bubble, Water Sport, Charm, Supersonic, Bubble Beam, Acid Armor, Whirlpool, Water Pulse, Aqua Ring, Dive, Rain Dance, Heart Swap

Does not evolve

MANDIBUZZ

Bone Vulture Pokémon

REGION
UNOVA

TYPE: DARK-FLYING

Mandibuzz flies in slow circles, high in the sky, to keep an eye out for a weak opponent. Then it swoops down in an aerial attack.

How to say it: MAN-dih-buz

Height: 3' 11" **Weight:** 87.1 lbs.

Possible Moves: Gust, Leer, Fury Attack, Pluck, Nasty Plot, Flatter, Feint Attack, Punishment, Defog, Tailwind, Air Slash, Dark Pulse, Embargo, Bone Rush, Whirlwind, Brave Bird, Mirror Move

MANECTRIC

Discharge Pokémon

REGIONS
HOENN, KALOS (COASTAL)

TYPE: ELECTRIC

When Manectric enters battle, thunderclouds follow. Its mane gives off a strong electric charge.

How to say it: mane-EK-trick

Height: 4' 11"
Weight: 88.6 lbs.

Possible Moves: Electric Terrain, Fire Fang, Tackle, Thunder Wave, Leer, Howl, Quick Attack, Spark, Odor Sleuth, Bite, Thunder Fang, Roar, Discharge, Charge, Wild Charge, Thunder

MEGA MANECTRIC

Discharge Pokémon

TYPE: ELECTRIC

Height: 5' 11"
Weight: 97.0 lbs.

Electrike → Manectric → Mega Manectric

MANKEY

Pig Monkey Pokémon

REGION
KANTO

TYPE: FIGHTING

Mankey flies into a rage at the slightest provocation. These fits of temper are usually preceded by violent tremors, but there's rarely enough time to get away.

How to say it: MANK-ee

Height: 1' 08" **Weight:** 61.7 lbs.

Possible Moves: Covet, Scratch, Low Kick, Leer, Focus Energy, Fury Swipes, Karate Chop, Seismic Toss, Screech, Assurance, Swagger, Cross Chop, Thrash, Punishment, Close Combat, Final Gambit

Mankey Primeape

MANTINE

Kite Pokémon

REGIONS
JOHTO, KALOS (COASTAL)

TYPE: WATER-FLYING

When the weather is nice, Mantine often leap gracefully out of the waves into the bright sunlight. Sometimes Remoraid go along for the ride.

How to say it: MAN-tine

Height: 6' 11"
Weight: 485.0 lbs.

Possible Moves: Psybeam, Bullet Seed, Signal Beam, Tackle, Bubble, Supersonic, Bubble Beam, Confuse Ray, Wing Attack, Headbutt, Water Pulse, Wide Guard, Take Down, Agility, Air Slash, Aqua Ring, Bounce, Hydro Pump

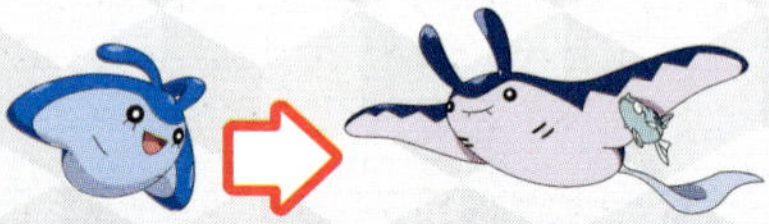

Mantyke Mantine

REGIONS
KALOS (COASTAL), SINNOH

MANTYKE

Kite Pokémon

TYPE: WATER-FLYING

Mantyke that live in different regions have different patterns on their backs. They're often found in the company of Remoraid.

How to say it: MAN-tike

Height: 3' 03"
Weight: 143.3 lbs.

Possible Moves: Tackle, Bubble, Supersonic, Bubble Beam, Confuse Ray, Wing Attack, Headbutt, Water Pulse, Wide Guard, Take Down, Agility, Air Slash, Aqua Ring, Bounce, Hydro Pump

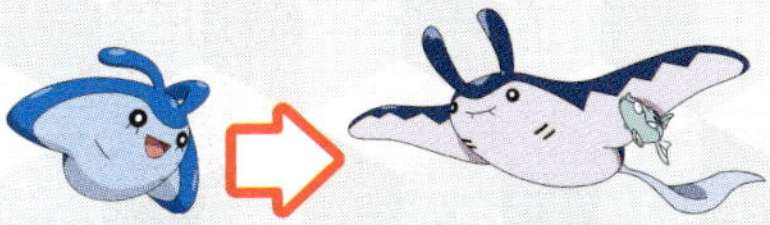

Mantyke → Mantine

REGION
UNOVA

MARACTUS

Cactus Pokémon

TYPE: GRASS

Maractus live in dry places, where they dance with rhythmic movements of their prickly limbs to keep others away. This motion gives off a sound like the shaking of maracas.

How to say it: mah-RAK-tus

Height: 3' 03" **Weight:** 61.7 lbs.

Possible Moves: Peck, Absorb, Sweet Scent, Growth, Pin Missile, Mega Drain, Synthesis, Cotton Spore, Needle Arm, Giga Drain, Acupressure, Ingrain, Petal Dance, Sucker Punch, Sunny Day, Solar Beam, Cotton Guard, After You

Does not evolve

MAREEP

Wool Pokémon

REGIONS
JOHTO, KALOS (COASTAL)

TYPE: ELECTRIC

When Mareep's woolly coat builds up static electricity, the end of its tail glows brightly. The static charge grows as Mareep moves and its wool rubs together.

How to say it: mah-REEP

Height: 2' 00" **Weight:** 17.2 lbs.

Possible Moves: Tackle, Growl, Thunder Wave, Thunder Shock, Cotton Spore, Charge, Take Down, Electro Ball, Confuse Ray, Power Gem, Discharge, Cotton Guard, Signal Beam, Light Screen, Thunder

Mareep → Flaaffy → Ampharos → Mega Ampharos

MARILL

Aqua Mouse Pokémon

REGIONS
JOHTO, KALOS (CENTRAL)

TYPE: WATER-FAIRY

When Marill dives underwater in search of plants to eat, its buoyant tail bobs on the surface. The tail is flexible enough to wrap around a tree as an anchor.

How to say it: MARE-rull

Height: 1' 04" **Weight:** 18.7 lbs.

Possible Moves: Tackle, Water Gun, Tail Whip, Water Sport, Bubble, Defense Curl, Rollout, Bubble Beam, Helping Hand, Aqua Tail, Double-Edge, Aqua Ring, Rain Dance, Superpower, Hydro Pump, Play Rough

Azurill → Marill → Azumarill

MAROWAK

REGIONS
KALOS (COASTAL), KANTO

Bone Keeper Pokémon

TYPE: GROUND

After overcoming its grief and evolving, Marowak has become extremely tough. Its spirit, tempered by adversity, can withstand just about anything.

How to say it: MAR-oh-wack

Height: 3' 03"
Weight: 99.2 lbs.

Possible Moves: Growl, Tail Whip, Bone Club, Headbutt, Leer, Focus Energy, Bonemerang, Rage, False Swipe, Thrash, Fling, Bone Rush, Endeavor, Double-Edge, Retaliate

MARSHTOMP

REGION
HOENN

Mud Fish Pokémon

TYPE: WATER-GROUND

When the tide goes out, Marshtomp loves to play in the mud. Its well-developed hind legs offer stability, so it can travel over mud faster than it can swim.

How to say it: MARSH-stomp

Height: 2' 04"
Weight: 61.7 lbs.

Possible Moves: Tackle, Growl, Mud-Slap, Water Gun, Bide, Mud Shot, Foresight, Mud Bomb, Take Down, Muddy Water, Protect, Earthquake, Endeavor

MASQUERAIN

Eyeball Pokémon

REGIONS
HOENN, KALOS (CENTRAL)

TYPE: BUG-FLYING

The eye patterns on Masquerain's large antennae usually have an angry expression, which sometimes scares would-be opponents. If the eyes look sad, it's a sign that heavy rain is coming.

How to say it: mas-ker-RAIN

Height: 2' 07" **Weight:** 7.9 lbs.

Possible Moves: Quiver Dance, Bug Buzz, Whirlwind, Ominous Wind, Bubble, Quick Attack, Sweet Scent, Water Sport, Gust, Scary Face, Stun Spore, Silver Wind, Air Slash

Surskit → Masquerain

MAWILE

Deceiver Pokémon

REGIONS
HOENN, KALOS (COASTAL)

TYPE: STEEL-FAIRY

An enemy fooled by Mawile's sweet face will quickly find itself in the crushing grip of the massive steel jaws on the back of this Pokémon's head.

How to say it: MAW-while

Height: 2' 00"
Weight: 25.4 lbs.

Possible Moves: Play Rough, Iron Head, Taunt, Growl, Fairy Wind, Astonish, Fake Tears, Bite, Sweet Scent, Vice Grip, Feint Attack, Baton Pass, Crunch, Iron Defense, Sucker Punch, Stockpile, Swallow, Spit Up

MEGA MAWILE

Deceiver Pokémon

TYPE: STEEL-FAIRY

Height: 3' 03"
Weight: 51.8 lbs.

Mawile → Mega Mawile

MEDICHAM

Meditate Pokémon

REGIONS
HOENN, KALOS (CENTRAL)

TYPE: FIGHTING-PSYCHIC

Medicham has developed a sixth sense and psychic powers through long meditation training. It can disappear into its mountain home if danger approaches.

How to say it: MED-uh-cham

Height: 4' 03"
Weight: 69.4 lbs.

Possible Moves: Zen Headbutt, Fire Punch, Thunder Punch, Ice Punch, Bide, Meditate, Confusion, Detect, Hidden Power, Mind Reader, Feint, Calm Mind, Force Palm, High Jump Kick, Psych Up, Acupressure, Power Trick, Reversal, Recover

MEGA MEDICHAM

Meditate Pokémon

TYPE: FIGHTING-PSYCHIC

Height: 4' 03"
Weight: 69.4 lbs.

MEDITITE

Meditate Pokémon

REGIONS
HOENN, KALOS (CENTRAL)

TYPE: FIGHTING-PSYCHIC

Through intense meditation and extreme hunger, Meditite works hard to train its mental powers.

How to say it: MED-uh-tite

Height: 2' 00" **Weight:** 24.7 lbs.

Possible Moves: Zen Headbutt, Fire Punch, Thunder Punch, Ice Punch, Bide, Meditate, Confusion, Detect, Hidden Power, Mind Reader, Feint, Calm Mind, Force Palm, High Jump Kick, Psych Up, Acupressure, Power Trick, Reversal, Recover

Meditite → Medicham → Mega Medicham

MEGANIUM

Herb Pokémon

REGION
JOHTO

TYPE: GRASS

Meganium's flower wafts a soothing aroma. During a battle, the fragrance grows stronger as this Pokémon attempts to calm its enemies.

How to say it: meg-GAY-nee-um

Height: 5' 11"
Weight: 221.6 lbs.

Possible Moves: Tackle, Growl, Razor Leaf, Poison Powder, Synthesis, Reflect, Magical Leaf, Natural Gift, Petal Dance, Sweet Scent, Light Screen, Body Slam, Safeguard, Aromatherapy, Solar Beam

Chikorita → Bayleef → Meganium

MELOETTA

Melody Pokémon

REGION
UNOVA

MYTHICAL POKÉMON

Aria Forme

Pirouette Forme

TYPE: NORMAL-PSYCHIC

When Meloetta sings, its voice can control the emotions of people or Pokémon. The beautiful melodies of this Mythical Pokémon can bring aching sadness or radiant joy.

How to say it: mell-oh-ET-uh

Height: 2' 00" **Weight:** 14.3 lbs.

Possible Moves: Round, Quick Attack, Confusion, Sing, Teeter Dance, Acrobatics, Psybeam, Echoed Voice, U-turn, Wake-Up Slap, Psychic, Hyper Voice, Role Play, Close Combat, Perish Song

Does not evolve

REGION
KALOS (CENTRAL)

MEOWSTIC

Constraint Pokémon

Male Form

Female Form

TYPE: PSYCHIC

When Meowstic unfolds its ears, the psychic blast created by the eyeball patterns inside can pulverize heavy machinery. It keeps its ears tightly folded unless it's in danger.

How to say it: MYOW-stik

Height: 2' 00" **Weight:** 18.7 lbs.

Possible Moves (male): Quick Guard, Mean Look, Helping Hand, Scratch, Leer, Covet, Confusion, Light Screen, Psybeam, Fake Out, Disarming Voice, Psyshock, Charm, Miracle Eye, Reflect, Psychic, Role Play, Imprison, Sucker Punch, Misty Terrain

Possible Moves (female): Stored Power, Me First, Magical Leaf, Scratch, Leer, Covet, Confusion, Light Screen, Psybeam, Fake Out, Disarming Voice, Psyshock, Charge Beam, Extrasensory, Psychic, Role Play, Signal Beam, Sucker Punch, Future Sight

Espurr

Meowstic (Male Form)

Meowstic (Female Form)

MEOWTH

Scratch Cat Pokémon

REGION
KANTO

TYPE: NORMAL

When Meowth retracts its sharp claws, it can move without making a sound or leaving a footprint. It's drawn to shiny things like coins.

How to say it: me-OUTH

Height: 1' 04"
Weight: 9.3 lbs.

Possible Moves: Scratch, Growl, Bite, Fake Out, Fury Swipes, Screech, Feint Attack, Taunt, Pay Day, Slash, Nasty Plot, Assurance, Captivate, Night Slash, Feint

MESPRIT

Emotion Pokémon

REGION
SINNOH

LEGENDARY POKÉMON

TYPE: PSYCHIC

According to legend, Mesprit brought the first taste of joy and sorrow to people's hearts. It is known as "the Being of Emotion."

How to say it: MES-prit

Height: 1' 00" **Weight:** 0.7 lbs.

Possible Moves: Rest, Confusion, Imprison, Protect, Swift, Lucky Chant, Future Sight, Charm, Extrasensory, Copycat, Natural Gift, Healing Wish

Does not evolve

TYPE: STEEL-PSYCHIC

Metagross is formed when two Metang combine, linking their four brains together. It is intimidating both physically and mentally—it can easily pin a foe underneath its massive steel body and perform complicated calculations in the blink of an eye.

How to say it: MET-uh-gross

Height: 5' 03"
Weight: 1,212.5 lbs.

Possible Moves: Magnet Rise, Take Down, Metal Claw, Confusion, Scary Face, Pursuit, Bullet Punch, Psychic, Iron Defense, Agility, Hammer Arm, Meteor Mash, Zen Headbutt, Hyper Beam

REGION
HOENN

METAGROSS

Iron Leg Pokémon

MEGA METAGROSS

Iron Leg Pokémon

TYPE: STEEL-PSYCHIC

Height: 8' 02"
Weight: 2,078.7 lbs.

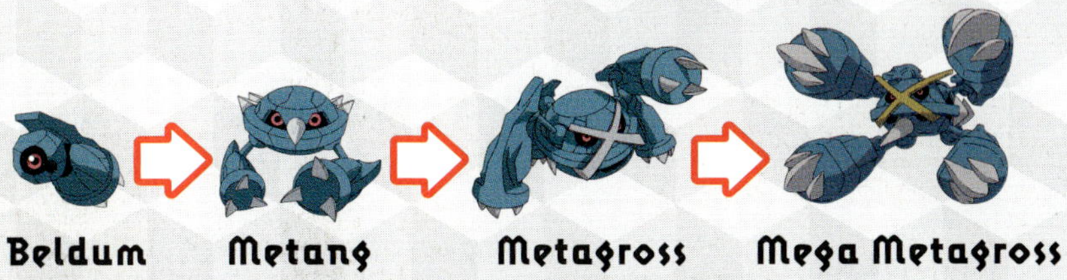

METANG

Iron Claw Pokémon

REGION
HOENN

TYPE: STEEL-PSYCHIC

Metang is formed when two Beldum combine, linking their brains and bodies. The power of its linked brains makes it capable of psychokinesis.

How to say it: met-TANG

Height: 3' 11" **Weight:** 446.4 lbs.

Possible Moves: Magnet Rise, Take Down, Metal Claw, Confusion, Scary Face, Pursuit, Bullet Punch, Psychic, Iron Defense, Agility, Meteor Mash, Zen Headbutt, Hyper Beam

METAPOD

Cocoon Pokémon

REGIONS
KALOS (CENTRAL), KANTO

TYPE: BUG

Inside its iron-hard shell, Metapod patiently prepares to evolve. It doesn't move much, so it relies on its shell for protection.

How to say it: MET-uh-pod

Height: 2' 04"
Weight: 21.8 lbs.

Possible Move: Harden

MYTHICAL POKÉMON

REGION
KANTO

MEW

New Species Pokémon

TYPE: PSYCHIC

It is said that within Mew's cells rests the entirety of the Pokémon genetic code. This Mythical Pokémon can turn invisible to keep others from noticing it.

How to say it: MUE

Height: 1' 04" **Weight:** 8.8 lbs.

Possible Moves: Pound, Reflect Type, Transform, Mega Punch, Metronome, Psychic, Barrier, Ancient Power, Amnesia, Me First, Baton Pass, Nasty Plot, Aura Sphere

Does not evolve

MEWTWO

Genetic Pokémon

REGIONS
KALOS (MOUNTAIN), KANTO

LEGENDARY POKÉMON

TYPE: PSYCHIC

Scientists created Mewtwo by manipulating its genes. If only they could have given it a sense of compassion . . .

How to say it: MUE-TOO

Height: 6' 07"   **Weight:** 269.0 lbs.

Possible Moves: Confusion, Disable, Barrier, Swift, Future Sight, Psych Up, Miracle Eye, Mist, Psycho Cut, Amnesia, Power Swap, Guard Swap, Psychic, Me First, Recover, Safeguard, Aura Sphere, Psystrike

MEGA MEWTWO X

Genetic Pokémon

TYPE: PSYCHIC-FIGHTING

Height: 7' 07"
Weight: 280.0 lbs.

MEGA MEWTWO Y

Genetic Pokémon

TYPE: PSYCHIC

Height: 4' 11"
Weight: 72.8 lbs.

MIENFOO

Martial Arts Pokémon

REGIONS
KALOS (COASTAL), UNOVA

TYPE: FIGHTING

In battle, Mienfoo never stops moving, flowing through one attack after another with grace and speed. Its claws are very sharp.

How to say it: MEEN-FOO

Height: 2' 11"
Weight: 44.1 lbs.

Possible Moves: Pound, Meditate, Detect, Fake Out, Double Slap, Swift, Calm Mind, Force Palm, Drain Punch, Jump Kick, U-turn, Quick Guard, Bounce, High Jump Kick, Reversal, Aura Sphere

MIENSHAO

Martial Arts Pokémon

REGIONS
KALOS (COASTAL), UNOVA

TYPE: FIGHTING

With the long, whiplike fur on its arms, Mienshao can unleash a flurry of attacks so fast they're almost invisible. Its battle combos are unstoppable.

How to say it: MEEN-SHOW

Height: 4' 07" **Weight:** 78.3 lbs.

Possible Moves: Aura Sphere, Reversal, Pound, Meditate, Detect, Fake Out, Double Slap, Swift, Calm Mind, Force Palm, Drain Punch, Jump Kick, U-turn, Wide Guard, Bounce, High Jump Kick

MIGHTYENA

Bite Pokémon

REGIONS
HOENN, KALOS (MOUNTAIN)

TYPE: DARK

Mightyena sounds a deep growl before attacking. In the wild, these Pokémon live together in packs.

How to say it: MY-tee-EH-nah

Height: 3' 03"
Weight: 81.6 lbs.

Possible Moves: Crunch, Tackle, Howl, Sand Attack, Bite, Howl, Odor Sleuth, Roar, Swagger, Assurance, Scary Face, Taunt, Embargo, Take Down, Thief, Sucker Punch

MILOTIC

Tender Pokémon

REGION
HOENN

TYPE: WATER

The astoundingly beautiful Milotic live on lake bottoms and radiate calming energy. When they give off a bright pink glow, people stop fighting.

How to say it: my-LOW-tic

Height: 20' 04"
Weight: 357.1 lbs.

Possible Moves: Water Gun, Wrap, Water Sport, Refresh, Water Pulse, Twister, Recover, Captivate, Aqua Tail, Rain Dance, Hydro Pump, Attract, Safeguard, Aqua Ring

MILTANK

Milk Cow Pokémon

REGIONS
JOHTO, KALOS (COASTAL)

TYPE: NORMAL

Miltank produces more than five gallons of milk every day! The milk has a sweet flavor that people of all ages enjoy.

How to say it: MILL-tank

Height: 3' 11"
Weight: 166.4 lbs.

Possible Moves: Tackle, Growl, Defense Curl, Stomp, Milk Drink, Bide, Rollout, Body Slam, Zen Headbutt, Captivate, Gyro Ball, Heal Bell, Wake-Up Slap

Does not evolve

MIME JR.

Mime Pokémon

REGIONS
KALOS (COASTAL), SINNOH

TYPE: PSYCHIC-FAIRY

To enthrall and confuse an attacker, Mime Jr. copies its movements. While the opponent is bewildered, it makes its escape.

How to say it: mime JOO-nyur

Height: 2' 00" **Weight:** 28.7 lbs.

Possible Moves: Tickle, Barrier, Confusion, Copycat, Meditate, Double Slap, Mimic, Encore, Light Screen, Reflect, Psybeam, Substitute, Recycle, Trick, Psychic, Role Play, Baton Pass, Safeguard

Mime Jr. Mr. Mime

MINCCINO

Chinchilla Pokémon

REGION
UNOVA

TYPE: NORMAL

The very tidy Minccino uses its tail as a broom to rid its habitat of any wayward dust or dirt. They even groom one another with their tails.

How to say it: min-CHEE-noh

Height: 1' 04"
Weight: 12.8 lbs.

Possible Moves: Pound, Growl, Helping Hand, Tickle, Double Slap, Encore, Swift, Sing, Tail Slap, Charm, Wake-Up Slap, Echoed Voice, Slam, Captivate, Hyper Voice, Last Resort, After You

Minccino → Cinccino

MINUN

Cheering Pokémon

REGIONS
HOENN, KALOS (CENTRAL)

TYPE: ELECTRIC

Minun shoots out sparks when cheering on its teammates. If the battle isn't going well, the spark showers get more intense.

How to say it: MIE-nun

Height: 1' 04" **Weight:** 9.3 lbs.

Possible Moves: Nasty Plot, Nuzzle, Entrainment, Play Nice, Growl, Thunder Wave, Quick Attack, Helping Hand, Spark, Encore, Charm, Copycat, Electro Ball, Swift, Fake Tears, Charge, Thunder, Baton Pass, Agility, Trump Card

Does not evolve

REGION
JOHTO

MISDREAVUS

Screech Pokémon

TYPE: GHOST

Misdreavus likes to scare people by making a dreadful wailing sound. The red spheres around its neck seem to soak up the fear so the Pokémon can use it for food.

How to say it: mis-DREE-vuss

Height: 2' 04"
Weight: 2.2 lbs.

Possible Moves: Growl, Psywave, Spite, Astonish, Confuse Ray, Mean Look, Hex, Psybeam, Pain Split, Payback, Shadow Ball, Perish Song, Grudge, Power Gem

Misdreavus Mismagius

REGION
SINNOH

MISMAGIUS

Magical Pokémon

TYPE: GHOST

Mismagius shows up unexpectedly, muttering in its chanting voice. Its chants often bring torment to those who listen.

How to say it: mis-MAG-ee-us

Height: 2' 11" **Weight:** 9.7 lbs.

Possible Moves: Lucky Chant, Magical Leaf, Growl, Psywave, Spite, Astonish

Misdreavus Mismagius

MOLTRES
Flame Pokémon

REGIONS
KALOS (COASTAL), KANTO

LEGENDARY POKÉMON

TYPE: FIRE-FLYING

When Moltres gets hurt, some say it dives into an active volcano and heals itself by bathing in lava. This Legendary Pokémon can give off flames and control fire.

How to say it: MOL-trays

Height: 6' 07" **Weight:** 132.3 lbs.

Possible Moves: Roost, Hurricane, Sky Attack, Heat Wave, Wing Attack, Ember, Fire Spin, Agility, Endure, Ancient Power, Flamethrower, Safeguard, Air Slash, Sunny Day, Solar Beam

Does not evolve

MONFERNO
Playful Pokémon

REGION
SINNOH

TYPE: FIRE-FIGHTING

An excellent climber, Monferno can strike from above. It can flare up its tail flame to keep enemies at bay.

How to say it: mon-FERN-oh

Height: 2' 11" **Weight:** 48.5 lbs.

Possible Moves: Scratch, Leer, Ember, Taunt, Mach Punch, Fury Swipes, Flame Wheel, Feint, Torment, Close Combat, Fire Spin, Acrobatics, Slack Off, Flare Blitz

Chimchar Monferno Infernape

REGIONS
KALOS (CENTRAL), SINNOH

MOTHIM

Moth Pokémon

TYPE: BUG-FLYING

Mothim loves the taste of Combee's honey. Sometimes it will raid a hive at night to steal the sweet substance.

How to say it: MOTH-im

Height: 2' 11" **Weight:** 51.4 lbs.

Possible Moves: Tackle, Protect, Bug Bite, Hidden Power, Confusion, Gust, Poison Powder, Psybeam, Camouflage, Silver Wind, Air Slash, Psychic, Bug Buzz, Quiver Dance

MR. MIME

Barrier Pokémon

REGIONS
KALOS (COASTAL), KANTO

TYPE: PSYCHIC-FAIRY

Sometimes, Mr. Mime's gestures convince an onlooker that the invisible thing it's miming actually exists. Then that thing becomes real.

How to say it: MIS-ter MIME

Height: 4' 03" **Weight:** 120.1 lbs.

Possible Moves: Misty Terrain, Magical Leaf, Quick Guard, Wide Guard, Power Swap, Guard Swap, Barrier, Confusion, Copycat, Meditate, Double Slap, Mimic, Psywave, Encore, Light Screen, Reflect, Psybeam, Substitute, Recycle, Trick, Psychic, Role Play, Baton Pass, Safeguard

MUDKIP

Mud Fish Pokémon

REGION
HOENN

TYPE: WATER

Because its fin is so sensitive to the motion of air and water, Mudkip knows what's going on nearby without opening its eyes. The flared gills on its cheeks allow it to breathe underwater.

How to say it: MUD-kip

Height: 1' 04"
Weight: 16.8 lbs.

Possible Moves: Tackle, Growl, Mud-Slap, Water Gun, Bide, Foresight, Mud Sport, Take Down, Whirlpool, Protect, Hydro Pump, Endeavor

REGION
KANTO

MUK
Sludge Pokémon

TYPE: POISON

Muk really stinks. The fluid it oozes gives off a terrible smell and pollutes clean water. Cities with a trash problem may also find they have a Muk problem.

How to say it: MUCK

Height: 3' 11"
Weight: 66.1 lbs.

Possible Moves: Poison Gas, Pound, Harden, Mud-Slap, Disable, Minimize, Sludge, Mud Bomb, Fling, Screech, Sludge Bomb, Acid Armor, Sludge Wave, Gunk Shot, Memento

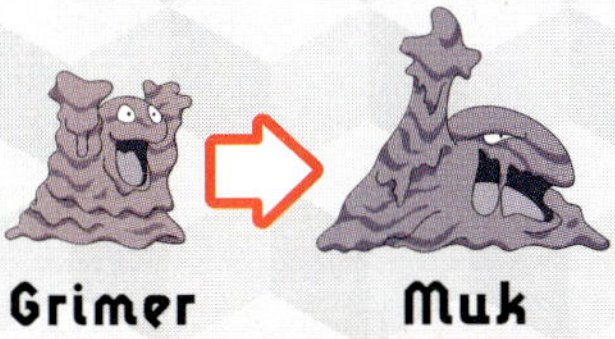

TYPE: NORMAL

Munchlax's long fur is a perfect place to hide snacks. With this permanent food stash, it never goes hungry.

How to say it: MUNCH-lax

Height: 2' 00"
Weight: 231.5 lbs.

Possible Moves: Last Resort, Snatch, Lick, Metronome, Odor Sleuth, Tackle, Defense Curl, Amnesia, Chip Away, Screech, Body Slam, Stockpile, Swallow, Rollout, Fling, Belly Drum, Natural Gift

REGIONS
KALOS (CENTRAL), SINNOH

MUNCHLAX
Big Eater Pokémon

MUNNA

Dream Eater Pokémon

REGION
UNOVA

TYPE: PSYCHIC

When people and Pokémon sleep, Munna appears to eat their dreams and nightmares. After eating a happy dream, it gives off pink mist.

How to say it: MOON-nuh

Height: 2' 00" **Weight:** 51.4 lbs.

Possible Moves: Psywave, Defense Curl, Lucky Chant, Yawn, Psybeam, Imprison, Moonlight, Hypnosis, Zen Headbutt, Synchronoise, Nightmare, Future Sight, Calm Mind, Psychic, Dream Eater, Telekinesis, Stored Power

Munna Musharna

REGIONS
JOHTO,
KALOS
(MOUNTAIN)

MURKROW

Darkness Pokémon

TYPE: DARK-FLYING

People used to think Murkrow brought bad luck, so they were afraid of it and kept their distance. It's drawn to sparkly things and sometimes tries to steal them.

How to say it: MUR-crow

Height: 1' 08"
Weight: 4.6 lbs.

Possible Moves: Peck, Astonish, Pursuit, Haze, Wing Attack, Night Shade, Assurance, Taunt, Feint Attack, Mean Look, Foul Play, Tailwind, Sucker Punch, Torment, Quash

Murkrow → Honchkrow

REGION
UNOVA

MUSHARNA

Drowsing Pokémon

TYPE: PSYCHIC

The dream mist that rises from Musharna's forehead is influenced by the dreams it eats. It can take on many different colors.

How to say it: moo-SHAHR-nuh

Height: 3' 07"
Weight: 133.4 lbs.

Possible Moves: Defense Curl, Lucky Chant, Psybeam, Hypnosis

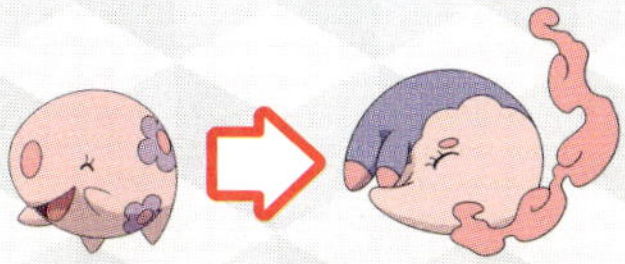

Munna → Musharna

NATU
Tiny Bird Pokémon

REGION
JOHTO

TYPE: PSYCHIC-FLYING

With its underdeveloped wings, Natu can't fly, but it's a great jumper, able to leap onto a tree branch higher than a grown man's head. It tends to engage in staring contests with those who meet its eyes.

How to say it: NAH-too

Height: 0' 08"   **Weight:** 4.4 lbs.

Possible Moves: Peck, Leer, Night Shade, Teleport, Lucky Chant, Miracle Eye, Me First, Confuse Ray, Wish, Psycho Shift, Future Sight, Stored Power, Ominous Wind, Power Swap, Guard Swap, Psychic

NIDOKING
Drill Pokémon

REGIONS
KALOS (COASTAL), KANTO

TYPE: POISON-GROUND

When Nidoking swings its massive tail, it can knock down a radio tower. Nothing can stand in the way of its furious rampage.

How to say it: NEE-doe-king

Height: 4' 07"
Weight: 136.7 lbs.

Possible Moves: Megahorn, Peck, Focus Energy, Double Kick, Poison Sting, Chip Away, Thrash, Earth Power

NIDOQUEEN

Drill Pokémon

REGIONS
KALOS (COASTAL), KANTO

TYPE: POISON-GROUND

When defending its nest, Nidoqueen hurls its hard-scaled body at an intruder. The impact is often enough to send the enemy flying through the air.

How to say it: NEE-doe-kween

Height: 4' 03"
Weight: 132.3 lbs.

Possible Moves: Superpower, Scratch, Tail Whip, Double Kick, Poison Sting, Chip Away, Body Slam, Earth Power

Nidoran ♀ Nidorina Nidoqueen

NIDORAN ♀

Poison Pin Pokémon

REGIONS
KALOS (COASTAL), KANTO

TYPE: POISON

Though Nidoran ♀ is small, it's quite dangerous. The barbs in its fur and the horn on its head are both extremely poisonous.

How to say it: NEE-doe-ran

Height: 1' 04"
Weight: 15.4 lbs.

Possible Moves: Growl, Scratch, Tail Whip, Double Kick, Poison Sting, Fury Swipes, Bite, Helping Hand, Toxic Spikes, Flatter, Crunch, Captivate, Poison Fang

Nidoran ♀ Nidorina Nidoqueen

NIDORAN ♂

Poison Pin Pokémon

REGIONS
KALOS (COASTAL), KANTO

TYPE: POISON

Nidoran ♂ has excellent hearing and, thanks to specialized muscles, it can move and rotate its ears to pick up the slightest sound.

How to say it: NEE-doe-ran

Height: 1' 04" **Weight:** 15.4 lbs.

Possible Moves: Leer, Peck, Focus Energy, Double Kick, Poison Sting, Fury Attack, Horn Attack, Helping Hand, Toxic Spikes, Flatter, Poison Jab, Captivate, Horn Drill

Nidoran ♂ Nidorino Nidoking

NIDORINA

Poison Pin Pokémon

REGIONS
KALOS (COASTAL), KANTO

TYPE: POISON

Nidorina are very social and become nervous on their own. When among friends, their poisonous barbs retract so they don't hurt anyone.

How to say it: NEE-doe-REE-na

Height: 2' 07"
Weight: 44.1 lbs.

Possible Moves: Growl, Scratch, Tail Whip, Double Kick, Poison Sting, Fury Swipes, Bite, Helping Hand, Toxic Spikes, Flatter, Crunch, Captivate, Poison Fang

Nidoran ♀ Nidorina Nidoqueen

REGIONS
KALOS (COASTAL), KANTO

NIDORINO

Poison Pin Pokémon

TYPE: POISON

The horn on Nidorino's forehead is made of an extremely hard substance. When challenged, its body bristles with poisonous barbs.

How to say it: NEE-doe-REE-no

Height: 2' 11"
Weight: 43.0 lbs.

Possible Moves: Leer, Peck, Focus Energy, Double Kick, Poison Sting, Fury Attack, Horn Attack, Helping Hand, Toxic Spikes, Flatter, Poison Jab, Captivate, Horn Drill

REGIONS
HOENN, KALOS (CENTRAL)

NINCADA

Trainee Pokémon

TYPE: BUG-GROUND

Nincada prefers to stay out of the sun, living underground and feeding on tree roots. When Evolution approaches, it stops moving altogether.

How to say it: nin-KAH-da

Height: 1' 08" **Weight:** 12.1 lbs.

Possible Moves: Scratch, Harden, Leech Life, Sand Attack, Fury Swipes, Mind Reader, False Swipe, Mud-Slap, Metal Claw, Dig

NINETALES

Fox Pokémon

REGION
KANTO

TYPE: FIRE

Ninetales can control an opponent's mind with the light from its red eyes. Stories say this Pokémon was formed when nine wizards merged into a single being.

How to say it: NINE-tails

Height: 3' 07"
Weight: 43.9 lbs.

Possible Moves: Nasty Plot, Ember, Quick Attack, Confuse Ray, Safeguard

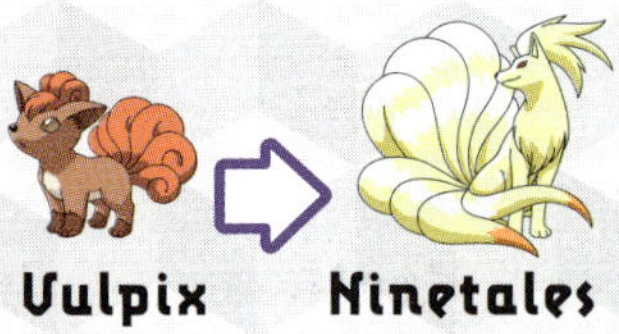

NINJASK

Ninja Pokémon

REGIONS
HOENN, KALOS (CENTRAL)

TYPE: BUG-FLYING

Ninjask moves so fast that it's hard to see, although its cry is quite audible. Proper training is a must to keep its defiant nature in check.

How to say it: NIN-jask

Height: 2' 07"   **Weight:** 26.5 lbs.

Possible Moves: Bug Bite, Scratch, Harden, Leech Life, Sand Attack, Fury Swipes, Mind Reader, Double Team, Fury Cutter, Screech, Swords Dance, Slash, Agility, Baton Pass, X-Scissor

REGIONS
JOHTO, KALOS (MOUNTAIN)

NOCTOWL

Owl Pokémon

TYPE: NORMAL-FLYING

With its excellent night vision and its silent wings, Noctowl is an expert when it comes to hunting in the darkness.

How to say it: NAHK-towl

Height: 5' 03" **Weight:** 89.9 lbs.

Possible Moves: Dream Eater, Sky Attack, Tackle, Growl, Foresight, Hypnosis, Peck, Uproar, Reflect, Confusion, Echoed Voice, Take Down, Air Slash, Zen Headbutt, Synchronoise, Extrasensory, Psycho Shift, Roost

Hoothoot → Noctowl

REGION
KALOS (MOUNTAIN)

NOIBAT

Sound Wave Pokémon

TYPE: FLYING-DRAGON

Noibat live in lightless caves and communicate with ultrasonic waves emitted from their ears. These waves can make a strong man dizzy.

How to say it: NOY-bat

Height: 1' 08"
Weight: 17.6 lbs.

Possible Moves: Screech, Supersonic, Tackle, Leech Life, Gust, Bite, Wing Attack, Agility, Air Cutter, Roost, Razor Wind, Tailwind, Whirlwind, Super Fang, Air Slash, Hurricane

Noibat → Noivern

NOIVERN

Sound Wave Pokémon

REGION
KALOS (MOUNTAIN)

Noibat Noivern

TYPE: FLYING-DRAGON

Noivern are masters when it comes to battling in the dark. The ultrasonic waves they release from their ears are powerful enough to crush a boulder.

How to say it: NOY-vurn

Height: 4' 11"
Weight: 187.4 lbs.

Possible Moves: Moonlight, Boomburst, Dragon Pulse, Hurricane, Screech, Supersonic, Tackle, Leech Life, Gust, Bite, Wing Attack, Agility, Air Cutter, Roost, Razor Wind, Tailwind, Whirlwind, Super Fang, Air Slash

NOSEPASS

Compass Pokémon

REGIONS
HOENN, KALOS (COASTAL)

TYPE: ROCK

It's impossible for two Nosepass to stand face-to-face because their magnetic noses repel each other. They move at a glacial pace.

How to say it: NOSE-pass

Height: 3' 03" **Weight:** 213.8 lbs.

Possible Moves: Tackle, Harden, Block, Rock Throw, Thunder Wave, Rock Blast, Rest, Spark, Rock Slide, Power Gem, Sandstorm, Discharge, Earth Power, Stone Edge, Lock-On, Zap Cannon

Nosepass Probopass

NUMEL

REGION
HOENN

Numb Pokémon

TYPE: FIRE-GROUND

The rather dull Numel sometimes doesn't notice when it's being attacked. Its body is full of magma, so Numel takes care to stay dry. Rain can make the magma cool and harden.

How to say it: NUM-mull

Height: 2' 04"
Weight: 52.9 lbs.

Possible Moves: Growl, Tackle, Ember, Magnitude, Focus Energy, Flame Burst, Take Down, Amnesia, Lava Plume, Earth Power, Earthquake, Flamethrower, Double-Edge

Numel Camerupt Mega Camerupt

NUZLEAF

REGION
HOENN

Wily Pokémon

TYPE: GRASS-DARK

Nuzleaf can play the leaf on its head like a flute, and the music makes listeners nervous. It lives in dense forests and doesn't like visitors.

How to say it: NUZ-leaf

Height: 3' 03"
Weight: 61.7 lbs.

Possible Moves: Razor Leaf, Pound, Harden, Growth, Nature Power, Fake Out, Torment, Feint Attack, Razor Wind, Swagger, Extrasensory

Seedot Nuzleaf Shiftry

OCTILLERY
Jet Pokémon

REGIONS
JOHTO, KALOS (COASTAL)

TYPE: WATER

In battle, Octillery wraps its opponent up in its tentacles to keep it from moving. If that doesn't work, it sprays a cloud of ink to cover its escape.

How to say it: ock-TILL-er-ree

Height: 2' 11"
Weight: 62.8 lbs.

Possible Moves: Gunk Shot, Rock Blast, Water Gun, Constrict, Psybeam, Aurora Beam, Bubble Beam, Focus Energy, Octazooka, Wring Out, Signal Beam, Ice Beam, Bullet Seed, Hydro Pump, Hyper Beam, Soak

ODDISH
Weed Pokémon

REGIONS
KALOS (CENTRAL), KANTO

TYPE: GRASS-POISON

Oddish seeks out fertile ground where it can absorb nutrients from the soil. When it finds the perfect spot, it buries itself, and its feet apparently become like tree roots.

How to say it: ODD-ish

Height: 1' 08" **Weight:** 11.9 lbs.

Possible Moves: Absorb, Sweet Scent, Acid, Poison Powder, Stun Spore, Sleep Powder, Mega Drain, Lucky Chant, Natural Gift, Moonlight, Giga Drain, Petal Dance, Grassy Terrain

REGION
KANTO

OMANYTE

Spiral Pokémon

TYPE: ROCK-WATER

Omanyte's sturdy shell protects it from enemy attacks. This ancient Pokémon was restored from a fossil.

How to say it: AH-man-ite

Height: 1' 04" **Weight:** 16.5 lbs.

Possible Moves: Constrict, Withdraw, Bite, Water Gun, Rollout, Leer, Mud Shot, Brine, Protect, Ancient Power, Tickle, Rock Blast, Shell Smash, Hydro Pump

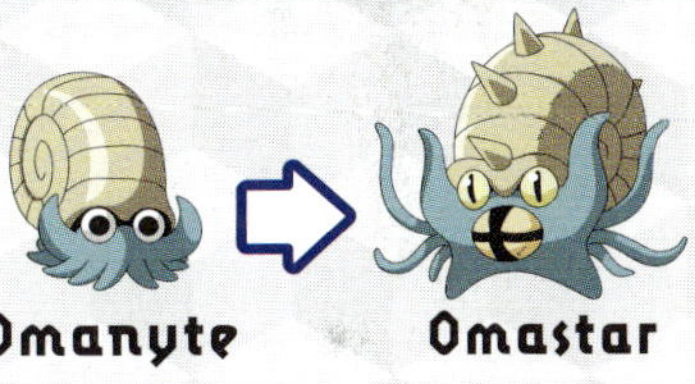

TYPE: ROCK-WATER

Some suspect that Omastar went extinct because it could no longer carry its heavy shell with ease. It seeks out food with its tentacles.

How to say it: AHM-uh-star

Height: 3' 03" **Weight:** 77.2 lbs.

Possible Moves: Constrict, Withdraw, Bite, Water Gun, Rollout, Leer, Mud Shot, Brine, Protect, Ancient Power, Spike Cannon, Tickle, Rock Blast, Shell Smash, Hydro Pump

REGION
KANTO

OMASTAR

Spiral Pokémon

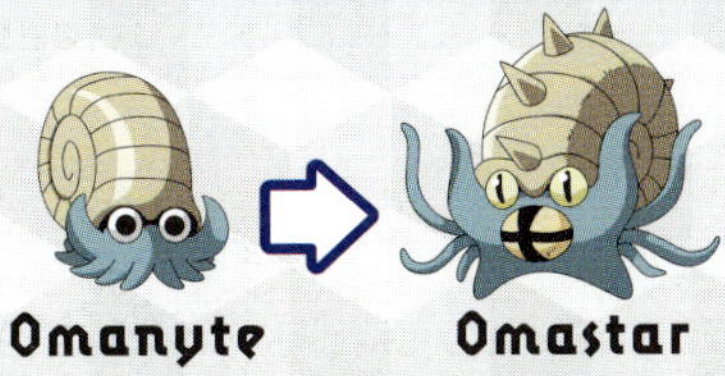

ONIX
Rock Snake Pokémon

REGIONS
KALOS (COASTAL), KANTO

TYPE: ROCK-GROUND

Thanks to its internal magnet, Onix never loses its way while boring through the ground. Its body grows smoother with age as the rough edges wear away.

How to say it: ON-icks

Height: 28' 10" **Weight:** 463.0 lbs.

Possible Moves: Mud Sport, Tackle, Harden, Bind, Curse, Rock Throw, Rock Tomb, Rage, Stealth Rock, Rock Polish, Gyro Ball, Smack Down, Dragon Breath, Slam, Screech, Rock Slide, Sand Tomb, Iron Tail, Dig, Stone Edge, Double-Edge, Sandstorm

OSHAWOTT
Sea Otter Pokémon

REGION
UNOVA

TYPE: WATER

Oshawott can detach the scalchop on its belly and use it as a weapon in battle or as a tool for cutting up food and other things.

How to say it: AH-shuh-wot

Height: 1' 08" **Weight:** 13.0 lbs.

Possible Moves: Tackle, Tail Whip, Water Gun, Water Sport, Focus Energy, Razor Shell, Fury Cutter, Water Pulse, Revenge, Aqua Jet, Encore, Aqua Tail, Retaliate, Swords Dance, Hydro Pump

REGIONS
KALOS (COASTAL), SINNOH

PACHIRISU

EleSquirrel Pokémon

TYPE: ELECTRIC

When Pachirisu affectionately rub their cheeks together, they're sharing electric energy with one another. The balls of fur they shed crackle with static.

How to say it: patch-ee-REE-sue

Height: 1' 04" **Weight:** 8.6 lbs.

Possible Moves: Growl, Bide, Quick Attack, Charm, Spark, Endure, Nuzzle, Swift, Electro Ball, Sweet Kiss, Thunder Wave, Super Fang, Discharge, Last Resort, Hyper Fang

Does not evolve

PALKIA

Spatial Pokémon

REGION
SINNOH

LEGENDARY POKÉMON

TYPE: WATER-DRAGON

It is said Palkia can cause rents and distortions in space. In ancient times, it was revered as a legend.

How to say it: PAL-kee-uh

Height: 13' 09" **Weight:** 740.8 lbs.

Possible Moves: Dragon Breath, Scary Face, Water Pulse, Ancient Power, Slash, Power Gem, Aqua Tail, Dragon Claw, Earth Power, Aura Sphere, Aqua Tail, Spacial Rend, Hydro Pump

Does not evolve

REGION
UNOVA

PALPITOAD

Vibration Pokémon

TYPE: WATER-GROUND

With the vibrations of its head bumps, Palpitoad can make ripples in the water or cause seismic activity. Its long tongue is coated in a sticky substance.

How to say it: PAL-pih-tohd

Height: 2' 07" **Weight:** 37.5 lbs.

Possible Moves: Bubble, Growl, Supersonic, Round, Bubble Beam, Mud Shot, Aqua Ring, Uproar, Muddy Water, Rain Dance, Flail, Echoed Voice, Hydro Pump, Hyper Voice

PANCHAM
Playful Pokémon

REGION
KALOS (CENTRAL)

TYPE: FIGHTING

Pancham tries to be intimidating, but it's just too cute. When someone pats it on the head, it drops the tough-guy act and grins.

How to say it: PAN-chum

Height: 2' 00" **Weight:** 17.6 lbs.

Possible Moves: Tackle, Leer, Arm Thrust, Work Up, Karate Chop, Comet Punch, Slash, Circle Throw, Vital Throw, Body Slam, Crunch, Entrainment, Parting Shot, Sky Uppercut

PANGORO
Daunting Pokémon

REGION
KALOS (CENTRAL)

TYPE: FIGHTING-DARK

The leafy sprig Pangoro holds in its mouth helps the Pokémon track its opponents' movements. Taking hits in battle doesn't seem to bother it at all.

How to say it: PAN-go-roh

Height: 6' 11" **Weight:** 299.8 lbs.

Possible Moves: Entrainment, Hammer Arm, Tackle, Leer, Arm Thrust, Work Up, Karate Chop, Comet Punch, Slash, Circle Throw, Vital Throw, Body Slam, Crunch, Parting Shot, Sky Uppercut, Taunt, Low Sweep

REGIONS
KALOS (CENTRAL), UNOVA

PANPOUR

Spray Pokémon

TYPE: WATER

Panpour's head tuft is full of nutrient-rich water. It uses its tail to water plants, which then grow big and healthy.

How to say it: PAN-por

Height: 2' 00"
Weight: 29.8 lbs.

Possible Moves: Scratch, Play Nice, Leer, Lick, Water Gun, Fury Swipes, Water Sport, Bite, Scald, Taunt, Fling, Acrobatics, Brine, Recycle, Natural Gift, Crunch

REGIONS
KALOS (CENTRAL), UNOVA

PANSAGE

Grass Monkey Pokémon

TYPE: GRASS

Chewing the leaf from Pansage's head is a known method of stress relief. It willingly shares its leaf—along with any berries it's collected—with those who need it.

How to say it: PAN-sayj

Height: 2' 00" **Weight:** 23.1 lbs.

Possible Moves: Scratch, Play Nice, Leer, Lick, Vine Whip, Fury Swipes, Leech Seed, Bite, Seed Bomb, Torment, Fling, Acrobatics, Grass Knot, Recycle, Natural Gift, Crunch

PANSEAR

High Temp Pokémon

REGIONS
KALOS (CENTRAL), UNOVA

TYPE: FIRE

Clever and helpful, Pansear prefers to cook its berries rather than eating them raw. Its natural habitat is volcanic caves, so it's no surprise that its fiery tuft burns at six hundred degrees Fahrenheit.

How to say it: PAN-seer

Height: 2' 00"
Weight: 24.3 lbs.

Possible Moves: Scratch, Play Nice, Leer, Lick, Incinerate, Fury Swipes, Yawn, Bite, Flame Burst, Amnesia, Fling, Acrobatics, Fire Blast, Recycle, Natural Gift, Crunch

Pansear Simisear

PARAS

Mushroom Pokémon

REGION
KANTO

TYPE: BUG-GRASS

Mushrooms called tochukaso grow on Paras's back. Some people use them in medicines.

How to say it: PAR-iss

Height: 1' 00"
Weight: 11.9 lbs.

Possible Moves: Scratch, Stun Spore, Poison Powder, Leech Life, Fury Cutter, Spore, Slash, Growth, Giga Drain, Aromatherapy, Rage Powder, X-Scissor

Paras Parasect

PARASECT

REGION
KANTO

Mushroom Pokémon

TYPE: BUG-GRASS

Parasect feed on the roots of trees. If a group of them infests the same tree, they can be very destructive.

How to say it: PAR-i-sect

Height: 3' 03"
Weight: 65.0 lbs.

Possible Moves: Cross Poison, Scratch, Stun Spore, Poison Powder, Leech Life, Fury Cutter, Spore, Slash, Growth, Giga Drain, Aromatherapy, Rage Powder, X-Scissor

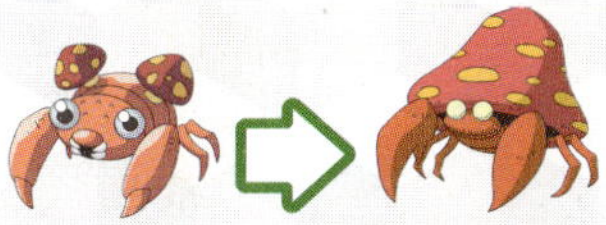

Paras → Parasect

PATRAT

REGIONS
KALOS (MOUNTAIN), UNOVA

Scout Pokémon

TYPE: NORMAL

Wary and cautious, Patrat are very serious about their job as lookouts. They store food in their cheeks so they don't have to leave their posts.

How to say it: pat-RAT

Height: 1' 08"
Weight: 25.6 lbs.

Possible Moves: Tackle, Leer, Bite, Bide, Detect, Sand Attack, Crunch, Hypnosis, Super Fang, After You, Work Up, Hyper Fang, Mean Look, Baton Pass, Slam

Patrat → Watchog

PAWNIARD

Sharp Blade Pokémon

REGIONS
KALOS (MOUNTAIN), UNOVA

TYPE: DARK-STEEL

Pawniard's body is covered in blades, which it keeps sharp by polishing them after battle. Even when hurt, it's a relentless hunter.

How to say it: PAWN-yard

Height: 1' 08"
Weight: 22.5 lbs.

Possible Moves: Scratch, Leer, Fury Cutter, Torment, Feint Attack, Scary Face, Metal Claw, Slash, Assurance, Metal Sound, Embargo, Iron Defense, Night Slash, Iron Head, Swords Dance, Guillotine

PELIPPER

Water Bird Pokémon

REGIONS
HOENN, KALOS (COASTAL)

TYPE: WATER-FLYING

Flying low over the waves, Pelipper catches food by dipping its huge bill into the water. Its bill is big enough that it can even carry small Pokémon from place to place.

How to say it: PEL-ip-purr

Height: 3' 11" **Weight:** 61.7 lbs.

Possible Moves: Hydro Pump, Tailwind, Soak, Growl, Water Gun, Water Sport, Wing Attack, Supersonic, Mist, Water Pulse, Payback, Protect, Roost, Brine, Stockpile, Swallow, Spit Up, Fling, Hurricane

PERSIAN

REGION KANTO

Classy Cat Pokémon

TYPE: NORMAL

Persian uses its distinctive whiskers as sensors to find out about its surroundings. Grabbing the whiskers makes it meek and docile.

How to say it: PURR-shin

Height: 3' 03"
Weight: 70.5 lbs.

Possible Moves: Switcheroo, Scratch, Growl, Bite, Fake Out, Fury Swipes, Screech, Feint Attack, Taunt, Power Gem, Slash, Nasty Plot, Assurance, Captivate, Night Slash, Feint

PETILIL

REGION UNOVA

Bulb Pokémon

TYPE: GRASS

When many Petilil settle in an area, gardeners and farmers pay attention, because these Pokémon seek out rich soil that's good for growing plants. Their leaves have healing properties.

How to say it: PEH-tih-lil

Height: 1' 08" **Weight:** 14.6 lbs.

Possible Moves: Absorb, Growth, Leech Seed, Sleep Powder, Mega Drain, Synthesis, Magical Leaf, Stun Spore, Giga Drain, Aromatherapy, Helping Hand, Energy Ball, Entrainment, Sunny Day, After You, Leaf Storm

PHANPY

Long Nose Pokémon

REGION
JOHTO

TYPE: GROUND

Phanpy sucks up water with its long trunk to spray itself for a bath or to playfully squirt others. It makes its nest by digging into a riverbank.

How to say it: FAN-pee

Height: 1' 08"
Weight: 73.9 lbs.

Possible Moves: Odor Sleuth, Tackle, Growl, Defense Curl, Flail, Take Down, Rollout, Natural Gift, Slam, Endure, Charm, Last Resort, Double-Edge

Phanpy Donphan

PHANTUMP

Stump Pokémon

REGION
KALOS (MOUNTAIN)

TYPE: GHOST-GRASS

It is said that when the spirits of wandering children inhabit old tree stumps, these Pokémon are created. Phantump dwell in lonely forests, far away from people.

How to say it: FAN-tump

Height: 1' 04" **Weight:** 15.4 lbs.

Possible Moves: Tackle, Confuse Ray, Astonish, Growth, Ingrain, Feint Attack, Leech Seed, Curse, Will-O-Wisp, Forest's Curse, Destiny Bond, Phantom Force, Wood Hammer, Horn Leech

Phantump Trevenant

MYTHICAL POKÉMON

REGION SINNOH

PHIONE

Sea Drifter Pokémon

TYPE: WATER

Phione gather in large groups as they drift with the current through warm seas. After floating for a time, they always return home, no matter how far they have traveled.

How to say it: fee-OWN-ay

Height: 1' 04" **Weight:** 6.8 lbs.

Possible Moves: Bubble, Water Sport, Charm, Supersonic, Bubble Beam, Acid Armor, Whirlpool, Water Pulse, Aqua Ring, Dive, Rain Dance

Does not evolve

PICHU

Tiny Mouse Pokémon

REGIONS
JOHTO, KALOS (CENTRAL)

TYPE: ELECTRIC

Sometimes, when two Pichu play together, the static electricity that crackles off their bodies produces an unexpected shower of sparks. This often startles them into crying.

How to say it: PEE-choo

Height: 1' 00" **Weight:** 4.4 lbs.

Possible Moves: Thunder Shock, Charm, Tail Whip, Sweet Kiss, Thunder Wave, Nasty Plot

REGIONS
KALOS (CENTRAL), KANTO

PIDGEOT

Bird Pokémon

TYPE: NORMAL-FLYING

Many Trainers are drawn to Pidgeot because of its lovely feathers. The beautiful colors of its crest are particularly striking.

How to say it: PIDG-ee-ott

Height: 4' 11"
Weight: 87.1 lbs.

Possible Moves: Hurricane, Tackle, Sand Attack, Gust, Quick Attack, Whirlwind, Twister, Feather Dance, Agility, Wing Attack, Roost, Tailwind, Mirror Move, Air Slash

MEGA PIDGEOT

Bird Pokémon

TYPE: NORMAL-FLYING

Height: 7' 03"
Weight: 111.3 lbs.

Pidgey Pidgeotto Pidgeot Mega Pidgeot

PIDGEOTTO

Bird Pokémon

REGIONS
KALOS (CENTRAL), KANTO

TYPE: NORMAL-FLYING

Very territorial, Pidgeotto keeps up a steady patrol of the large area it claims as its own. Any intruder will be driven off with merciless attacks from its sharp claws.

How to say it: PIDG-ee-OH-toe

Height: 3' 07" **Weight:** 66.1 lbs.

Possible Moves: Tackle, Sand Attack, Gust, Quick Attack, Whirlwind, Twister, Feather Dance, Agility, Wing Attack, Roost, Tailwind, Mirror Move, Air Slash, Hurricane

Pidgey Pidgeotto Pidgeot Mega Pidgeot

PIDGEY

Tiny Bird Pokémon

REGIONS
KALOS (CENTRAL), KANTO

TYPE: NORMAL-FLYING

Thanks to Pidgey's excellent sense of direction, it can always find its way home, no matter how far it has traveled.

How to say it: PIDG-ee

Height: 1' 00" **Weight:** 4.0 lbs.

Possible Moves: Tackle, Sand Attack, Gust, Quick Attack, Whirlwind, Twister, Feather Dance, Agility, Wing Attack, Roost, Tailwind, Mirror Move, Air Slash, Hurricane

Pidgey Pidgeotto Pidgeot Mega Pidgeot

TYPE: NORMAL-FLYING

Even wild Pidove are used to having people around. They live in cities and often flock to places where people spend time like plazas and parks.

How to say it: pih-DUV

Height: 1' 00" **Weight:** 4.6 lbs.

Possible Moves: Gust, Growl, Leer, Quick Attack, Air Cutter, Roost, Detect, Taunt, Air Slash, Razor Wind, Feather Dance, Swagger, Facade, Tailwind, Sky Attack

REGION UNOVA

PIDOVE

Tiny Pigeon Pokémon

Pidove Tranquill Unfezant

TYPE: FIRE-FIGHTING

"Food is fuel"—for Pignite, that common phrase is a bit more literal. When it eats, its internal fire is stoked, which increases its power and speed.

How to say it: pig-NYTE

Height: 3' 03" **Weight:** 122.4 lbs.

Possible Moves: Tackle, Tail Whip, Ember, Odor Sleuth, Defense Curl, Flame Charge, Arm Thrust, Smog, Rollout, Take Down, Heat Crash, Assurance, Flamethrower, Head Smash, Roar, Flare Blitz

REGION UNOVA

PIGNITE

Fire Pig Pokémon

Tepig Pignite Emboar

PIKACHU
Mouse Pokémon

REGIONS
KALOS (CENTRAL), KANTO

Pichu Pikachu Raichu

TYPE: ELECTRIC

The red pouches on Pikachu's cheeks store up electricity while it sleeps. It often delivers a zap when encountering something unfamiliar.

How to say it: PEE-ka-choo

Height: 1' 04" **Weight:** 13.2 lbs.

Possible Moves: Tail Whip, Thunder Shock, Growl, Play Nice, Quick Attack, Thunder Wave, Electro Ball, Double Team, Nuzzle, Slam, Thunderbolt, Feint, Agility, Discharge, Light Screen, Thunder

REGION
HOENN

Pikachu Libre
Special Move:
Flying Press

Pikachu Belle
Special Move:
Icicle Crash

Pikachu PhD
Special Move:
Electric Terrain

Pikachu Pop Star
Special Move:
Draining Kiss

Pikachu Rock Star
Special Move:
Meteor Mash

Does not evolve

REGIONS
JOHTO, KALOS (MOUNTAIN)

PILOSWINE

Swine Pokémon

TYPE: ICE-GROUND

Piloswine's long, thick hair helps protect it from the intense cold of its surroundings. Its tusks can dig through the ice to find buried food.

How to say it: PILE-oh-swine

Height: 3' 07"
Weight: 123.0 lbs.

Possible Moves: Ancient Power, Peck, Odor Sleuth, Mud Sport, Powder Snow, Mud-Slap, Endure, Mud Bomb, Icy Wind, Ice Fang, Take Down, Fury Attack, Mist, Thrash, Earthquake, Blizzard, Amnesia

Swinub → Piloswine → Mamoswine

REGION
JOHTO

PINECO

Bagworm Pokémon

TYPE: BUG

Don't disturb Pineco while it's eating! Most of the time it patiently hangs onto a branch, but if it's dislodged during a meal, it will fall to the ground and explode.

How to say it: PINE-co

Height: 2' 00" **Weight:** 15.9 lbs.

Possible Moves: Tackle, Protect, Self-Destruct, Bug Bite, Take Down, Rapid Spin, Bide, Natural Gift, Spikes, Payback, Explosion, Iron Defense, Gyro Ball, Double-Edge

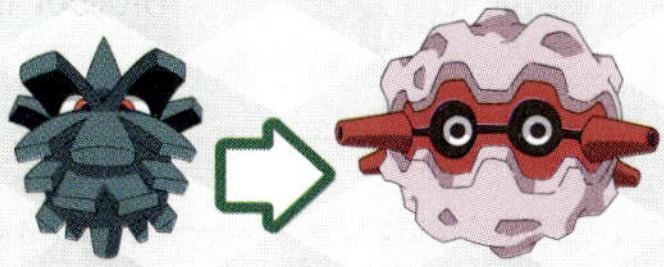

Pineco → Forretress

PINSIR

Stag Beetle Pokémon

REGIONS
KALOS (COASTAL), KANTO

TYPE: BUG

When its strong pincer gets a grip, Pinsir can lift an enemy much bigger than itself. The thorns that line its horns dig into its opponent, making it hard to get away.

How to say it: PIN-sir

Height: 4' 11"
Weight: 121.3 lbs.

Possible Moves: Vice Grip, Focus Energy, Bind, Seismic Toss, Harden, Revenge, Brick Break, Vital Throw, Submission, X-Scissor, Storm Throw, Thrash, Swords Dance, Superpower, Guillotine

MEGA PINSIR

Stag Beetle Pokémon

TYPE: BUG-FLYING

Height: 5' 07"
Weight: 130.1 lbs.

Pinsir → Mega Pinsir

PIPLUP

Penguin Pokémon

REGION
SINNOH

TYPE: WATER

Proud and stubborn, Piplup can be a challenge to train. It's quite independent, preferring to take care of itself and find its own food.

How to say it: PIP-plup

Height: 1' 04"
Weight: 11.5 lbs.

Possible Moves: Pound, Growl, Bubble, Water Sport, Peck, Bubble Beam, Bide, Fury Attack, Brine, Whirlpool, Mist, Drill Peck, Hydro Pump

Piplup   Prinplup   Empoleon

PLUSLE

Cheering Pokémon

REGIONS
HOENN,
KALOS
(CENTRAL)

TYPE: ELECTRIC

Plusle can short out the electricity in its body to create a crackling shower of sparks! It always cheers on its friends in battle.

How to say it: PLUS-ull

Height: 1' 04"
Weight: 9.3 lbs.

Possible Moves: Nasty Plot, Nuzzle, Entrainment, Play Nice, Growl, Thunder Wave, Quick Attack, Helping Hand, Spark, Encore, Copycat, Electro Ball, Swift, Fake Tears, Charge, Thunder, Baton Pass, Agility, Last Resort

Does not evolve

POLITOED

Frog Pokémon

REGIONS
JOHTO, KALOS (MOUNTAIN)

TYPE: WATER

Politoed has a single long, curly hair on the top of its head, which marks it as a ruler. Apparently, a longer hair with more curl is more respected by others.

How to say it: PAUL-lee-TOED

Height: 3' 07"
Weight: 74.7 lbs.

Possible Moves: Bubble Beam, Hypnosis, Double Slap, Perish Song, Swagger, Bounce, Hyper Voice

POLIWAG

Tadpole Pokémon

REGIONS
KALOS (MOUNTAIN), KANTO

TYPE: WATER

Poliwag's skin is so thin that you can see right through it to the Pokémon's spiral-shaped insides. Fortunately, it's also very resilient and flexible.

How to say it: PAUL-lee-wag

Height: 2' 00" **Weight:** 27.3 lbs.

Possible Moves: Water Sport, Water Gun, Hypnosis, Bubble, Double Slap, Rain Dance, Body Slam, Bubble Beam, Mud Shot, Belly Drum, Wake-Up Slap, Hydro Pump, Mud Bomb

POLIWHIRL

REGIONS
KALOS (MOUNTAIN), KANTO

Tadpole Pokémon

TYPE: WATER

Poliwhirl is covered with a slick, slippery, slimy fluid that allows it to wriggle out of sticky situations.

How to say it: PAUL-lee-wirl

Height: 3' 03"
Weight: 44.1 lbs.

Possible Moves: Water Sport, Water Gun, Hypnosis, Bubble, Double Slap, Rain Dance, Body Slam, Bubble Beam, Mud Shot, Belly Drum, Wake-Up Slap, Hydro Pump, Mud Bomb

POLIWRATH

REGIONS
KALOS (MOUNTAIN), KANTO

Tadpole Pokémon

TYPE: WATER-FIGHTING

Burly and muscular, Poliwrath can exercise for hours without getting tired. It swims effortlessly through the ocean.

How to say it: PAUL-lee-rath

Height: 4' 03"
Weight: 119.0 lbs.

Possible Moves: Circle Throw, Bubble Beam, Hypnosis, Double Slap, Submission, Dynamic Punch, Mind Reader

PONYTA

Fire Horse Pokémon

REGION
KANTO

TYPE: FIRE

At the beginning of its life, Ponyta's legs are too weak to hold it up. It quickly learns to run by chasing after its elders.

How to say it: PO-nee-tuh

Height: 3' 03"
Weight: 66.1 lbs.

Possible Moves: Growl, Tackle, Tail Whip, Ember, Flame Wheel, Stomp, Flame Charge, Fire Spin, Take Down, Inferno, Agility, Fire Blast, Bounce, Flare Blitz

POOCHYENA

Bite Pokémon

REGIONS
HOENN, KALOS (MOUNTAIN)

TYPE: DARK

Poochyena tries to look bigger than it is by bristling up its tail. It tends to react to unexpected movement by biting, and it easily chases prey to exhaustion.

How to say it: POO-chee-EH-nah

Height: 1' 08" **Weight:** 30.0 lbs.

Possible Moves: Tackle, Howl, Sand Attack, Bite, Odor Sleuth, Roar, Swagger, Assurance, Scary Face, Taunt, Embargo, Take Down, Sucker Punch, Crunch

REGION KANTO

PORYGON

Virtual Pokémon

TYPE: NORMAL

Porygon was created from programming code, and it can return to that form to navigate cyberspace. It can't be copied like regular data.

How to say it: POR-ee-gon

Height: 2' 07"
Weight: 80.5 lbs.

Possible Moves: Conversion 2, Tackle, Conversion, Sharpen, Psybeam, Agility, Recover, Magnet Rise, Signal Beam, Recycle, Discharge, Lock-On, Tri Attack, Magic Coat, Zap Cannon

Porygon → Porygon2 → Porygon-Z

REGION JOHTO

PORYGON2

Virtual Pokémon

TYPE: NORMAL

Porygon2 is the product of human ingenuity. Programmed with artificial intelligence, it is capable of learning new things.

How to say it: POR-ee-gon TOO

Height: 2' 00" **Weight:** 71.6 lbs.

Possible Moves: Conversion 2, Tackle, Conversion, Defense Curl, Psybeam, Agility, Recover, Magnet Rise, Signal Beam, Recycle, Discharge, Lock-On, Tri Attack, Magic Coat, Zap Cannon, Hyper Beam

Porygon → Porygon2 → Porygon-Z

PORYGON-Z

Virtual Pokémon

REGION
SINNOH

TYPE: NORMAL

Changes in its programming were intended to allow Porygon-Z to travel to other dimensions, but something went awry during the upgrade, and it began behaving erratically.

How to say it: POR-ee-gon ZEE

Height: 2' 11" **Weight:** 75.0 lbs.

Possible Moves: Trick Room, Conversion 2, Tackle, Conversion, Nasty Plot, Psybeam, Agility, Recover, Magnet Rise, Signal Beam, Embargo, Discharge, Lock-On, Tri Attack, Magic Coat, Zap Cannon, Hyper Beam

PRIMEAPE

Pig Monkey Pokémon

REGION
KANTO

TYPE: FIGHTING

Fury increases Primeape's blood flow and powers up its muscles. Its intelligence drops sharply during a rage.

How to say it: PRIME-ape

Height: 3' 03" **Weight:** 70.5 lbs.

Possible Moves: Fling, Scratch, Low Kick, Leer, Focus Energy, Fury Swipes, Karate Chop, Seismic Toss, Screech, Assurance, Rage, Swagger, Cross Chop, Thrash, Punishment, Close Combat, Final Gambit

PRINPLUP

REGION
SINNOH

Penguin Pokémon

TYPE: WATER

Because Prinplup have a strong sense of self-importance, they tend to live alone. They can topple trees by striking with their wings.

How to say it: PRIN-plup

Height: 2' 07"
Weight: 50.7 lbs.

Possible Moves: Tackle, Growl, Bubble, Water Sport, Peck, Metal Claw, Bubble Beam, Bide, Fury Attack, Brine, Whirlpool, Mist, Drill Peck, Hydro Pump

Piplup Prinplup Empoleon

PROBOPASS

REGIONS
KALOS (COASTAL), SINNOH

Compass Pokémon

TYPE: ROCK-STEEL

Probopass uses the strong magnetic field it generates to control the three smaller Mini-Noses attached to the sides of its body.

How to say it: PRO-bow-pass

Height: 4' 07" **Weight:** 749.6 lbs.

Possible Moves: Magnet Rise, Gravity, Tackle, Iron Defense, Block, Magnet Bomb, Thunder Wave, Rock Blast, Rest, Spark, Rock Slide, Power Gem, Sandstorm, Discharge, Earth Power, Stone Edge, Lock-On, Zap Cannon

Nosepass Probopass

PSYDUCK
Duck Pokémon

REGIONS
KALOS (CENTRAL), KANTO

TYPE: WATER

Though Psyduck can use mysterious psychic powers, it can never remember doing so. Apparently, this power creates strange brain waves that resemble deep slumber.

How to say it: SY-duck

Height: 2' 07" **Weight:** 43.2 lbs.

Possible Moves: Water Sport, Scratch, Tail Whip, Water Gun, Disable, Confusion, Water Pulse, Fury Swipes, Screech, Zen Headbutt, Aqua Tail, Soak, Psych Up, Amnesia, Hydro Pump, Wonder Room

PUMPKABOO
Pumpkin Pokémon

REGION
KALOS (MOUNTAIN)

TYPE: GHOST-GRASS

The nocturnal Pumpkaboo tends to get restless as darkness falls. Stories say it serves as a guide for wandering spirits, leading them through the night to find their true home.

How to say it: PUMP-kuh-boo

Height: 1' 04" **Weight:** 11.0 lbs.

Possible Moves: Trick, Astonish, Confuse Ray, Scary Face, Trick-or-Treat, Worry Seed, Razor Leaf, Leech Seed, Bullet Seed, Shadow Sneak, Shadow Ball, Pain Split, Seed Bomb

PUPITAR

Hard Shell Pokémon

REGIONS
JOHTO, KALOS (MOUNTAIN)

TYPE: ROCK-GROUND

Pupitar moves by propulsion, expelling compressed gases to launch itself forward. Its hard surface protects it when it hits solid objects.

How to say it: PUE-puh-tar

Height: 3' 11"
Weight: 335.1 lbs.

Possible Moves: Bite, Leer, Sandstorm, Screech, Chip Away, Rock Slide, Scary Face, Thrash, Dark Pulse, Payback, Crunch, Earthquake, Stone Edge, Hyper Beam

Larvitar Pupitar Tyranitar Mega Tyranitar

PURRLOIN

Devious Pokémon

REGIONS
KALOS (MOUNTAIN), UNOVA

TYPE: DARK

Purrloin acts cute and innocent to trick people into trusting it. Then it steals their stuff.

How to say it: PUR-loyn

Height: 1' 04"
Weight: 22.3 lbs.

Possible Moves: Scratch, Growl, Assist, Sand Attack, Fury Swipes, Pursuit, Torment, Fake Out, Hone Claws, Assurance, Slash, Captivate, Night Slash, Snatch, Nasty Plot, Sucker Punch, Play Rough

Purrloin Liepard

PURUGLY

Tiger Cat Pokémon

REGION
SINNOH

TYPE: NORMAL

Purugly wraps its two tails around its waist to make itself look bigger. It's been known to kick other Pokémon out of their comfortable nests and take over.

How to say it: purr-UG-lee

Height: 3' 03"
Weight: 96.6 lbs.

Possible Moves: Fake Out, Scratch, Growl, Hypnosis, Feint Attack, Fury Swipes, Charm, Assist, Captivate, Slash, Swagger, Body Slam, Attract, Hone Claws

Glameow Purugly

PYROAR

Royal Pokémon

REGION
KALOS
(CENTRAL)

TYPE: FIRE-NORMAL

Pyroar live together in prides, led by the male whose fiery mane is the biggest. The females of the pride guard the young.

How to say it: PIE-roar

Height: 4' 11" **Weight:** 179.7 lbs.

Possible Moves: Hyper Beam, Tackle, Leer, Ember, Work Up, Headbutt, Noble Roar, Take Down, Fire Fang, Endeavor, Echoed Voice, Flamethrower, Crunch, Hyper Voice, Incinerate, Overheat

Male Form

Female Form

Litleo Pyroar

QUAGSIRE

Water Fish Pokémon

REGIONS
JOHTO, KALOS (MOUNTAIN)

TYPE: WATER-GROUND

Quagsire doesn't exactly hunt for food—it hangs out in the water with its mouth open and waits for something to drift in. Fortunately, this lack of movement means it doesn't need to eat much.

How to say it: KWAG-sire

Height: 4' 07" **Weight:** 165.3 lbs.

Possible Moves: Water Gun, Tail Whip, Mud Sport, Mud Shot, Slam, Mud Bomb, Amnesia, Yawn, Earthquake, Rain Dance, Mist, Haze, Muddy Water

Wooper Quagsire

QUILAVA

Volcano Pokémon

REGION
JOHTO

TYPE: FIRE

To keep opponents from getting too close, Quilava heats up the air around it by flaring the flames on its body. It's extremely nimble and good at dodging.

How to say it: kwil-LA-va

Height: 2' 11" **Weight:** 41.9 lbs.

Possible Moves: Tackle, Leer, Smokescreen, Ember, Quick Attack, Flame Wheel, Defense Curl, Swift, Flame Charge, Lava Plume, Flamethrower, Inferno, Rollout, Double-Edge, Eruption

Cyndaquil Quilava Typhlosion

QUILLADIN

Spiny Armor Pokémon

REGION
KALOS (CENTRAL)

TYPE: GRASS

Quilladin often train for battle by charging forcefully into one another. Despite their spiky appearance, they have a gentle nature and don't like confrontation.

How to say it: QUILL-uh-din

Height: 2' 04"
Weight: 63.9 lbs.

Possible Moves: Tackle, Growl, Vine Whip, Rollout, Bite, Leech Seed, Pin Missile, Needle Arm, Take Down, Seed Bomb, Mud Shot, Bulk Up, Body Slam, Pain Split, Wood Hammer

Chespin Quilladin Chesnaught

QWILFISH

Balloon Pokémon

REGIONS
JOHTO, KALOS (COASTAL)

TYPE: WATER-POISON

Qwilfish puffs up its body by sucking in water, and then uses that water pressure to send the poisonous spikes that cover it shooting outward at an opponent.

How to say it: KWILL-fish

Height: 1' 08" **Weight:** 8.6 lbs.

Possible Moves: Fell Stinger, Hydro Pump, Destiny Bond, Water Gun, Spikes, Tackle, Poison Sting, Harden, Minimize, Bubble, Rollout, Toxic Spikes, Stockpile, Spit Up, Revenge, Brine, Pin Missile, Take Down, Aqua Tail, Poison Jab

Does not evolve

REGIONS
KALOS (CENTRAL), KANTO

RAICHU

Mouse Pokémon

TYPE: ELECTRIC

When overcharged with electricity, Raichu sinks its tail into the ground to get rid of the excess. The charge makes it glow faintly in the dark.

How to say it: RYE-choo

Height: 2' 07" **Weight:** 66.1 lbs.

Possible Moves: Thunder Shock, Tail Whip, Quick Attack, Thunderbolt

Pichu Pikachu Raichu

RAIKOU

Thunder Pokémon

REGION
JOHTO

LEGENDARY POKÉMON

TYPE: ELECTRIC

When Raikou roars, the air and land shudder. This Legendary Pokémon moves with lightning speed.

How to say it: RYE-coo

Height: 6' 03" **Weight:** 392.4 lbs.

Possible Moves: Bite, Leer, Thunder Shock, Roar, Quick Attack, Spark, Reflect, Crunch, Thunder Fang, Discharge, Extrasensory, Rain Dance, Calm Mind, Thunder

Does not evolve

RALTS

Feeling Pokémon

REGIONS
HOENN, KALOS (CENTRAL)

TYPE: PSYCHIC-FAIRY

With its horns, Ralts can sense people's emotions. Its own mood tends to reflect what it senses, and it's drawn to people with a positive attitude.

How to say it: RALTS

Height: 1' 04"
Weight: 14.6 lbs.

Possible Moves: Growl, Confusion, Double Team, Teleport, Lucky Chant, Magical Leaf, Heal Pulse, Calm Mind, Psychic, Imprison, Future Sight, Charm, Hypnosis, Dream Eater, Stored Power

RAMPARDOS

Head Butt Pokémon

REGION
SINNOH

TYPE: ROCK

Rampardos can smash through anything with its skull, which is iron-hard and incredibly thick. Unfortunately, this means its brain has no room to grow.

How to say it: ram-PAR-dose

Height: 5' 03"
Weight: 226.0 lbs.

Possible Moves: Headbutt, Leer, Focus Energy, Pursuit, Take Down, Scary Face, Assurance, Chip Away, Endeavor, Ancient Power, Zen Headbutt, Screech, Head Smash

RAPIDASH

Fire Horse Pokémon

REGION
KANTO

TYPE: FIRE

Most of the time, Rapidash travels at a casual canter across the flat lands where it lives. When it breaks into a gallop, its mane blazes brightly.

How to say it: RAP-i-dash

Height: 3' 11"
Weight: 69.7 lbs.

Possible Moves: Poison Jab, Megahorn, Growl, Quick Attack, Tail Whip, Ember, Flame Wheel, Stomp, Flame Charge, Fire Spin, Take Down, Inferno, Agility, Fury Attack, Fire Blast, Bounce, Flare Blitz

RATICATE

REGION KANTO

Mouse Pokémon

TYPE: NORMAL

Because Raticate's fangs never stop growing, it has to gnaw on hard objects to whittle them down. Logs and rocks often serve this purpose, but sometimes it chews on houses!

How to say it: RAT-i-kate

Height: 2' 04"
Weight: 40.8 lbs.

Possible Moves: Swords Dance, Tackle, Tail Whip, Quick Attack, Focus Energy, Bite, Pursuit, Hyper Fang, Sucker Punch, Scary Face, Crunch, Assurance, Super Fang, Double-Edge, Endeavor

Rattata Raticate

RATTATA

REGION KANTO

Mouse Pokémon

TYPE: NORMAL

Rattata is always on the alert, keeping an ear out for the slightest sound even in its sleep. It's happy to nest just about anywhere.

How to say it: ruh-TA-tah

Height: 1' 00"
Weight: 7.7 lbs.

Possible Moves: Tackle, Tail Whip, Quick Attack, Focus Energy, Bite, Pursuit, Hyper Fang, Sucker Punch, Crunch, Assurance, Super Fang, Double-Edge, Endeavor

Rattata Raticate

RAYQUAZA

Sky High Pokémon

REGION
HOENN

LEGENDARY POKÉMON

TYPE: DRAGON-FLYING

Legends say the ancient Pokémon Rayquaza flies through the upper atmosphere and feeds on meteoroids. It's known for stopping the endless battles between Kyogre and Groudon.

How to say it: ray-KWAZ-uh

Height: 23' 00"
Weight: 455.2 lbs.

Possible Moves: Twister, Scary Face, Crunch, Hyper Voice, Rest, Air Slash, Ancient Power, Outrage, Dragon Dance, Fly, Extreme Speed, Hyper Beam, Dragon Pulse

MEGA RAYQUAZA

Sky High Pokémon

TYPE: DRAGON-FLYING

Height: 35' 05"
Weight: 864.2 lbs.

LEGENDARY POKÉMON

REGION
HOENN

REGICE

Iceberg Pokémon

TYPE: ICE

Created during an ice age, Regice's body is frozen solid, and even lava can't melt it. It can lower the temperature of the air around it by several hundred degrees.

How to say it: REDGE-ice

Height: 5' 11" **Weight:** 385.8 lbs.

Possible Moves: Explosion, Stomp, Icy Wind, Curse, Superpower, Ancient Power, Amnesia, Charge Beam, Lock-On, Zap Cannon, Ice Beam, Hammer Arm, Hyper Beam

Does not evolve

REGIGIGAS

Colossal Pokémon

REGION
SINNOH

LEGENDARY POKÉMON

TYPE: NORMAL

According to legend, Regigigas built smaller models of itself out of rock, ice, and magma. It's so enormous that it could tow an entire continent behind it.

How to say it: REDGE-ee-gee-gus

Height: 12' 02" **Weight:** 925.9 lbs.

Possible Moves: Fire Punch, Ice Punch, Thunder Punch, Dizzy Punch, Knock Off, Confuse Ray, Foresight, Revenge, Wide Guard, Zen Headbutt, Payback, Crush Grip, Heavy Slam, Giga Impact

Does not evolve

LEGENDARY POKÉMON

REGION
HOENN

REGIROCK

Rock Peak Pokémon

TYPE: ROCK

Regirock's body is made entirely of rocks, and these rocks were recently discovered to be from all around the world. It repairs itself after battle by seeking out new rocks.

How to say it: REDGE-ee-rock

Height: 5' 07" **Weight:** 507.1 lbs.

Possible Moves: Explosion, Stomp, Rock Throw, Curse, Superpower, Ancient Power, Iron Defense, Charge Beam, Lock-On, Zap Cannon, Stone Edge, Hammer Arm, Hyper Beam

Does not evolve

REGISTEEL

Iron Pokémon

REGION
HOENN

LEGENDARY POKÉMON

TYPE: STEEL

Registeel isn't actually made of steel—it's a strange substance harder than any known metal. Ancient people sealed it away in a prison.

How to say it: REDGE-ee-steel

Height: 6' 03" **Weight:** 451.9 lbs.

Possible Moves: Explosion, Stomp, Metal Claw, Curse, Superpower, Ancient Power, Iron Defense, Amnesia, Charge Beam, Lock-On, Zap Cannon, Iron Head, Flash Cannon, Hammer Arm, Hyper Beam

Does not evolve

RELICANTH

Longevity Pokémon

REGIONS
HOENN, KALOS (COASTAL)

TYPE: WATER-ROCK

Relicanth today look much the same as they did one hundred million years ago. These ancient Pokémon are covered in rocky scales to protect them in the ocean depths.

How to say it: REL-uh-canth

Height: 3' 03"
Weight: 51.6 lbs.

Possible Moves: Head Smash, Hydro Pump, Ancient Power, Mud Sport, Tackle, Harden, Water Gun, Rock Tomb, Yawn, Take Down, Double-Edge, Dive, Rest

Does not evolve

REMORAID

Jet Pokémon

REGIONS
JOHTO, KALOS (COASTAL)

TYPE: WATER

Remoraid can knock flying targets out of the air with precise jets of high-velocity water. It swims downstream when it's time to evolve.

How to say it: REM-oh-raid

Height: 2' 00"
Weight: 26.5 lbs.

Possible Moves: Water Gun, Lock-On, Psybeam, Aurora Beam, Bubble Beam, Focus Energy, Water Pulse, Signal Beam, Ice Beam, Bullet Seed, Hydro Pump, Hyper Beam, Soak

Remoraid → Octillery

RESHIRAM
Vast White Pokémon

REGION
UNOVA

LEGENDARY POKÉMON

TYPE: DRAGON-FIRE

Legends say Reshiram is drawn to those who value the truth. The flare of its fiery tail can disrupt the atmosphere and cause strange weather patterns.

How to say it: RESH-i-ram

Height: 10' 06" **Weight:** 6,727.5 lbs.

Possible Moves: Fire Fang, Dragon Rage, Imprison, Ancient Power, Flamethrower, Dragon Breath, Slash, Extrasensory, Fusion Flare, Dragon Pulse, Imprison, Crunch, Fire Blast, Outrage, Hyper Voice, Blue Flare

Does not evolve

REUNICLUS

Multiplying Pokémon

REGIONS
KALOS (COASTAL), UNOVA

TYPE: PSYCHIC

Reuniclus shake hands with one another to create a network between their brains. Working together boosts their psychic power, and they can crush huge rocks with their minds.

How to say it: ree-yoo-NIH-klus

Height: 3' 03"
Weight: 44.3 lbs.

Possible Moves: Psywave, Reflect, Rollout, Snatch, Hidden Power, Light Screen, Charm, Recover, Psyshock, Endeavor, Future Sight, Pain Split, Psychic, Dizzy Punch, Skill Swap, Heal Block, Wonder Room

Solosis Duosion Reuniclus

RHYDON

Drill Pokémon

REGIONS
KALOS (COASTAL), KANTO

TYPE: GROUND-ROCK

Rhydon's horn, which it uses as a drill, is hard enough to crush diamonds. Its hide is like armor, and it can run right through molten lava without feeling a thing.

How to say it: RYE-don

Height: 6' 03" **Weight:** 264.6 lbs.

Possible Moves: Megahorn, Horn Drill, Horn Attack, Tail Whip, Stomp, Fury Attack, Scary Face, Rock Blast, Bulldoze, Chip Away, Take Down, Hammer Arm, Drill Run, Stone Edge, Earthquake

Rhyhorn Rhydon Rhyperior

RHYHORN

Spikes Pokémon

REGIONS
KALOS (COASTAL), KANTO

TYPE: GROUND-ROCK

A charging Rhyhorn is so single-minded that it doesn't think about anything else until it demolishes its target.

How to say it: RYE-horn

Height: 3' 03"
Weight: 253.5 lbs.

Possible Moves: Horn Attack, Tail Whip, Stomp, Fury Attack, Scary Face, Rock Blast, Bulldoze, Chip Away, Take Down, Drill Run, Stone Edge, Earthquake, Horn Drill, Megahorn

Rhyhorn Rhydon Rhyperior

RHYPERIOR

Drill Pokémon

REGIONS
KALOS (COASTAL), SINNOH

TYPE: GROUND-ROCK

Rhyperior uses the holes in its hands to bombard its opponents with rocks. Sometimes it even hurls a Geodude! Rhyperior's rocky hide is thick enough to protect it from molten lava.

How to say it: rye-PEER-ee-or

Height: 7' 10"
Weight: 623.5 lbs.

Possible Moves: Rock Wrecker, Megahorn, Horn Drill, Poison Jab, Horn Attack, Tail Whip, Stomp, Fury Attack, Scary Face, Rock Blast, Chip Away, Take Down, Hammer Arm, Drill Run, Stone Edge, Earthquake

Rhyhorn Rhydon Rhyperior

REGIONS
KALOS (CENTRAL), SINNOH

RIOLU

Emanation Pokémon

TYPE: FIGHTING

The aura surrounding Riolu's body indicates its emotional state. It alters the shape of this aura to communicate.

How to say it: ree-OH-loo

Height: 2' 04"
Weight: 44.5 lbs.

Possible Moves: Foresight, Quick Attack, Endure, Counter, Feint, Force Palm, Copycat, Screech, Reversal, Nasty Plot, Final Gambit

Riolu → Lucario → Mega Lucario

REGIONS
KALOS (COASTAL), UNOVA

ROGGENROLA

Mantle Pokémon

TYPE: ROCK

Each Roggenrola has an energy core at its center. The intense pressure in their underground home has compressed their bodies into a steely toughness.

How to say it: rah-gen-ROH-lah

Height: 1' 04" **Weight:** 39.7 lbs.

Possible Moves: Tackle, Harden, Sand Attack, Headbutt, Rock Blast, Mud-Slap, Iron Defense, Smack Down, Rock Slide, Stealth Rock, Sandstorm, Stone Edge, Explosion

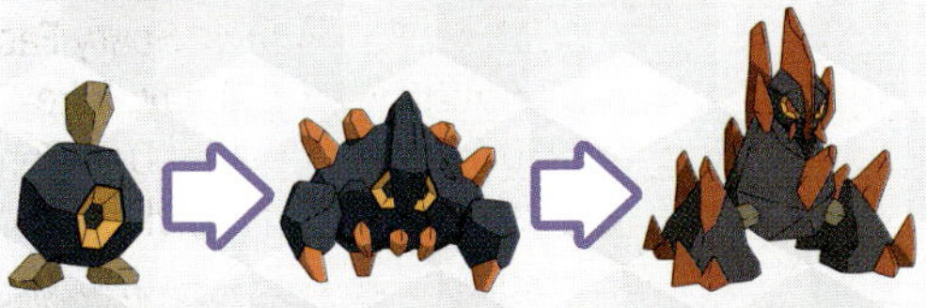

Roggenrola → Boldore → Gigalith

ROSELIA

Thorn Pokémon

REGIONS
HOENN, KALOS (CENTRAL)

TYPE: GRASS-POISON

Thieves sometimes try to swipe the lovely blossoms Roselia grows. It responds with a shower of sharp, poisonous thorns.

How to say it: roh-ZEH-lee-uh

Height: 1' 00" **Weight:** 4.4 lbs.

Possible Moves: Absorb, Growth, Poison Sting, Stun Spore, Mega Drain, Leech Seed, Magical Leaf, Grass Whistle, Giga Drain, Toxic Spikes, Sweet Scent, Ingrain, Petal Dance, Toxic, Aromatherapy, Synthesis, Petal Blizzard

Budew Roselia Roserade

ROSERADE

Bouquet Pokémon

REGIONS
KALOS (CENTRAL), SINNOH

TYPE: GRASS-POISON

With its beautiful blooms, enticing aroma, and graceful movements, Roserade is quite enchanting—but watch out! Its arms conceal thorny whips, and the thorns carry poison.

How to say it: ROSE-raid

Height: 2' 11"
Weight: 32.0 lbs.

Possible Moves: Venom Drench, Grassy Terrain, Weather Ball, Poison Sting, Mega Drain, Magical Leaf, Sweet Scent

Budew Roselia Roserade

ROTOM

Plasma Pokémon

REGIONS
KALOS (MOUNTAIN), SINNOH

TYPE: ELECTRIC-GHOST

Scientists are conducting ongoing research on Rotom, which shows potential as a power source. Sometimes it sneaks into electrical appliances and causes trouble.

How to say it: ROW-tom

Height: 1' 00"
Weight: 0.7 lbs.

Possible Moves: Discharge, Charge, Trick, Astonish, Thunder Wave, Thunder Shock, Confuse Ray, Uproar, Double Team, Shock Wave, Ominous Wind, Substitute, Electro Ball, Hex

Does not evolve

RUFFLET

Eaglet Pokémon

REGION
UNOVA

TYPE: NORMAL-FLYING

Rufflet is absolutely fearless when challenging opponents. It will pick a fight with just about anyone, becoming stronger in the process.

How to say it: RUF-lit

Height: 21' 08" **Weight:** 23.1 lbs.

Possible Moves: Peck, Leer, Fury Attack, Wing Attack, Hone Claws, Scary Face, Aerial Ace, Slash, Defog, Tailwind, Air Slash, Crush Claw, Sky Drop, Whirlwind, Brave Bird, Thrash

Rufflet → Braviary

SABLEYE

Darkness Pokémon

REGIONS
HOENN, KALOS (COASTAL)

TYPE: DARK-GHOST

Sableye lives deep in a cave, where it uses its sharp claws to dig up rocks for food. Minerals from these rocks then become part of its gemstone eyes and the crystals on its body.

How to say it: SAY-bull-eye

Height: 1' 08" **Weight:** 24.3 lbs.

Possible Moves: Mean Look, Zen Headbutt, Leer, Scratch, Foresight, Night Shade, Astonish, Fury Swipes, Fake Out, Detect, Shadow Sneak, Knock Off, Feint Attack, Punishment, Shadow Claw, Power Gem, Confuse Ray, Foul Play, Shadow Ball

MEGA SABLEYE

Darkness Pokémon

TYPE: DARK-GHOST

Height: 1' 08"
Weight: 24.3 lbs.

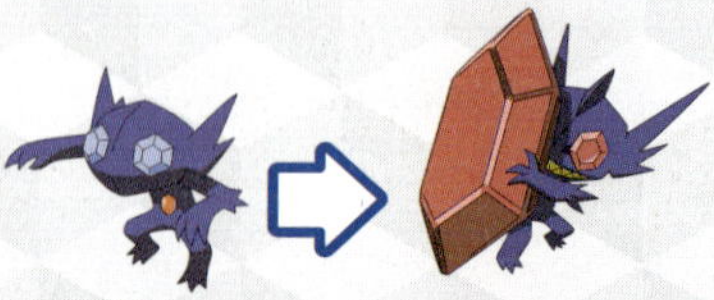

Sableye Mega Sableye

SALAMENCE

Dragon Pokémon

REGIONS
HOENN, KALOS (COASTAL)

TYPE: DRAGON-FLYING

When it evolves, Salamence finally grows the wings it's always dreamed of. It trails fire across the sky in a soaring celebration.

How to say it: SAL-uh-mence

Height: 4' 11"
Weight: 226.2 lbs.

Possible Moves: Double-Edge, Fire Fang, Thunder Fang, Rage, Bite, Leer, Headbutt, Focus Energy, Ember, Protect, Dragon Breath, Zen Headbutt, Scary Face, Fly, Crunch, Dragon Claw, Dragon Tail

MEGA SALAMENCE

Dragon Pokémon

TYPE: DRAGON-FLYING

Height: 5' 11"
Weight: 248.2 lbs.

Bagon → Shelgon → Salamence → Mega Salamence

SAMUROTT

Formidable Pokémon

REGION
UNOVA

Oshawott Dewott Samurott

TYPE: WATER

From the armor on its front legs, Samurott can draw its swordlike seamitars in a heartbeat. Its glare can make everyone behave.

How to say it: SAM-uh-rot

Height: 4' 11" **Weight:** 208.6 lbs.

Possible Moves: Megahorn, Tackle, Tail Whip, Water Gun, Water Sport, Focus Energy, Razor Shell, Fury Cutter, Water Pulse, Revenge, Aqua Jet, Slash, Encore, Aqua Tail, Retaliate, Swords Dance, Hydro Pump

SANDILE

Desert Croc

REGIONS
KALOS (COASTAL), UNOVA

Sandile Krokorok Krookodile

TYPE: GROUND-DARK

Sandile travels just below the surface of the desert sand, with only its nose and eyes sticking out. The warmth of the sand keeps it from getting too cold.

How to say it: SAN-dyle

Height: 2' 04"
Weight: 33.5 lbs.

Possible Moves: Leer, Rage, Bite, Sand Attack, Torment, Sand Tomb, Assurance, Mud-Slap, Embargo, Swagger, Crunch, Dig, Scary Face, Foul Play, Sandstorm, Earthquake, Thrash

SANDSHREW

Mouse Pokémon

REGIONS
KALOS (MOUNTAIN), KANTO

TYPE: GROUND

When Sandshrew rolls up into a ball, its tough hide helps keep it safe. It lives in the desert and sleeps in a burrow under the sand.

How to say it: SAND-shroo

Height: 2' 00"
Weight: 26.5 lbs.

Possible Moves: Scratch, Defense Curl, Sand Attack, Poison Sting, Rollout, Rapid Spin, Swift, Fury Cutter, Magnitude, Fury Swipes, Sand Tomb, Slash, Dig, Gyro Ball, Swords Dance, Sandstorm, Earthquake

Sandshrew

Sandslash

SANDSLASH

Mouse Pokémon

REGIONS
KALOS (MOUNTAIN), KANTO

TYPE: GROUND

Sections of hardened hide form the spikes that cover Sandslash's body. The spikes protect it in battle and can also be used as a weapon.

How to say it: SAND-slash

Height: 3' 03" **Weight:** 65.0 lbs.

Possible Moves: Scratch, Defense Curl, Sand Attack, Poison Sting, Rollout, Rapid Spin, Swift, Fury Cutter, Magnitude, Fury Swipes, Crush Claw, Sand Tomb, Slash, Dig, Gyro Ball, Swords Dance, Sandstorm, Earthquake

Sandshrew

Sandslash

SAWK
Karate Pokémon

REGIONS
KALOS (COASTAL), UNOVA

TYPE: FIGHTING

Sawk go deep into the mountains to train their fighting skills relentlessly. If they are disturbed during this training, they become very angry.

How to say it: SAWK

Height: 4' 07"
Weight: 112.4 lbs.

Possible Moves: Rock Smash, Leer, Bide, Focus Energy, Double Kick, Low Sweep, Counter, Karate Chop, Brick Break, Bulk Up, Retaliate, Endure, Quick Guard, Close Combat, Reversal

Does not evolve

SAWSBUCK
Season Pokémon

REGION
UNOVA

Winter Form

Spring Form

Summer Form

Autumn Form

Deerling Sawsbuck

TYPE: NORMAL-GRASS

As the seasons change, their horns display different kinds of plant growth. Because of their seasonal migration, some people regard Sawsbuck's appearance as a sign of spring.

How to say it: SAWZ-buk

Height: 6' 03"
Weight: 203.9 lbs.

Possible Moves: Megahorn, Tackle, Camouflage, Growl, Sand Attack, Double Kick, Leech Seed, Feint Attack, Take Down, Jump Kick, Aromatherapy, Energy Ball, Charm, Horn Leech, Nature Power, Double-Edge, Solar Beam

REGION
KALOS
(CENTRAL)

SCATTERBUG

Scatterdust Pokémon

TYPE: BUG

When threatened, Scatterbug protects itself with a cloud of black powder that can paralyze its attacker. This powder also serves as protection from the elements.

How to say it: SCAT-ter-BUG

Height: 1' 00" **Weight:** 5.5 lbs.

Possible Moves: Tackle, String Shot, Stun Spore, Bug Bite

SCEPTILE

Forest Pokémon

REGION
HOENN

TYPE: GRASS

Razor-edged leaves and nutritious seeds sprout from Sceptile's back. It wields the leaves in battle, and cares for trees by planting its seeds nearby to enrich the soil.

How to say it: SEP-tile

Height: 5' 07"
Weight: 115.1 lbs.

Possible Moves: Night Slash, Pound, Leer, Absorb, Quick Attack, X-Scissor, Pursuit, Screech, Leaf Blade, Agility, Slam, Detect, False Swipe, Leaf Storm

MEGA SCEPTILE

Forest Pokémon

TYPE: GRASS

Height: 6' 03"
Weight: 121.7 lbs.

Treecko → Grovyle → Sceptile → Mega Sceptile

SCIZOR

Pincer Pokémon

TYPE: BUG-STEEL

Scizor's exoskeleton is as hard as steel, easily shrugging off most ordinary attacks. It controls its internal temperature by flapping its wings.

How to say it: SI-zor

Height: 5' 11" **Weight:** 260.1 lbs.

Possible Moves: Feint, Bullet Punch, Quick Attack, Leer, Focus Energy, Pursuit, False Swipe, Agility, Metal Claw, Fury Cutter, Slash, Razor Wind, Iron Defense, X-Scissor, Night Slash, Double Hit, Iron Head, Swords Dance

MEGA SCIZOR

Pincer Pokémon

TYPE: BUG-STEEL

Height: 6' 07"
Weight: 275.6 lbs.

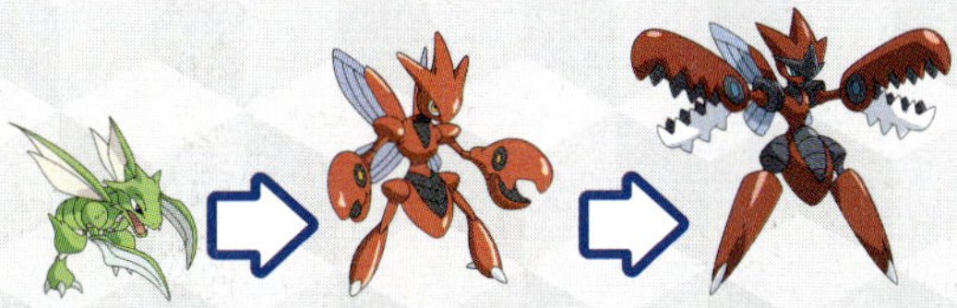

SCOLIPEDE

Megapede Pokémon

REGIONS
KALOS (CENTRAL), UNOVA

TYPE: BUG-POISON

The claws near Scolipede's head can be used to grab, immobilize, and poison its opponent. Scolipede moves quickly when chasing down enemies.

How to say it: SKOH-lih-peed

Height: 8' 02"
Weight: 442.0 lbs.

Possible Moves: Megahorn, Defense Curl, Rollout, Poison Sting, Screech, Pursuit, Protect, Poison Tail, Bug Bite, Venoshock, Baton Pass, Agility, Steamroller, Toxic, Venom Drench, Rock Climb, Double-Edge

Venipede Whirlipede Scolipede

SCRAFTY

Hoodlum Pokémon

REGIONS
KALOS (CENTRAL), UNOVA

TYPE: DARK-FIGHTING

A group of Scrafty is led by the one with the biggest crest. Their powerful kicks can shatter concrete.

How to say it: SKRAF-tee

Height: 3' 07"
Weight: 66.1 lbs.

Possible Moves: Leer, Low Kick, Sand Attack, Feint Attack, Headbutt, Swagger, Brick Break, Payback, Chip Away, High Jump Kick, Scary Face, Crunch, Facade, Rock Climb, Focus Punch, Head Smash

Scraggy Scrafty

REGIONS
KALOS (CENTRAL), UNOVA

SCRAGGY

Shedding Pokémon

TYPE: DARK-FIGHTING

Scraggy can pull its loose, rubbery skin up around its neck to protect itself from attacks. With its tough skull, it delivers headbutts without warning.

How to say it: SKRAG-ee

Height: 2' 00" **Weight:** 26.0 lbs.

Possible Moves: Leer, Low Kick, Sand Attack, Feint Attack, Headbutt, Swagger, Brick Break, Payback, Chip Away, High Jump Kick, Scary Face, Crunch, Facade, Rock Climb, Focus Punch, Head Smash

Scraggy → Scrafty

REGIONS
KALOS (MOUNTAIN), KANTO

SCYTHER

Mantis Pokémon

TYPE: BUG-FLYING

With its impressive speed and razor-sharp scythes, Scyther is a formidable opponent. It can slash through a log with one blow.

How to say it: SY-thur

Height: 4' 11" **Weight:** 123.5 lbs.

Possible Moves: Vacuum Wave, Quick Attack, Leer, Focus Energy, Pursuit, False Swipe, Agility, Wing Attack, Fury Cutter, Slash, Razor Wind, Double Team, X-Scissor, Night Slash, Double Hit, Air Slash, Swords Dance, Feint

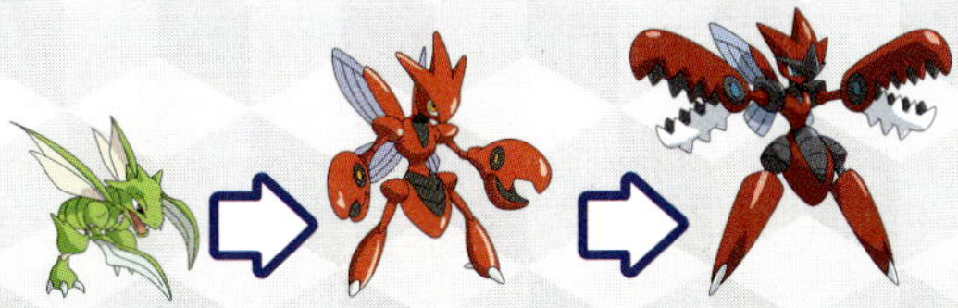

Scyther → Scizor → Mega Scizor

SEADRA

Dragon Pokémon

REGIONS
KALOS (COASTAL), KANTO

TYPE: WATER

When Seadra spins around in the water, it can cause a whirlpool with enough force to capsize a small boat. It sleeps among coral branches.

How to say it: SEE-dra

Height: 3' 11"
Weight: 55.1 lbs.

Possible Moves: Water Gun, Smokescreen, Leer, Bubble, Focus Energy, Bubble Beam, Agility, Twister, Brine, Hydro Pump, Dragon Dance, Dragon Pulse

Horsea Seadra Kingdra

SEAKING

Goldfish Pokémon

REGIONS
KALOS (COASTAL), KANTO

TYPE: WATER

Male Seaking become brilliantly colored during the autumn, when they perform their courtship dance. The pair take turns keeping watch over their nests.

How to say it: SEE-king

Height: 4' 03"
Weight: 86.0 lbs.

Possible Moves: Megahorn, Poison Jab, Peck, Tail Whip, Water Sport, Supersonic, Horn Attack, Water Pulse, Flail, Aqua Ring, Fury Attack, Waterfall, Horn Drill, Agility, Soak

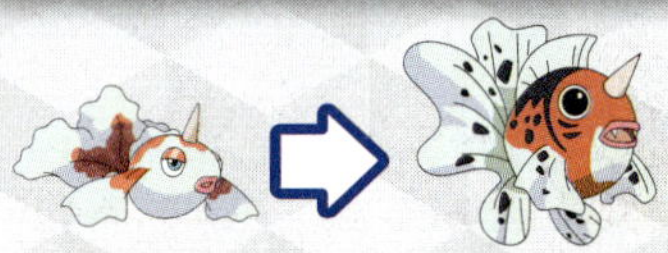

Goldeen Seaking

REGION
HOENN

SEALEO

Ball Roll Pokémon

TYPE: ICE-WATER

Sealeo learns about new things by exploring them with its nose, examining the fragrance and texture. It particularly enjoys spinning round objects on its nose.

How to say it: SEEL-ee-oh

Height: 3' 07"
Weight: 193.1 lbs.

Possible Moves: Powder Snow, Growl, Water Gun, Encore, Ice Ball, Body Slam, Aurora Beam, Hall, Swagger, Rest, Snore, Blizzard, Sheer Cold

REGION
HOENN

SEEDOT

Acorn Pokémon

TYPE: GRASS

Because Seedot hangs from branches by the top of its head, it looks just like an acorn when it isn't moving. For a glossy finish, it drinks plenty of water and polishes itself with leaves.

How to say it: SEE-dot

Height: 1' 08"
Weight: 8.8 lbs.

Possible Moves: Bide, Harden, Growth, Nature Power, Synthesis, Sunny Day, Explosion

SEEL

Sea Lion Pokémon

REGION
KANTO

TYPE: WATER

In frozen seas, Seel swims under the ice in search of food. It uses the point on its head to break through the ice when it comes up for air.

How to say it: SEEL

Height: 3' 07"
Weight: 198.4 lbs.

Possible Moves: Headbutt, Growl, Water Sport, Icy Wind, Encore, Ice Shard, Rest, Aqua Ring, Aurora Beam, Aqua Jet, Brine, Take Down, Dive, Aqua Tail, Ice Beam, Safeguard, Hail

Seel Dewgong

SEISMITOAD

Vibration Pokémon

REGION
UNOVA

TYPE: WATER-GROUND

When Seismitoad vibrates the bumps on its hands, its punches get a serious power boost—enough to pulverize a boulder with a single hit.

How to say it: SYZ-mih-tohd

Height: 4' 11"
Weight: 136.7 lbs.

Possible Moves: Bubble, Growl, Supersonic, Round, Bubble Beam, Mud Shot, Aqua Ring, Uproar, Muddy Water, Rain Dance, Acid, Flail, Drain Punch, Echoed Voice, Hydro Pump, Hyper Voice

Tympole Palpitoad Seismitoad

REGIONS
JOHTO, KALOS (CENTRAL)

SENTRET

Scout Pokémon

TYPE: NORMAL

Sentret always sleep in groups of two or more so one of them can keep watch and alert its friends if danger threatens. When alone, they're too nervous to sleep.

How to say it: SEN-tret

Height: 2' 07" **Weight:** 13.2 lbs.

Possible Moves: Scratch, Foresight, Defense Curl, Quick Attack, Fury Swipes, Helping Hand, Follow Me, Slam, Rest, Sucker Punch, Amnesia, Baton Pass, Me First, Hyper Voice

Sentret → Furret

REGION
UNOVA

SERPERIOR

Regal Pokémon

TYPE: GRASS

A single glare from Serperior can stop most opponents in their tracks. The energy it absorbs from the sun gets a boost inside its body.

How to say it: sur-PEER-ee-ur

Height: 10' 10"
Weight: 138.9 lbs.

Possible Moves: Tackle, Leer, Vine Whip, Wrap, Growth, Leaf Tornado, Leech Seed, Mega Drain, Slam, Leaf Blade, Coil, Giga Drain, Wring Out, Gastro Acid, Leaf Storm

Snivy → Servine → Serperior

SERVINE

Grass Snake Pokémon

REGION
UNOVA

TYPE: GRASS

Dirt on its leaves blocks its photosynthesis, so Servine is fussy about staying clean. It confounds its enemies with quick movements before it strikes with its whiplike vines.

How to say it: SUR-vine

Height: 2' 07"
Weight: 35.3 lbs.

Possible Moves: Tackle, Leer, Vine Whip, Wrap, Growth, Leaf Tornado, Leech Seed, Mega Drain, Slam, Leaf Blade, Coil, Giga Drain, Wring Out, Gastro Acid, Leaf Storm

SEVIPER

Fang Snake Pokémon

REGIONS
HOENN, KALOS (COASTAL)

TYPE: POISON

The sharp blade on Seviper's tail also gives off a powerful poison. These Pokémon constantly feud with Zangoose.

How to say it: seh-VIE-per

Height: 8' 10"
Weight: 115.7 lbs.

Possible Moves: Wrap, Swagger, Bite, Lick, Poison Tail, Screech, Venoshock, Glare, Poison Fang, Venom Drench, Night Slash, Gastro Acid, Haze, Poison Jab, Crunch, Belch, Coil, Wring Out

Does not evolve

REGION
UNOVA

SEWADDLE

Sewing Pokémon

TYPE: BUG-GRASS

Sewaddle makes clothing for itself by sewing leaves together with the sticky thread it produces from its mouth. Fashion designers often use it as a mascot.

How to say it: seh-WAH-dul

Height: 1' 00" **Weight:** 5.5 lbs.

Possible Moves: Tackle, String Shot, Bug Bite, Razor Leaf, Struggle Bug, Endure, Bug Buzz, Flail

Sewaddle Swadloon Leavanny

SHARPEDO

Brutal Pokémon

REGIONS
HOENN, KALOS (CENTRAL)

TYPE: WATER-DARK

Though Sharpedo isn't great at swimming long distances, it can shoot forward at seventy-five MPH by propelling seawater through its body. If a tooth falls out, it grows back immediately.

How to say it: shar-PEE-do

Height: 5' 11"
Weight: 195.8 lbs.

Possible Moves: Night Slash, Feint, Leer, Bite, Rage, Focus Energy, Scary Face, Ice Fang, Screech, Swagger, Assurance, Crunch, Slash, Aqua Jet, Taunt, Agility, Skull Bash

MEGA SHARPEDO

Brutal Pokémon

TYPE: WATER-DARK

Height: 8' 02"
Weight: 287.3 lbs.

REGION
SINNOH

SHAYMIN (LAND FORME)

Gratitude Pokémon

TYPE: GRASS

When the Gracidea flower blooms, Shaymin gains the power of flight. Wherever it goes, it clears the air of toxins and brings feelings of gratitude.

How to say it: SHAY-min

Height: 0' 08" **Weight:** 4.6 lbs.

Possible Moves: Growth, Magical Leaf, Leech Seed, Synthesis, Sweet Scent, Natural Gift, Worry Seed, Aromatherapy, Energy Ball, Sweet Kiss, Healing Wish, Seed Flare

MYTHICAL POKÉMON

Does not evolve

REGION
SINNOH

SHAYMIN (SKY FORME)

Gratitude Pokémon

TYPE: GRASS-FLYING

Shaymin has the power to clean the environment in this forme, too. Once it has transformed, Shaymin Sky Forme flies off to find a new home.

How to say it: SHAY-min

Height: 1' 04" **Weight:** 11.5 lbs.

Possible Moves: Growth, Magical Leaf, Leech Seed, Quick Attack, Sweet Scent, Natural Gift, Worry Seed, Air Slash, Energy Ball, Sweet Kiss, Leaf Storm, Seed Flare

MYTHICAL POKÉMON

Does not evolve

SHEDINJA
Shed Pokémon

REGIONS
HOENN, KALOS (CENTRAL)

TYPE: BUG-GHOST

Shedinja is a strange Pokémon. It doesn't move, it doesn't breathe, and no one really knows where it came from. Its body seems to be nothing more than a hollow shell.

How to say it: sheh-DIN-ja

Height: 2' 07" **Weight:** 2.6 lbs.

Possible Moves: Scratch, Harden, Leech Life, Sand Attack, Fury Swipes, Mind Reader, Spite, Confuse Ray, Shadow Sneak, Grudge, Phantom Force, Heal Block, Shadow Ball

SHELGON
Endurance Pokémon

REGIONS
HOENN, KALOS (COASTAL)

TYPE: DRAGON

A shell of thick armor protects Shelgon while it prepares to evolve. It's hard enough to repel enemy attacks, and so heavy that it makes the Pokémon move slowly.

How to say it: SHELL-gon

Height: 3' 07" **Weight:** 243.6 lbs.

Possible Moves: Rage, Bite, Leer, Headbutt, Focus Energy, Ember, Protect, Dragon Breath, Zen Headbutt, Scary Face, Crunch, Dragon Claw, Double-Edge

SHELLDER
Bivalve Pokémon

REGIONS
KALOS (COASTAL), KANTO

TYPE: WATER

When Shellder's shell is closed, its large tongue tends to hang out. It uses its tongue as a shovel to dig a nest in the sand.

How to say it: SHELL-der

Height: 1' 00"
Weight: 8.8 lbs.

Possible Moves: Tackle, Withdraw, Supersonic, Icicle Spear, Protect, Leer, Clamp, Ice Shard, Razor Shell, Aurora Beam, Whirlpool, Brine, Iron Defense, Ice Beam, Shell Smash, Hydro Pump

SHELLOS (EAST SEA)
Sea Slug Pokémon

REGION
SINNOH

TYPE: WATER

Shellos come in different colors and shapes, depending on where they live. Their squishy bodies give off a strange purple fluid when pressure is applied.

How to say it: SHELL-oss

Height: 1' 00"
Weight: 13.9 lbs.

Possible Moves: Mud-Slap, Mud Sport, Harden, Water Pulse, Mud Bomb, Hidden Power, Rain Dance, Body Slam, Muddy Water, Recover

SHELLOS (WEST SEA)

Sea Slug Pokémon

REGION
SINNOH

TYPE: WATER

Like Gastrodon, Shellos will look quite different depending upon where it lives.

How to say it: SHELL-oss

Height: 1' 00"
Weight: 13.9 lbs.

Possible Moves: Mud-Slap, Mud Sport, Harden, Water Pulse, Mud Bomb, Hidden Power, Rain Dance, Body Slam, Muddy Water, Recover

Shellos (West Sea) → Gastrodon (West Sea)

SHELMET

Snail Pokémon

REGIONS
KALOS (MOUNTAIN), UNOVA

TYPE: BUG

Shelmet evolves when exposed to electricity, but only if Karrablast is nearby. It's unclear why this is the case.

How to say it: SHELL-mett

Height: 1' 04"
Weight: 17.0 lbs.

Possible Moves: Leech Life, Acid, Bide, Curse, Struggle Bug, Mega Drain, Yawn, Protect, Acid Armor, Giga Drain, Body Slam, Bug Buzz, Recover, Guard Swap, Final Gambit

Shelmet → Accelgor

REGION
SINNOH

SHIELDON

Shield Pokémon

TYPE: ROCK-STEEL

Though Shieldon's face is well protected by its polished armor, it's vulnerable if a foe strikes from behind. It was restored from a fossil.

How to say it: SHEEL-donn

Height: 1' 08"
Weight: 125.7 lbs.

Possible Moves: Tackle, Protect, Taunt, Metal Sound, Take Down, Iron Defense, Swagger, Ancient Power, Endure, Metal Burst, Iron Head, Heavy Slam

Shieldon Bastiodon

REGION
HOENN

SHIFTRY

Wicked Pokémon

TYPE: GRASS-DARK

Shiftry makes its home in the tops of ancient trees. Its leafy fans can stir up powerful gusts of wind.

How to say it: SHIFF-tree

Height: 4' 03"
Weight: 131.4 lbs.

Possible Moves: Feint Attack, Whirlwind, Nasty Plot, Razor Leaf, Leaf Tornado, Leaf Storm

Seedot Nuzleaf Shiftry

SHINX

Flash Pokémon

REGION
SINNOH

TYPE: ELECTRIC

When Shinx senses danger, its fur gives off a bright flash. This brilliant light blinds its attacker so Shinx can make a hasty escape.

How to say it: SHINKS

Height: 1' 08"
Weight: 20.9 lbs.

Possible Moves: Tackle, Leer, Charge, Spark, Bite, Roar, Swagger, Thunder Fang, Crunch, Scary Face, Discharge, Wild Charge

SHROOMISH

Mushroom Pokémon

REGION
HOENN

TYPE: GRASS

Shroomish live deep in the forest and make their home in moist soil, using rotted plant material as food. The spores it shakes from its cap are poisonous.

How to say it: SHROOM-ish

Height: 1' 04" **Weight:** 9.9 lbs.

Possible Moves: Absorb, Tackle, Stun Spore, Leech Seed, Mega Drain, Headbutt, Poison Powder, Worry Seed, Growth, Giga Drain, Seed Bomb, Spore

SHUCKLE

Mold Pokémon

REGIONS
JOHTO, KALOS (MOUNTAIN)

TYPE: BUG-ROCK

Shuckle stores berries in its shell so it always has a food supply. This comes in handy when it hides away under the rocks.

How to say it: SHUCK-kull

Height: 2' 00"
Weight: 45.2 lbs.

Possible Moves: Sticky Web, Withdraw, Constrict, Bide, Rollout, Encore, Wrap, Struggle Bug, Safeguard, Rest, Rock Throw, Gastro Acid, Power Trick, Shell Smash, Rock Slide, Bug Bite, Power Split, Guard Split, Stone Edge

Does not evolve

SHUPPET

Puppet Pokémon

REGIONS
HOENN, KALOS (MOUNTAIN)

TYPE: GHOST

If someone is consumed by thoughts of revenge, it's likely a Shuppet is lurking nearby, drawing energy from those dark feelings.

How to say it: SHUP-pett

Height: 2' 00"
Weight: 5.1 lbs.

Possible Moves: Knock Off, Screech, Night Shade, Spite, Will-O-Wisp, Shadow Sneak, Curse, Feint Attack, Hex, Shadow Ball, Sucker Punch, Embargo, Snatch, Grudge, Trick

Shuppet → Banette → Mega Banette

SIGILYPH

Avianoid Pokémon

REGIONS
KALOS (COASTAL), UNOVA

TYPE: PSYCHIC-FLYING

Sigilyph were appointed to keep watch over an ancient city. Their patrol route never varies.

How to say it: SIH-jih-liff

Height: 4' 07"
Weight: 30.9 lbs.

Possible Moves: Gust, Miracle Eye, Hypnosis, Psywave, Tailwind, Whirlwind, Psybeam, Air Cutter, Light Screen, Reflect, Synchronoise, Mirror Move, Gravity, Air Slash, Psychic, Cosmic Power, Sky Attack

Does not evolve

SILCOON

Cocoon Pokémon

REGION
HOENN

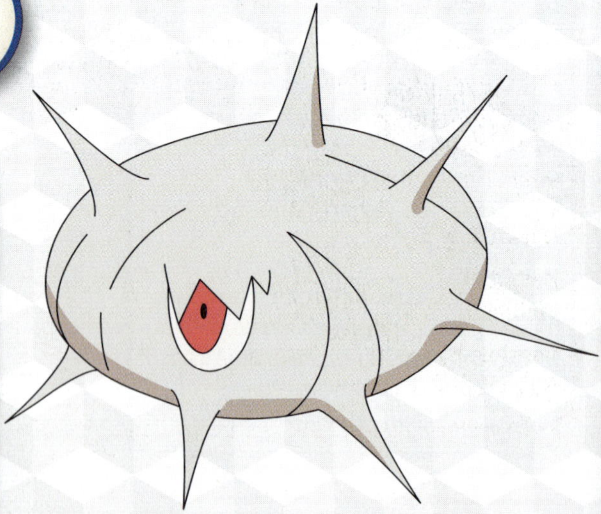

TYPE: BUG

While waiting to evolve, Silcoon wraps its body in silk and attaches itself to a branch. It leaves a tiny hole so it can see. The cocoon protects the Pokémon and collects rainwater so it can drink.

How to say it: sill-COON

Height: 2' 00"
Weight: 22.0 lbs.

Possible Move: Harden

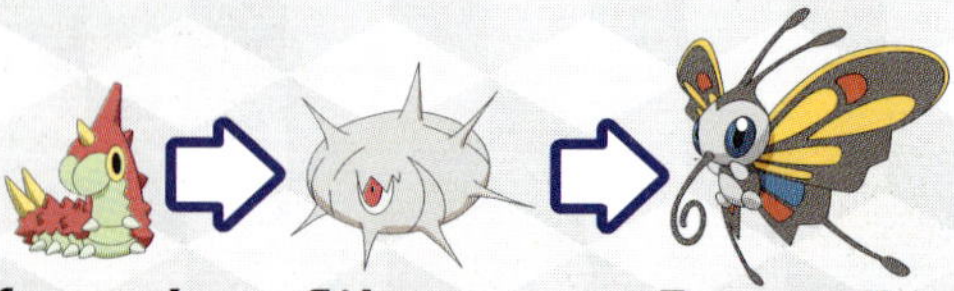

Wurmple → Silcoon → Beautifly

REGIONS
KALOS (CENTRAL), UNOVA

SIMIPOUR

Geyser Pokémon

TYPE: WATER

Simipour can shoot water out of its tail with such force that it can punch right through a concrete wall. When its stores run low, it dips its tail into clean water to suck up a refill.

How to say it: SIH-mee-por

Height: 3' 03"
Weight: 63.9 lbs.

Possible Moves: Leer, Lick, Fury Swipes, Scald

REGIONS
KALOS (CENTRAL), UNOVA

SIMISAGE

Thorn Monkey Pokémon

TYPE: GRASS

Simisage's tail is covered in thorns, and it uses the tail like a whip to lash out at opponents. It always seems to be in a bad mood.

How to say it: SIH-mee-sayj

Height: 3' 07"
Weight: 67.2 lbs.

Possible Moves: Leer, Lick, Fury Swipes, Seed Bomb

SIMISEAR

Ember Pokémon

REGIONS
KALOS (CENTRAL), UNOVA

TYPE: FIRE

Simisear's head and tail give off embers in the heat of battle . . . or any time it's excited. It has quite a sweet tooth.

How to say it: SIH-mee-seer

Height: 3' 03"
Weight: 61.7 lbs.

Possible Moves: Leer, Lick, Fury Swipes, Flame Burst

Pansear → Simisear

SKARMORY

Armor Bird Pokémon

REGIONS
JOHTO, KALOS (MOUNTAIN)

TYPE: STEEL-FLYING

The steel that makes up Skarmory's wings gets dinged up and dented during battles. Every year, the sharp edges renew themselves.

How to say it: SKAR-more-ree

Height: 5' 07"
Weight: 111.3 lbs.

Possible Moves: Leer, Peck, Sand Attack, Swift, Agility, Fury Attack, Feint, Air Cutter, Spikes, Metal Sound, Steel Wing, Autotomize, Air Slash, Slash, Night Slash

Does not evolve

SKIDDO

Mount Pokémon

REGION
KALOS (CENTRAL)

TYPE: GRASS

Calm and gentle, Skiddo have been living side by side with people for many generations. They can create energy via photosynthesis.

How to say it: skid-OO

Height: 2' 11"
Weight: 68.3 lbs.

Possible Moves: Tackle, Growth, Vine Whip, Tail Whip, Leech Seed, Razor Leaf, Worry Seed, Synthesis, Take Down, Bulldoze, Seed Bomb, Bulk Up, Double-Edge, Horn Leech, Leaf Blade, Milk Drink

SKIPLOOM

Cottonweed Pokémon

REGIONS
JOHTO, KALOS (CENTRAL)

TYPE: GRASS-FLYING

In mild temperatures, the flower on Skiploom's head begins to bloom. The petals start to open at just above sixty-four degrees Fahrenheit, and warmer temperatures coax them into full blossom.

How to say it: SKIP-loom

Height: 2' 00"
Weight: 2.2 lbs.

Possible Moves: Splash, Synthesis, Tail Whip, Tackle, Fairy Wind, Poison Powder, Stun Spore, Sleep Powder, Bullet Seed, Leech Seed, Mega Drain, Acrobatics, Rage Powder, Cotton Spore, U-turn, Worry Seed, Giga Drain, Bounce, Memento

SKITTY
Kitten Pokémon

REGIONS
HOENN, KALOS (CENTRAL)

TYPE: NORMAL

Anything that moves, including its own tail, draws Skitty's attention and starts a playful game of chase. Wild Skitty live in trees.

How to say it: SKIT-tee

Height: 2' 00"
Weight: 24.3 lbs.

Possible Moves: Fake Out, Growl, Tail Whip, Tackle, Foresight, Attract, Sing, Double Slap, Copycat, Assist, Charm, Feint Attack, Wake-Up Slap, Covet, Heal Bell, Double-Edge, Captivate, Play Rough

Skitty → Delcatty

SKORUPI
Scorpion Pokémon

REGIONS
KALOS (MOUNTAIN), SINNOH

TYPE: POISON-BUG

After burying itself in the sand, Skorupi lurks in hiding. If an intruder gets too close, it latches on with the poisonous claws on its tail.

How to say it: skor-ROOP-ee

Height: 2' 07" **Weight:** 26.5 lbs.

Possible Moves: Bite, Poison Sting, Leer, Knock Off, Pin Missile, Acupressure, Pursuit, Bug Bite, Poison Fang, Venoshock, Hone Claws, Toxic Spikes, Night Slash, Scary Face, Crunch, Fell Stinger, Cross Poison

Skorupi → Drapion

SKRELP

Mock Kelp Pokémon

REGION
KALOS (COASTAL)

TYPE: POISON-WATER

Skrelp disguises itself as rotten kelp to hide from enemies. It defends itself by spraying a poisonous liquid.

How to say it: Skrelp

Height: 1' 08"
Weight: 16.1 lbs.

Possible Moves: Tackle, Smokescreen, Water Gun, Feint Attack, Tail Whip, Bubble, Acid, Camouflage, Poison Tail, Water Pulse, Double Team, Toxic, Aqua Tail, Sludge Bomb, Hydro Pump, Dragon Pulse

SKUNTANK

Skunk Pokémon

REGIONS
KALOS (COASTAL), SINNOH

TYPE: POISON-DARK

From the end of its tail, Skuntank can shoot a noxious fluid more than 160 feet. This fluid smells awful, and the stench only gets worse if it's not cleaned up immediately.

How to say it: SKUN-tank

Height: 3' 03" **Weight:** 83.8 lbs.

Possible Moves: Scratch, Focus Energy, Poison Gas, Screech, Fury Swipes, Smokescreen, Feint, Slash, Toxic, Acid Spray, Flamethrower, Night Slash, Memento, Belch, Explosion

SLAKING
Lazy Pokémon

REGION
HOENN

TYPE: NORMAL

Slaking lies in one place and pulls up grass to eat. Circular bare spots in a meadow might be a sign that a Slaking lives nearby. After eating everything within reach, it moves to another spot, but it's not happy about that.

How to say it: SLAH-king

Height: 6' 07" **Weight:** 287.7 lbs.

Possible Moves: Scratch, Yawn, Encore, Slack Off, Feint Attack, Amnesia, Covet, Swagger, Chip Away, Counter, Flail, Fling, Punishment, Hammer Arm

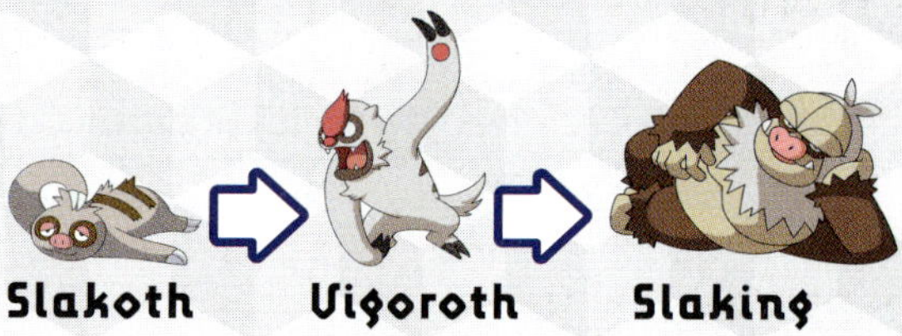

SLAKOTH
Slacker Pokémon

REGION
HOENN

TYPE: NORMAL

It's rare to see a Slakoth move. It's awake for only a few hours per day, its heart beats extremely slowly, and it doesn't require much food.

How to say it: SLAH-koth

Height: 2' 07" **Weight:** 52.9 lbs.

Possible Moves: Scratch, Yawn, Encore, Slack Off, Feint Attack, Amnesia, Covet, Chip Away, Counter, Flail

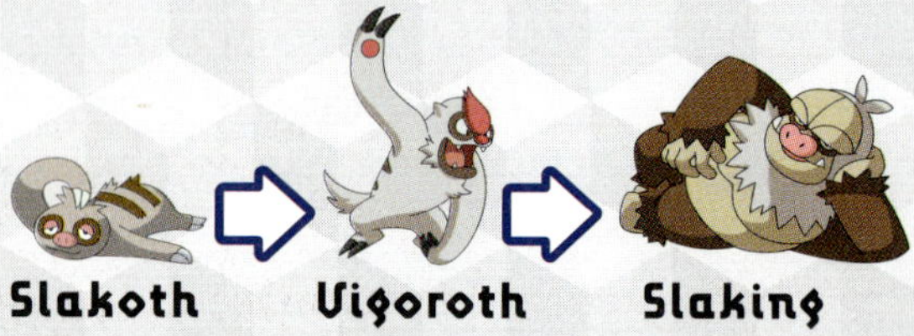

REGION
KALOS (MOUNTAIN)

SLIGGOO

Soft Tissue Pokémon

TYPE: DRAGON

The four horns on Sliggoo's head are sense organs that allow the Pokémon to find its way by sound and smell.

How to say it: SLIH-goo

Height: 2' 07"   **Weight:** 38.6 lbs.

Possible Moves: Tackle, Bubble, Absorb, Protect, Bide, Dragon Breath, Rain Dance, Flail, Body Slam, Muddy Water, Dragon Pulse

Goomy → Sliggoo → Goodra

SLOWBRO

Hermit Crab Pokémon

REGIONS
KALOS (COASTAL), KANTO

TYPE: WATER-PSYCHIC

Because of the Shellder chomping on its tail, Slowbro can no longer spend its days fishing. It can swim to catch food, but it's not happy about that.

How to say it: SLOW-bro

Height: 5' 03"
Weight: 173.1 lbs.

Possible Moves: Heal Pulse, Curse, Yawn, Tackle, Growl, Water Gun, Confusion, Disable, Headbutt, Water Pulse, Zen Headbutt, Slack Off, Withdraw, Amnesia, Psychic, Rain Dance, Psych Up

MEGA SLOWBRO

Hermit Crab Pokémon

TYPE: WATER-PSYCHIC

Height: 6' 07"
Weight: 264.6 lbs.

SLOWKING
Royal Pokémon

REGIONS
JOHTO, KALOS (COASTAL)

TYPE: WATER-PSYCHIC

If the Shellder on its head were to let go, Slowking would forget all its knowledge. It spends time in research every day, trying to solve the world's greatest mysteries.

How to say it: SLOW-king

Height: 6' 07" **Weight:** 175.3 lbs.

Possible Moves: Heal Pulse, Power Gem, Hidden Power, Curse, Yawn, Tackle, Growl, Water Gun, Confusion, Disable, Headbutt, Water Pulse, Zen Headbutt, Nasty Plot, Swagger, Psychic, Trump Card, Psych Up

SLOWPOKE
Dopey Pokémon

REGIONS
KALOS (COASTAL), KANTO

TYPE: WATER-PSYCHIC

Slowpoke spends much of its time along the riverbank, where it uses its tail for fishing. Often, its mind wanders and it spends the whole day lazing about.

How to say it: SLOW-poke

Height: 3' 11" **Weight:** 79.4 lbs.

Possible Moves: Curse, Yawn, Tackle, Growl, Water Gun, Confusion, Disable, Headbutt, Water Pulse, Zen Headbutt, Slack Off, Amnesia, Psychic, Rain Dance, Psych Up, Heal Pulse

SLUGMA

Lava Pokémon

REGIONS
JOHTO, KALOS (MOUNTAIN)

TYPE: FIRE

The magma that circulates within Slugma's body serves as its blood, supplying its organs with oxygen and nutrients. It has to stay warm, or the magma will harden.

How to say it: SLUG-ma

Height: 2' 04"
Weight: 77.2 lbs.

Possible Moves: Yawn, Smog, Ember, Rock Throw, Harden, Recover, Flame Burst, Ancient Power, Amnesia, Lava Plume, Rock Slide, Body Slam, Flamethrower, Earth Power

Slugma Magcargo

SLURPUFF

Meringue Pokémon

REGION
KALOS (CENTRAL)

TYPE: FAIRY

Pastry chefs love having a Slurpuff in the kitchen. With its incredibly sensitive nose, it can tell exactly when a dessert is baked to perfection.

How to say it: SLUR-puff

Height: 2' 07" **Weight:** 11.0 lbs.

Possible Moves: Sweet Scent, Tackle, Fairy Wind, Play Nice, Fake Tears, Round, Cotton Spore, Endeavor, Aromatherapy, Draining Kiss, Energy Ball, Cotton Guard, Wish, Play Rough, Light Screen, Safeguard

Swirlix Slurpuff

SMEARGLE

Painter Pokémon

REGIONS
JOHTO, KALOS (CENTRAL)

TYPE: NORMAL

Smeargle's tail tip produces a fluid that it uses like paint to draw thousands of different territorial markings.

How to say it: SMEAR-gull

Height: 3' 11"
Weight: 127.9 lbs.

Possible Move: Sketch

Does not evolve

SMOOCHUM

Kiss Pokémon

REGIONS
JOHTO, KALOS (MOUNTAIN)

TYPE: ICE-PSYCHIC

Very active but a little clumsy, Smoochum falls down a lot when it runs. After falling, it seeks out a reflective surface so it can make sure its face isn't smudged.

How to say it: SMOO-chum

Height: 1' 04" **Weight:** 13.2 lbs.

Possible Moves: Pound, Lick, Sweet Kiss, Powder Snow, Confusion, Sing, Heart Stamp, Mean Look, Fake Tears, Lucky Chant, Avalanche, Psychic, Copycat, Perish Song, Blizzard

Smoochum

Jynx

SNEASEL

Sharp Claw Pokémon

REGIONS
JOHTO, KALOS (MOUNTAIN)

TYPE: DARK-ICE

When Sneasel climbs trees, its hooklike claws sink into the bark to give it a good grip. It sometimes raids unprotected nests for food.

How to say it: SNEE-zul

Height: 2' 11"
Weight: 61.7 lbs.

Possible Moves: Scratch, Leer, Taunt, Quick Attack, Feint Attack, Icy Wind, Fury Swipes, Agility, Metal Claw, Hone Claws, Beat Up, Screech, Slash, Snatch, Punishment, Ice Shard

SNIVY

Grass Snake Pokémon

REGION
UNOVA

TYPE: GRASS

Soaking up sunlight with its tail increases Snivy's speed. Though it has hands, it generally uses the vines that extend from its neck instead.

How to say it: SNY-vee

Height: 2' 00" **Weight:** 17.9 lbs.

Possible Moves: Tackle, Leer, Vine Whip, Wrap, Growth, Leaf Tornado, Leech Seed, Mega Drain, Slam, Leaf Blade, Coil, Giga Drain, Wring Out, Gastro Acid, Leaf Storm

SNORLAX
Sleeping Pokémon

REGIONS
KALOS (CENTRAL), KANTO

TYPE: NORMAL

Snorlax spends most of its time eating and sleeping. Small children sometimes play by bouncing on this gentle Pokémon's vast belly.

How to say it: SNOR-lacks

Height: 6' 11"
Weight: 1,014.1 lbs.

Possible Moves: Tackle, Defense Curl, Amnesia, Lick, Chip Away, Yawn, Body Slam, Rest, Snore, Sleep Talk, Rollout, Block, Belly Drum, Crunch, Heavy Slam, Giga Impact

SNORUNT
Snow Hat Pokémon

REGION
HOENN

TYPE: ICE

They say that when a Snorunt visits your home, it brings good fortune that will last. It eats snow and spends the warmer seasons hidden deep in caves.

How to say it: SNOW-runt

Height: 2' 04" **Weight:** 37.0 lbs.

Possible Moves: Powder Snow, Leer, Double Team, Bite, Icy Wind, Headbutt, Protect, Ice Fang, Crunch, Ice Shard, Hail, Blizzard

SNOVER

Frost Tree Pokémon

REGIONS
KALOS (MOUNTAIN), SINNOH

TYPE: GRASS-ICE

Snover live high in the mountains most of the year, but in the winter, they migrate to lower elevations.

How to say it: SNOW-vur

Height: 3' 03"
Weight: 111.3 lbs.

Possible Moves: Powder Snow, Leer, Razor Leaf, Icy Wind, Grass Whistle, Swagger, Mist, Ice Shard, Ingrain, Wood Hammer, Blizzard, Sheer Cold

SNUBBULL

Fairy Pokémon

REGIONS
JOHTO, KALOS (COASTAL)

TYPE: FAIRY

Snubbull can drive off smaller Pokémon by making scary faces at them. After they run away, it seems to regret its behavior.

How to say it: SNUB-bull

Height: 2' 00"
Weight: 17.2 lbs.

Possible Moves: Ice Fang, Fire Fang, Thunder Fang, Tackle, Scary Face, Tail Whip, Charm, Bite, Lick, Headbutt, Roar, Rage, Play Rough, Payback, Crunch

SOLOSIS
Cell Pokémon

REGIONS
KALOS (COASTAL), UNOVA

TYPE: PSYCHIC

The special liquid that surrounds Solosis protects it from any harsh conditions. They communicate with telepathy.

How to say it: soh-LOH-sis

Height: 1' 00"
Weight: 2.2 lbs.

Possible Moves: Psywave, Reflect, Rollout, Snatch, Hidden Power, Light Screen, Charm, Recover, Psyshock, Endeavor, Future Sight, Pain Split, Psychic, Skill Swap, Heal Block, Wonder Room

Solosis → Duosion → Reuniclus

SOLROCK
Meteorite Pokémon

REGIONS
HOENN, KALOS (COASTAL)

TYPE: ROCK-PSYCHIC

When Solrock spins, it gives off heat and light. It uses sunlight for energy and can apparently pick up on others' emotions.

How to say it: SOLE-rock

Height: 3' 11" **Weight:** 339.5 lbs.

Possible Moves: Wonder Room, Rock Throw, Tackle, Harden, Confusion, Fire Spin, Rock Polish, Psywave, Embargo, Rock Slide, Cosmic Power, Psychic, Heal Block, Stone Edge, Solar Beam, Explosion

Does not evolve

SPEAROW
Tiny Bird Pokémon

REGIONS
KALOS (MOUNTAIN), KANTO

TYPE: NORMAL-FLYING

When many Spearow sound their loud, high-pitched cry all at once, it usually means danger is nearby.

How to say it: SPEAR-oh

Height: 1' 00"
Weight: 4.4 lbs.

Possible Moves: Peck, Growl, Leer, Fury Attack, Pursuit, Aerial Ace, Mirror Move, Agility, Assurance, Roost, Drill Peck

SPEWPA
Scatterdust Pokémon

REGION
KALOS (CENTRAL)

TYPE: BUG

Like Scatterbug, Spewpa releases a protective cloud of powder when attacked. It can also bristle up its thick fur in an attempt to scare off any aggressors.

How to say it: SPEW-puh

Height: 1' 00"
Weight: 18.5 lbs.

Possible Moves: Harden, Protect

REGION
HOENN

SPHEAL
Clap Pokémon

TYPE: ICE-WATER

Spheal can roll across the ice faster than it can walk. When it's happy, it bursts into applause by clapping its fins together, so a group of joyful Spheal is rather noisy.

How to say it: SFEEL

Height: 2' 07"
Weight: 87.1 lbs.

Possible Moves: Defense Curl, Powder Snow, Growl, Water Gun, Encore, Ice Ball, Body Slam, Aurora Beam, Hail, Rest, Snore, Blizzard, Sheer Cold

REGIONS
JOHTO, KALOS (MOUNTAIN)

SPINARAK
String Spit Pokémon

TYPE: BUG-POISON

Spinarak uses its web like another sensory organ. It can read the vibration of the strands to tell what's happening nearby.

How to say it: SPIN-uh-rack

Height: 1' 08" **Weight:** 18.7 lbs.

Possible Moves: Poison Sting, String Shot, Scary Face, Constrict, Leech Life, Night Shade, Shadow Sneak, Fury Swipes, Sucker Punch, Spider Web, Agility, Pin Missile, Psychic, Poison Jab, Cross Poison, Sticky Web

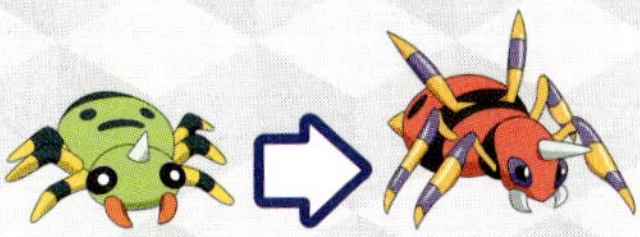

SPINDA

Spot Panda Pokémon

REGIONS
HOENN, KALOS (MOUNTAIN)

TYPE: NORMAL

It's said that no two Spinda have the same pattern of spots. They stumble and totter when they walk, making their opponents dizzy.

How to say it: SPIN-dah

Height: 3' 07"
Weight: 11.0 lbs.

Possible Moves: Tackle, Uproar, Copycat, Feint Attack, Psybeam, Hypnosis, Dizzy Punch, Sucker Punch, Teeter Dance, Psych Up, Double-Edge, Flail, Thrash

Does not evolve

SPIRITOMB

Forbidden Pokémon

REGION
SINNOH

TYPE: GHOST-DARK

Long ago, Spiritomb was bound to an odd keystone as punishment for bad behavior. Its body is formed of more than a hundred spirits.

How to say it: SPIRI-toom

Height: 3' 03"
Weight: 238.1 lbs.

Possible Moves: Curse, Pursuit, Confuse Ray, Spite, Shadow Sneak, Feint Attack, Hypnosis, Dream Eater, Ominous Wind, Sucker Punch, Nasty Plot, Memento, Dark Pulse

Does not evolve

SPOINK

REGIONS
HOENN, KALOS (COASTAL)

Bounce Pokémon

TYPE: PSYCHIC

The constant bouncing motion of Spoink's springy tail regulates its heartbeat. It's always looking for a bigger pearl for its head, because the jewel focuses its psychic powers.

How to say it: SPOINK

Height: 2' 04" **Weight:** 67.5 lbs.

Possible Moves: Splash, Psywave, Odor Sleuth, Psybeam, Psych Up, Confuse Ray, Magic Coat, Zen Headbutt, Rest, Snore, Power Gem, Psyshock, Payback, Psychic, Bounce

Spoink → Grumpig

SPRITZEE

REGION
KALOS (CENTRAL)

Perfume Pokémon

TYPE: FAIRY

Long ago, this Pokémon was popular among the nobility for its lovely scent. Instead of spraying perfume, ladies would keep a Spritzee close at hand.

How to say it: SPRIT-zee

Height: 0' 08" **Weight:** 1.1 lbs.

Possible Moves: Sweet Scent, Fairy Wind, Sweet Kiss, Odor Sleuth, Echoed Voice, Calm Mind, Draining Kiss, Aromatherapy, Attract, Moonblast, Charm, Flail, Misty Terrain, Skill Swap, Psychic, Disarming Voice

Spritzee → Aromatisse

SQUIRTLE

Tiny Turtle Pokémon

REGIONS
KALOS (CENTRAL), KANTO

TYPE: WATER

With its aerodynamic shape and grooved surface, Squirtle's shell helps it cut through the water very quickly. It also offers protection in battle.

How to say it: SKWIR-tul

Height: 1' 08" **Weight:** 19.8 lbs.

Possible Moves: Tackle, Tail Whip, Water Gun, Withdraw, Bubble, Bite, Rapid Spin, Protect, Water Pulse, Aqua Tail, Skull Bash, Iron Defense, Rain Dance, Hydro Pump

Squirtle → Wartortle → Blastoise → Mega Blastoise

STANTLER

Big Horn Pokémon

REGION
JOHTO

TYPE: NORMAL

The intricately curved antlers that grow from Stantler's head have been regarded as priceless works of art by collectors.

How to say it: STAN-tler

Height: 4' 07"
Weight: 157.0 lbs.

Possible Moves: Tackle, Leer, Astonish, Hypnosis, Stomp, Sand Attack, Take Down, Confuse Ray, Calm Mind, Role Play, Zen Headbutt, Jump Kick, Imprison, Captivate, Me First

Does not evolve

STARAPTOR

Predator Pokémon

REGIONS
KALOS (COASTAL), SINNOH

TYPE: NORMAL-FLYING

After evolving, Staraptor go off on their own, leaving their flocks behind. With their strong wings, they can fly with ease even when carrying a burden.

How to say it: star-RAP-tor

Height: 3' 11"
Weight: 54.9 lbs.

Possible Moves: Tackle, Growl, Quick Attack, Wing Attack, Double Team, Endeavor, Whirlwind, Aerial Ace, Take Down, Close Combat, Agility, Brave Bird, Final Gambit

STARAVIA

Starling Pokémon

REGIONS
KALOS (COASTAL), SINNOH

TYPE: NORMAL-FLYING

Staravia travel in large flocks that can be very territorial. Battles sometimes break out between two competing flocks.

How to say it: star-AY-vee-ah

Height: 2' 00"
Weight: 34.2 lbs.

Possible Moves: Tackle, Growl, Quick Attack, Wing Attack, Double Team, Endeavor, Whirlwind, Aerial Ace, Take Down, Agility, Brave Bird, Final Gambit

STARLY

Starling Pokémon

REGIONS
KALOS (COASTAL), SINNOH

TYPE: NORMAL-FLYING

Huge flocks of Starly gather in fields and mountains. In such large numbers, their wings flap with impressive power . . . and their noisy singing is quite a nuisance!

How to say it: STAR-lee

Height: 1' 00"
Weight: 4.4 lbs.

Possible Moves: Tackle, Growl, Quick Attack, Wing Attack, Double Team, Endeavor, Whirlwind, Aerial Ace, Take Down, Agility, Brave Bird, Final Gambit

STARMIE

Mysterious Pokémon

REGIONS
KALOS (COASTAL), KANTO

TYPE: WATER-PSYCHIC

Because of the glowing rainbow of colors produced by Starmie's core, this Pokémon is known as "the Gem of the Sea." It spins its body like a propeller to swim.

How to say it: STAR-mee

Height: 3' 07"
Weight: 176.4 lbs.

Possible Moves: Hydro Pump, Water Gun, Rapid Spin, Recover, Swift, Confuse Ray

REGIONS
KALOS (COASTAL), KANTO

STARYU

Star Shape Pokémon

TYPE: WATER

Staryu's red core glows brightly in the dark. When it flashes this light, it is said to be communing with the stars.

How to say it: STAR-you

Height: 2' 07" **Weight:** 76.1 lbs.

Possible Moves: Tackle, Harden, Water Gun, Rapid Spin, Recover, Camouflage, Swift, Bubble Beam, Minimize, Gyro Ball, Light Screen, Brine, Reflect Type, Power Gem, Cosmic Power, Hydro Pump

STEELIX

Iron Snake Pokémon

REGIONS
JOHTO, KALOS (COASTAL)

TYPE: STEEL-GROUND

Steelix lives deep underground and can tunnel straight down more than half a mile below the surface.

How to say it: STEE-licks

Height: 30' 02"
Weight: 881.8 lbs.

Possible Moves: Thunder Fang, Ice Fang, Fire Fang, Mud Sport, Tackle, Harden, Bind, Curse, Rock Throw, Rock Tomb, Rage, Stealth Rock, Autotomize, Gyro Ball, Smack Down, Dragon Breath, Slam, Screech, Rock Slide, Crunch, Iron Tail, Dig, Stone Edge, Double-Edge, Sandstorm

MEGA STEELIX

Iron Snake Pokémon

TYPE: STEEL-GROUND

Height: 34' 05"
Weight: 1,631.4 lbs.

Onix → Steelix → Mega Steelix

REGION
UNOVA

STOUTLAND

Big-Hearted Pokémon

TYPE: NORMAL

Stoutland excels at cold-weather rescues. Wrapped up in its warm, shaggy fur, someone could even spend the night on a snowy mountain and be okay.

How to say it: STOWT-lund

Height: 3' 11"
Weight: 134.5 lbs.

Possible Moves: Ice Fang, Fire Fang, Thunder Fang, Leer, Tackle, Odor Sleuth, Bite, Helping Hand, Take Down, Work Up, Crunch, Roar, Retaliate, Reversal, Last Resort, Giga Impact

REGIONS
KALOS (MOUNTAIN), UNOVA

STUNFISK

Trap Pokémon

TYPE: GROUND-ELECTRIC

Stunfisk buries its flat body in mud, so it's hard to see and often gets stepped on. When that happens, its thick skin keeps it from being hurt, and Stunfisk zaps the offender with a cheery smile.

How to say it: STUN-fisk

Height: 2' 04"
Weight: 24.3 lbs.

Possible Moves: Fissure, Flail, Tackle, Water Gun, Mud-Slap, Mud Sport, Bide, Thunder Shock, Mud Shot, Camouflage, Mud Bomb, Discharge, Endure, Bounce, Muddy Water, Thunderbolt, Revenge

Does not evolve

STUNKY

Skunk Pokémon

REGIONS
KALOS (COASTAL), SINNOH

TYPE: POISON-DARK

The terrible-smelling fluid that Stunky sprays from its rear can keep others far away from it for a whole day.

How to say it: STUNK-ee

Height: 1' 04"
Weight: 42.3 lbs.

Possible Moves: Scratch, Focus Energy, Poison Gas, Screech, Fury Swipes, Smokescreen, Feint, Slash, Toxic, Acid Spray, Night Slash, Memento, Belch, Explosion

Stunky → Skuntank

SUDOWOODO

Imitation Pokémon

REGIONS
JOHTO, KALOS (MOUNTAIN)

TYPE: ROCK

For most of the year, Sudowoodo can easily disguise itself as a tree for protection. However, in the winter, its green hands give it away.

How to say it: SOO-doe-WOO-doe

Height: 3' 11" **Weight:** 83.8 lbs.

Possible Moves: Wood Hammer, Copycat, Flail, Low Kick, Rock Throw, Mimic, Slam, Feint Attack, Rock Tomb, Block, Rock Slide, Counter, Sucker Punch, Double-Edge, Stone Edge, Hammer Arm

Bonsly → Sudowoodo

LEGENDARY POKÉMON

REGION
JOHTO

SUICUNE

Aurora Pokémon

TYPE: WATER

Suicune can clear pollution from lakes and rivers. This Legendary Pokémon's heart is as pure as clear water.

How to say it: SWEE-koon

Height: 6' 07"   **Weight:** 412.3 lbs.

Possible Moves: Bite, Leer, Bubble Beam, Rain Dance, Gust, Aurora Beam, Mist, Mirror Coat, Ice Fang, Tailwind, Extrasensory, Hydro Pump, Calm Mind, Blizzard

Does not evolve

SUNFLORA

Sun Pokémon

REGION
JOHTO

TYPE: GRASS

Sunflora soaks up the sun's rays and transforms that energy into nutrients. It's very active during the warmth of the day, but when sunset arrives, it stops moving.

How to say it: sun-FLOR-a

Height: 2' 07"
Weight: 18.7 lbs.

Possible Moves: Absorb, Pound, Growth, Mega Drain, Ingrain, Grass Whistle, Leech Seed, Bullet Seed, Worry Seed, Razor Leaf, Petal Dance, Sunny Day, Solar Beam, Leaf Storm

SUNKERN

Seed Pokémon

REGION
JOHTO

TYPE: GRASS

Sunkern doesn't consume food but lives entirely on dewdrops. It avoids movement as much as possible so it doesn't use up its stored energy.

How to say it: SUN-kurn

Height: 1' 00"
Weight: 4.0 lbs.

Possible Moves: Absorb, Growth, Mega Drain, Ingrain, Grass Whistle, Leech Seed, Endeavor, Worry Seed, Razor Leaf, Synthesis, Sunny Day, Giga Drain, Seed Bomb

SURSKIT

REGIONS
HOENN,
KALOS
(CENTRAL)

Pond Skater Pokémon

TYPE: BUG-WATER

The point on Surskit's head produces a sweet syrup that attracts some Pokémon. The points on its feet give off an oil that lets it skate across the surface of the water.

How to say it: SUR-skit

Height: 1' 08"
Weight: 3.7 lbs.

Possible Moves: Bubble, Quick Attack, Sweet Scent, Water Sport, Bubble Beam, Agility, Mist, Haze, Baton Pass, Sticky Web

Surskit → Masquerain

SWABLU

REGIONS
HOENN,
KALOS
(MOUNTAIN)

Cotton Bird Pokémon

TYPE: NORMAL-FLYING

Swablu uses its cottony wings to polish everything around it. It also likes to land on people's heads, so a woman walking down the sidewalk could suddenly discover she's wearing a fluffy Swablu hat.

How to say it: swah-BLUE

Height: 1' 04" **Weight:** 2.6 lbs.

Possible Moves: Peck, Growl, Astonish, Sing, Fury Attack, Safeguard, Mist, Round, Natural Gift, Take Down, Refresh, Mirror Move, Cotton Guard, Dragon Pulse, Perish Song, Moonblast

Swablu → Altaria → Mega Altaria

SWADLOON

Leaf-Wrapped Pokémon

REGION
UNOVA

TYPE: BUG-GRASS

When many Swadloon live in a forest, the plants grow strong and healthy. These Pokémon eat fallen leaves and give off nutrients that enrich the soil.

How to say it: swahd-LOON

Height: 1' 08"
Weight: 16.1 lbs.

Possible Moves: Grass Whistle, Tackle, String Shot, Bug Bite, Razor Leaf, Protect

Sewaddle Swadloon Leavanny

SWALOT

Poison Bag Pokémon

REGIONS
HOENN, KALOS (COASTAL)

TYPE: POISON

Swalot's mouth can open wide enough to swallow a car tire easily. It defends itself by secreting a poisonous fluid.

How to say it: SWAH-lot

Height: 5' 07" **Weight:** 176.4 lbs.

Possible Moves: Gunk Shot, Wring Out, Pound, Yawn, Poison Gas, Sludge, Amnesia, Encore, Body Slam, Toxic, Acid Spray, Stockpile, Spit Up, Swallow, Belch, Sludge Bomb, Gastro Acid

Gulpin Swalot

SWAMPERT

REGION HOENN

Mud Fish Pokémon

TYPE: WATER-GROUND

Swampert can tell when a storm is coming by shifts in the winds and waves. It's strong enough to drag and lift heavy boulders, so it builds a fort to take shelter.

How to say it: SWAM-pert

Height: 4' 11"
Weight: 180.6 lbs.

Possible Moves: Tackle, Growl, Mud-Slap, Water Gun, Bide, Mud Shot, Foresight, Mud Bomb, Take Down, Muddy Water, Protect, Earthquake, Endeavor, Hammer Arm

MEGA SWAMPERT

Mud Fish Pokémon

TYPE: WATER-GROUND

Height: 6' 03"
Weight: 224.9 lbs.

SWANNA
White Bird Pokémon

REGIONS
KALOS (CENTRAL), UNOVA

TYPE: WATER-FLYING

In the evening, a flock of Swanna performs an elegant dance around its leader. Their exceptional stamina and wing strength allow them to fly thousands of miles at a time.

How to say it: SWAH-nuh

Height: 4' 03"
Weight: 53.4 lbs.

Possible Moves: Water Gun, Water Sport, Defog, Wing Attack, Water Pulse, Aerial Ace, Bubble Beam, Feather Dance, Aqua Ring, Air Slash, Roost, Rain Dance, Tailwind, Brave Bird, Hurricane

SWELLOW
Swallow Pokémon

REGIONS
HOENN, KALOS (COASTAL)

TYPE: NORMAL-FLYING

Soaring gracefully through the sky, Swellow will go into a steep dive if it spots food on the ground. It's very vain about keeping its wings properly groomed.

How to say it: SWELL-low

Height: 2' 04"
Weight: 43.7 lbs.

Possible Moves: Air Slash, Pluck, Peck, Growl, Focus Energy, Quick Attack, Wing Attack, Double Team, Endeavor, Aerial Ace, Agility

REGIONS
JOHTO, KALOS (MOUNTAIN)

SWINUB

Pig Pokémon

TYPE: ICE-GROUND

Swinub keeps its nose to the ground in search of food. Its favorite thing to eat is a certain kind of mushroom found under dead grass. Sometimes, it finds a hot spring while it's sniffing about.

How to say it: SWY-nub

Height: 1' 04" **Weight:** 14.3 lbs.

Possible Moves: Tackle, Odor Sleuth, Mud Sport, Powder Snow, Mud-Slap, Endure, Mud Bomb, Icy Wind, Ice Shard, Take Down, Mist, Earthquake, Flail, Blizzard, Amnesia

REGION
KALOS (CENTRAL)

SWIRLIX

Cotton Candy Pokémon

TYPE: FAIRY

Swirlix loves to snack on sweets. Its sugary eating habits have made its white fur sweet and sticky, just like cotton candy.

How to say it: SWUR-licks

Height: 1' 04"
Weight: 7.7 lbs.

Possible Moves: Sweet Scent, Tackle, Fairy Wind, Play Nice, Fake Tears, Round, Cotton Spore, Endeavor, Aromatherapy, Draining Kiss, Energy Ball, Cotton Guard, Wish, Play Rough, Light Screen, Safeguard

SWOOBAT

Courting Pokémon

REGIONS
KALOS (COASTAL), UNOVA

TYPE: PSYCHIC-FLYING

When a male Swoobat is trying to impress a female, it gives off ultrasonic waves that put everyone in a good mood. Under other circumstances, Swoobat's waves can pulverize concrete.

How to say it: SWOO-bat

Height: 2' 11"
Weight: 23.1 lbs.

Possible Moves: Confusion, Odor Sleuth, Gust, Assurance, Heart Stamp, Imprison, Air Cutter, Attract, Amnesia, Calm Mind, Air Slash, Future Sight, Psychic, Endeavor

SYLVEON

Intertwining Pokémon

REGION
KALOS (COASTAL)

TYPE: FAIRY

To keep others from fighting, Sylveon projects a calming aura from its feelers, which look like flowing ribbons. It wraps those ribbons around its Trainer's arm when they walk together.

How to say it: SIL-vee-on

Height: 3' 03" **Weight:** 51.8 lbs.

Possible Moves: Disarming Voice, Tail Whip, Tackle, Helping Hand, Sand Attack, Fairy Wind, Quick Attack, Swift, Draining Kiss, Skill Swap, Misty Terrain, Light Screen, Moonblast, Last Resort, Psych Up

TAILLOW

Tiny Swallow Pokémon

REGIONS
HOENN, KALOS (COASTAL)

TYPE: NORMAL-FLYING

Although Taillow is fierce and courageous in battle, even against stronger foes, hunger or loneliness sometimes makes it cry.

How to say it: TAY-low

Height: 1' 00"
Weight: 5.1 lbs.

Possible Moves: Peck, Growl, Focus Energy, Quick Attack, Wing Attack, Double Team, Endeavor, Aerial Ace, Agility, Air Slash

TALONFLAME

Scorching Pokémon

REGION
KALOS (CENTRAL)

TYPE: FIRE-FLYING

Talonflame can swoop at incredible speeds when attacking. During intense battles, its wings give off showers of embers as it flies.

How to say it: TAL-un-flame

Height: 3' 11" **Weight:** 54.0 lbs.

Possible Moves: Brave Bird, Flare Blitz, Tackle, Growl, Quick Attack, Peck, Agility, Flail, Ember, Roost, Razor Wind, Natural Gift, Flame Charge, Acrobatics, Me First, Tailwind, Steel Wing

TANGELA

Vine Pokémon

REGION
KANTO

TYPE: GRASS

If grabbed by an attacker, Tangela can break away and leave the foe with a handful of vines. The vines grow back within a day.

How to say it: TANG-guh-luh

Height: 3' 03"
Weight: 77.2 lbs.

Possible Moves: Ingrain, Constrict, Sleep Powder, Absorb, Growth, Poison Powder, Vine Whip, Bind, Mega Drain, Stun Spore, Knock Off, Ancient Power, Natural Gift, Slam, Tickle, Wring Out, Power Whip

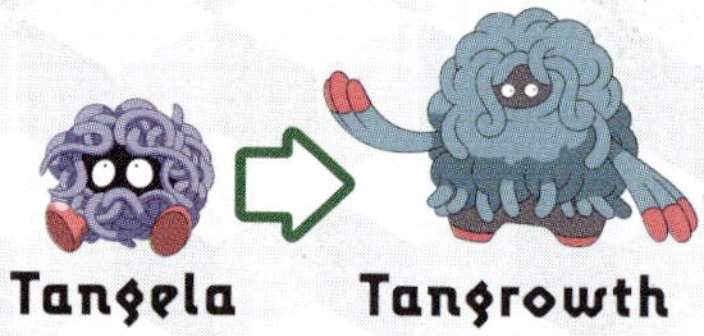

TANGROWTH

Vine Pokémon

REGION
SINNOH

TYPE: GRASS

During warmer times of the year, Tangrowth's vines grow so rapidly that they cover its eyes. It can control its vines like arms.

How to say it: TANG-growth

Height: 6' 07"
Weight: 283.5 lbs.

Possible Moves: Ingrain, Constrict, Sleep Powder, Absorb, Growth, Poison Powder, Vine Whip, Bind, Mega Drain, Stun Spore, Ancient Power, Knock Off, Natural Gift, Slam, Tickle, Wring Out, Power Whip, Block

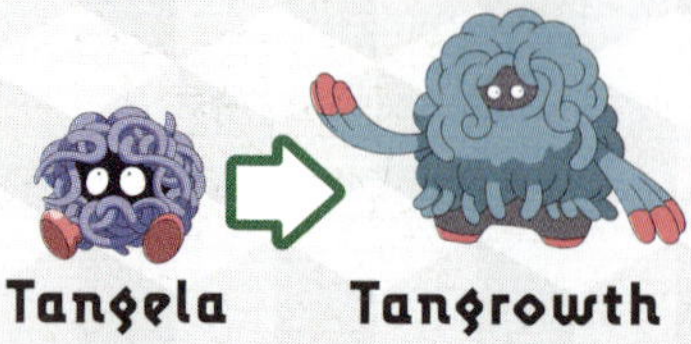

REGIONS
KALOS (COASTAL), KANTO

TAUROS

Wild Bull Pokémon

TYPE: NORMAL

Tauros just isn't happy unless it's battling. If nobody's up for the challenge, it blows off steam by charging at trees and knocking them over.

How to say it: TORE-ros

Height: 4' 07"
Weight: 194.9 lbs.

Possible Moves: Tackle, Tail Whip, Rage, Horn Attack, Scary Face, Pursuit, Rest, Payback, Work Up, Zen Headbutt, Take Down, Swagger, Thrash, Giga Impact

Does not evolve

REGIONS
JOHTO, KALOS (MOUNTAIN)

TEDDIURSA

Little Bear Pokémon

TYPE: NORMAL

Teddiursa changes the flavor of its honey-soaked paws by incorporating different kinds of berries and pollen.

How to say it: TED-dy-UR-sa

Height: 2' 00"
Weight: 19.4 lbs.

Possible Moves: Fling, Covet, Scratch, Baby-Doll Eyes, Lick, Fake Tears, Fury Swipes, Feint Attack, Sweet Scent, Play Nice, Slash, Charm, Rest, Snore, Thrash

Teddiursa Ursaring

TENTACOOL
Jellyfish Pokémon

REGIONS
KALOS (COASTAL), KANTO

TYPE: WATER-POISON

If a Tentacool spends too much time out of water, its body will dry out. In the sea, it can focus and redirect sunlight into energy beams.

How to say it: TEN-ta-cool

Height: 2' 11"
Weight: 100.3 lbs.

Possible Moves: Poison Sting, Supersonic, Constrict, Acid, Toxic Spikes, Bubble Beam, Wrap, Acid Spray, Barrier, Water Pulse, Poison Jab, Screech, Hex, Hydro Pump, Sludge Wave, Wring Out

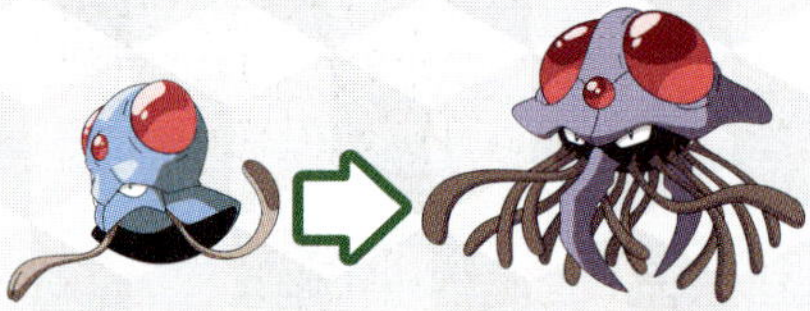

Tentacool Tentacruel

TENTACRUEL
Jellyfish Pokémon

REGIONS
KALOS (COASTAL), KANTO

TYPE: WATER-POISON

When the red orbs on Tentacruel's head glow, it's about to unleash a sonic blast that stirs up the sea. Its poisonous tentacles can extend to catch food.

How to say it: TEN-ta-crool

Height: 5' 03" **Weight:** 121.3 lbs.

Possible Moves: Reflect Type, Wring Out, Poison Sting, Supersonic, Constrict, Acid, Toxic Spikes, Bubble Beam, Wrap, Acid Spray, Barrier, Water Pulse, Poison Jab, Screech, Hex, Hydro Pump, Sludge Wave

Tentacool Tentacruel

TEPIG

Fire Pig Pokémon

TYPE: FIRE

Tepig uses the fireballs from its nose in battle—and in cooking! It likes to roast berries rather than eating them raw, though sometimes they get a little overdone.

How to say it: TEH-pig

Height: 1' 08" **Weight:** 21.8 lbs.

Possible Moves: Tackle, Tail Whip, Ember, Odor Sleuth, Defense Curl, Flame Charge, Smog, Rollout, Take Down, Heat Crash, Assurance, Flamethrower, Head Smash, Roar, Flare Blitz

TERRAKION
Cavern Pokémon

REGION
UNOVA

LEGENDARY POKÉMON

TYPE: ROCK-FIGHTING

Legends tell of a time when Terrakion attacked a mighty castle to protect its Pokémon friends. They say it knocked down a giant wall with the force of its charge.

How to say it: tur-RAK-ee-un

Height: 6' 03" **Weight:** 573.2 lbs.

Possible Moves: Quick Attack, Leer, Double Kick, Smack Down, Take Down, Helping Hand, Retaliate, Rock Slide, Sacred Sword, Swords Dance, Quick Guard, Work Up, Stone Edge, Close Combat

Does not evolve

REGIONS
KALOS (COASTAL), UNOVA

THROH

Judo Pokémon

TYPE: FIGHTING

Throh make belts for themselves out of vines, and pull those belts tight to power up their muscles. They can't resist the challenge of throwing a bigger opponent.

How to say it: THROH

Height: 4' 03" **Weight:** 122.4 lbs.

Possible Moves: Bind, Leer, Bide, Focus Energy, Seismic Toss, Vital Throw, Revenge, Storm Throw, Body Slam, Bulk Up, Circle Throw, Endure, Wide Guard, Superpower, Reversal

Does not evolve

THUNDURUS

Bolt Strike Pokémon

REGION
UNOVA

LEGENDARY POKÉMON

TYPE: ELECTRIC-FLYING

Thundurus can discharge powerful electric bolts from the spikes on its tail. This Legendary Pokémon causes terrible lightning storms, which often result in forest fires.

How to say it: THUN-duh-rus

Height: 4' 11" **Weight:** 134.5 lbs.

Possible Moves: Uproar, Astonish, Thunder Shock, Swagger, Bite, Revenge, Shock Wave, Heal Block, Agility, Discharge, Crunch, Charge, Nasty Plot, Thunder, Dark Pulse, Hammer Arm, Thrash

Does not evolve

REGION
SINNOH

TORTERRA

Continent Pokémon

TYPE: GRASS-GROUND

There's enough room on Torterra's enormous back for several small Pokémon to make their nests. According to ancient folklore, a particularly large one lived under the ground.

How to say it: tor-TERR-uh

Height: 7' 03" **Weight:** 683.4 lbs.

Possible Moves: Wood Hammer, Tackle, Withdraw, Absorb, Razor Leaf, Curse, Bite, Mega Drain, Earthquake, Leech Seed, Synthesis, Crunch, Giga Drain, Leaf Storm

Turtwig Grotle Torterra

TYPE: WATER

Be careful around a playful Totodile! It tends to nibble on friends as a sign of affection, but its jaws are strong enough to cause serious harm.

How to say it: TOE-toe-dyle

Height: 2' 00"
Weight: 20.9 lbs.

Possible Moves: Scratch, Leer, Water Gun, Rage, Bite, Scary Face, Ice Fang, Flail, Crunch, Chip Away, Slash, Screech, Thrash, Aqua Tail, Superpower, Hydro Pump

REGION
JOHTO

TOTODILE

Big Jaw Pokémon

Totodile Croconaw Feraligatr

TOXICROAK

Toxic Mouth Pokémon

REGIONS
KALOS (CENTRAL), SINNOH

TYPE: POISON-FIGHTING

Toxicroak's dangerous poison is stored in its throat sac and delivered through the claws on its knuckles.

How to say it: TOX-uh-croak

Height: 4' 03" **Weight:** 97.9 lbs.

Possible Moves: Astonish, Mud-Slap, Poison Sting, Taunt, Pursuit, Feint Attack, Revenge, Swagger, Mud Bomb, Sucker Punch, Venoshock, Nasty Plot, Poison Jab, Sludge Bomb, Belch, Flatter

TRANQUILL

Wild Pigeon Pokémon

REGION
UNOVA

TYPE: NORMAL-FLYING

Tranquill can always find its way back home, whether to its nest deep in the forest or to its Trainer's side. It's said that when these Pokémon nest together, peace surrounds the area.

How to say it: TRAN-kwil

Height: 2' 00" **Weight:** 33.1 lbs.

Possible Moves: Gust, Growl, Leer, Quick Attack, Air Cutter, Roost, Detect, Taunt, Air Slash, Razor Wind, Feather Dance, Swagger, Facade, Tailwind, Sky Attack

REGIONS
HOENN,
KALOS
(MOUNTAIN)

TRAPINCH

Ant Pit Pokémon

TYPE: GROUND

Trapinch lives in the desert, where it can go without water for several days. It digs a bowl-shaped pit in the sand and hides at the bottom, waiting for something to fall in.

How to say it: TRAP-inch

Height: 2' 04"
Weight: 33.1 lbs.

Possible Moves: Fissure, Superpower, Feint, Bite, Sand Attack, Feint Attack, Sand Tomb, Mud-Slap, Bide, Bulldoze, Rock Slide, Dig, Crunch, Earth Power, Sandstorm, Hyper Beam, Earthquake

REGION
HOENN

TREECKO

Wood Gecko Pokémon

TYPE: GRASS

The tiny hooks on Treecko's feet allow it to climb straight up walls. With its calm attitude, it coolly stands up to bigger opponents.

How to say it: TREE-ko

Height: 1' 08" **Weight:** 11.0 lbs.

Possible Moves: Pound, Leer, Absorb, Quick Attack, Pursuit, Screech, Mega Drain, Agility, Slam, Detect, Giga Drain, Energy Ball

TREVENANT

Elder Tree Pokémon

REGION
KALOS (MOUNTAIN)

TYPE: GHOST-GRASS

Using its roots, Trevenant can control the trees around it to protect its forest home. Smaller Pokémon sometimes live in its hollow body.

How to say it: TREV-uh-nunt

Height: 4' 11"
Weight: 156.5 lbs.

Possible Moves: Horn Leech, Tackle, Confuse Ray, Astonish, Growth, Ingrain, Feint Attack, Leech Seed, Curse, Will-O-Wisp, Forest's Curse, Destiny Bond, Phantom Force, Wood Hammer, Shadow Claw

TROPIUS

Fruit Pokémon

REGION
HOENN

TYPE: GRASS-FLYING

Tropius eats so much fruit that it started to grow its own fruit around its neck. The fruit is a popular snack for youngsters.

How to say it: TROH-pee-us

Height: 6' 07"
Weight: 220.5 lbs.

Possible Moves: Leer, Gust, Growth, Razor Leaf, Stomp, Sweet Scent, Whirlwind, Magical Leaf, Body Slam, Synthesis, Leaf Tornado, Air Slash, Bestow, Solar Beam, Natural Gift, Leaf Storm

Does not evolve

TRUBBISH

Trash Bag Pokémon

REGIONS
KALOS (MOUNTAIN), UNOVA

TYPE: POISON

Trubbish live in grungy, germy, grimy places and release a gas that induces sleep in anyone who breathes it. They were created when household garbage reacted with chemical waste.

How to say it: TRUB-bish

Height: 2' 00" **Weight:** 68.3 lbs.

Possible Moves: Pound, Poison Gas, Recycle, Toxic Spikes, Acid Spray, Double Slap, Sludge, Stockpile, Swallow, Take Down, Sludge Bomb, Clear Smog, Toxic, Amnesia, Belch, Gunk Shot, Explosion

TURTWIG

Tiny Leaf Pokémon

REGION
SINNOH

TYPE: GRASS

Turtwig's shell is made of soil, and its whole body can produce energy via photosynthesis. If it goes too long without water, its leaf wilts.

How to say it: TUR-twig

Height: 1' 04"
Weight: 22.5 lbs.

Possible Moves: Tackle, Withdraw, Absorb, Razor Leaf, Curse, Bite, Mega Drain, Leech Seed, Synthesis, Crunch, Giga Drain, Leaf Storm

TYMPOLE

Tadpole Pokémon

REGION
UNOVA

TYPE: WATER

Tympole creates sound waves with the vibrations of its cheeks. People can't hear these sounds, so it can communicate with others undetected.

How to say it: TIM-pohl

Height: 1' 08"
Weight: 9.9 lbs.

Possible Moves: Bubble, Growl, Supersonic, Round, Bubble Beam, Mud Shot, Aqua Ring, Uproar, Muddy Water, Rain Dance, Flail, Echoed Voice, Hydro Pump, Hyper Voice

Tympole → Palpitoad → Seismitoad

TYNAMO

Elefish Pokémon

REGION
UNOVA

TYPE: ELECTRIC

A single Tynamo can't generate much power, but when several of them join forces, they can unleash an electric shock with the force of a lightning strike.

How to say it: TY-nuh-moh

Height: 0' 08"
Weight: 0.7 lbs.

Possible Moves: Tackle, Thunder Wave, Spark, Charge Beam

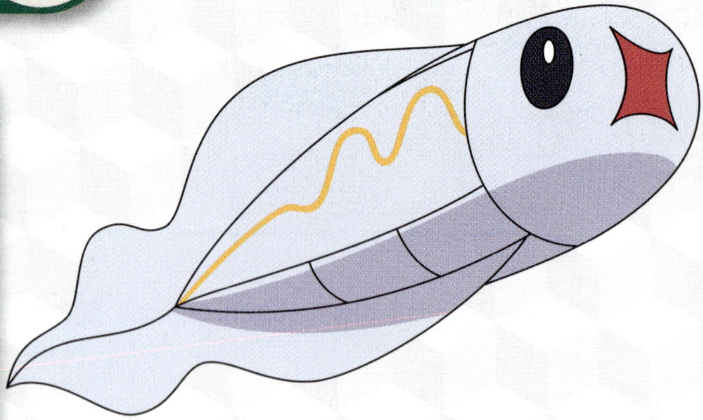

Tynamo → Eelektrik → Eelektross

REGION
JOHTO

TYPHLOSION

Volcano Pokémon

TYPE: FIRE

The heat shimmer given off by Typhlosion's flames serves to conceal the Pokémon's movements. It can unleash a fiery explosion to scorch everything around it.

How to say it: tie-FLOW-zhun

Height: 5' 07" **Weight:** 175.3 lbs.

Possible Moves: Gyro Ball, Tackle, Leer, Smokescreen, Ember, Quick Attack, Flame Wheel, Defense Curl, Swift, Flame Charge, Lava Plume, Flamethrower, Inferno, Rollout, Double-Edge, Eruption

TYRANITAR

Armor Pokémon

REGIONS
JOHTO, KALOS (MOUNTAIN)

TYPE: ROCK-DARK

Tyranitar lives in the mountains, where it often goes wandering in search of battle opponents. It has been known to topple a mountain when building a nest.

How to say it: tie-RAN-uh-tar

Height: 6' 07"
Weight: 445.3 lbs.

Possible Moves: Thunder Fang, Ice Fang, Fire Fang, Bite, Leer, Sandstorm, Screech, Chip Away, Rock Slide, Scary Face, Thrash, Dark Pulse, Payback, Crunch, Earthquake, Stone Edge, Hyper Beam, Giga Impact

MEGA TYRANITAR

Armor Pokémon

TYPE: ROCK-DARK

Height: 8' 02"
Weight: 562.2 lbs.

Larvitar → Pupitar → Tyranitar → Mega Tyranitar

TYRANTRUM

REGION
KALOS (COASTAL)

Despot Pokémon

TYPE: ROCK-DRAGON

Tyrantrum's enormous and powerful jaws made it the boss of its ancient world. Nothing could challenge its rule.

How to say it: tie-RAN-trum

Height: 8' 02"
Weight: 595.2 lbs.

Possible Moves: Head Smash, Tail Whip, Tackle, Roar, Stomp, Bide, Stealth Rock, Bite, Charm, Ancient Power, Dragon Tail, Crunch, Dragon Claw, Thrash, Earthquake, Horn Drill, Head Smash, Rock Slide, Giga Impact

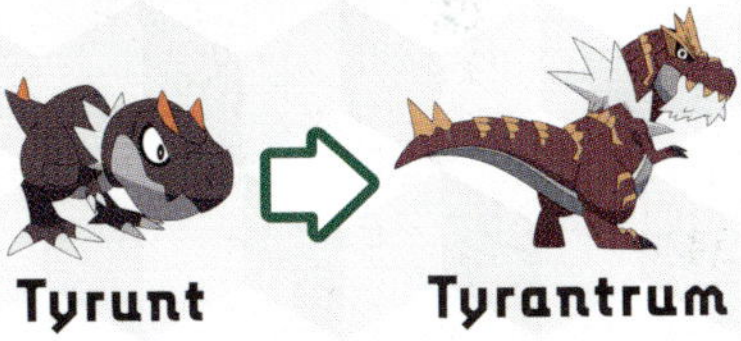

TYROGUE

REGION
JOHTO

Scuffle Pokémon

TYPE: FIGHTING

Training and working out every day is a must for keeping Tyrogue's stress levels under control. Its Trainer must take a disciplined approach.

How to say it: tie-ROAG

Height: 2' 04" **Weight:** 46.3 lbs.

Possible Moves: Tackle, Helping Hand, Fake Out, Foresight

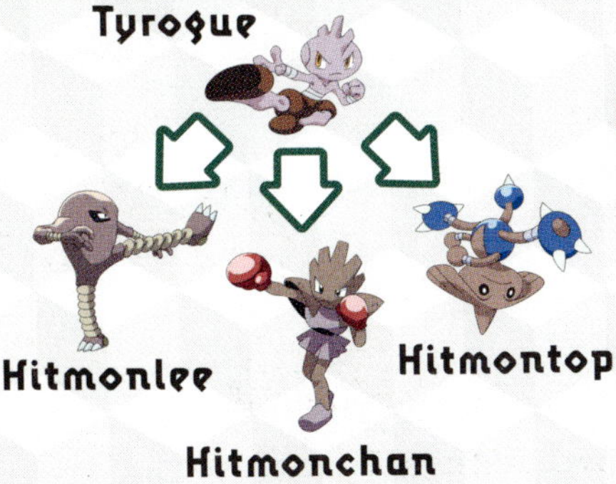

TYRUNT

Royal Heir Pokémon

REGION
KALOS (COASTAL)

TYPE: ROCK-DRAGON

Tyrunt often responds to frustration by pitching a fit. This ancient Pokémon lived millions of years ago.

How to say it: TIE-runt

Height: 2' 07" **Weight:** 57.3 lbs.

Possible Moves: Tail Whip, Tackle, Roar, Stomp, Bide, Stealth Rock, Bite, Charm, Ancient Power, Dragon Tail, Crunch, Dragon Claw, Thrash, Earthquake, Horn Drill

Tyrunt Tyrantrum

UMBREON
Moonlight Pokémon

REGIONS
JOHTO, KALOS (COASTAL)

TYPE: DARK

When Umbreon springs into battle, the ring pattern in its fur begins to glow. The influence of moonlight caused it to evolve.

How to say it: UM-bree-on

Height: 3' 03"
Weight: 59.5 lbs.

Possible Moves: Helping Hand, Tackle, Tail Whip, Sand Attack, Pursuit, Quick Attack, Confuse Ray, Feint Attack, Assurance, Screech, Moonlight, Mean Look, Last Resort, Guard Swap

UNFEZANT
Proud Pokémon

REGION
UNOVA

TYPE: NORMAL-FLYING

Unfezant has a prickly personality and rarely bonds with anyone other than its Trainer. The males have impressive head plumage, and the females are better at flying.

How to say it: un-FEZ-ent

Height: 3' 11" **Weight:** 63.9 lbs.

Possible Moves: Gust, Growl, Leer, Quick Attack, Air Cutter, Roost, Detect, Taunt, Air Slash, Razor Wind, Feather Dance, Swagger, Facade, Tailwind, Sky Attack

UNOWN

Symbol Pokémon

REGION
JOHTO

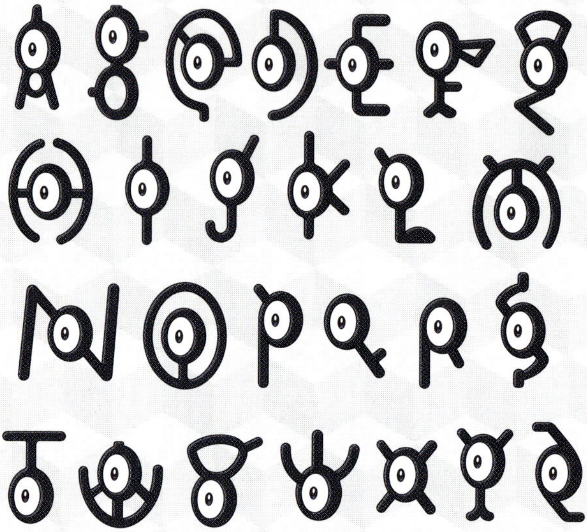

TYPE: PSYCHIC

Unown can be found in many different shapes that resemble ancient writing. It's not known which came first.

How to say it: un-KNOWN

Height: 1' 08"
Weight: 11.0 lbs.

Possible Move: Hidden Power

Does not evolve

URSARING

Hibernator Pokémon

REGIONS
JOHTO, KALOS (MOUNTAIN)

TYPE: NORMAL

Ursaring makes daily rounds through the forest where it lives, climbing high into the trees and splashing through the streams to find food.

How to say it: UR-sa-ring

Height: 5' 11" **Weight:** 277.3 lbs.

Possible Moves: Hammer Arm, Covet, Scratch, Leer, Lick, Fake Tears, Fury Swipes, Feint Attack, Sweet Scent, Play Nice, Slash, Scary Face, Rest, Snore, Thrash

Teddiursa → Ursaring

LEGENDARY POKÉMON

REGION
SINNOH

UXIE

Knowledge Pokémon

TYPE: PSYCHIC

According to legend, Uxie brought the gift of intelligence to humankind. It is known as "the Being of Knowledge."

How to say it: YUKE-see

Height: 1' 00" **Weight:** 0.7 lbs.

Possible Moves: Rest, Confusion, Imprison, Endure, Swift, Yawn, Future Sight, Amnesia, Extrasensory, Flail, Natural Gift, Memento

Does not evolve

VANILLISH

Icy Snow Pokémon

REGIONS
KALOS (MOUNTAIN), UNOVA

TYPE: ICE

Vanillish live in snow-covered mountains and battle using particles of ice they create by chilling the air around them.

How to say it: vuh-NIHL-lish

Height: 3' 07"
Weight: 90.4 lbs.

Possible Moves: Icicle Spear, Harden, Astonish, Uproar, Icy Wind, Mist, Avalanche, Taunt, Mirror Shot, Acid Armor, Ice Beam, Hail, Mirror Coat, Blizzard, Sheer Cold

Vanillite Vanillish Vanilluxe

VANILLITE

Fresh Snow Pokémon

REGIONS
KALOS (MOUNTAIN), UNOVA

TYPE: ICE

When the sun rose and cast its light on icicles, Vanillite were created. With their icy breath, they can surround themselves with snow showers.

How to say it: vuh-NIHL-lyte

Height: 1' 04"
Weight: 12.6 lbs.

Possible Moves: Icicle Spear, Harden, Astonish, Uproar, Icy Wind, Mist, Avalanche, Taunt, Mirror Shot, Acid Armor, Ice Beam, Hail, Mirror Coat, Blizzard, Sheer Cold

Vanillite Vanillish Vanilluxe

REGIONS
KALOS (MOUNTAIN), UNOVA

VANILLUXE

Snowstorm Pokémon

TYPE: ICE

From the water it gulps down, Vanilluxe creates snowy stormclouds inside its body. When it becomes angry, it uses those clouds to form a raging blizzard.

How to say it: vuh-NIHL-lux

Height: 4' 03" **Weight:** 126.8 lbs.

Possible Moves: Sheer Cold, Freeze-Dry, Weather Ball, Icicle Spear, Harden, Astonish, Uproar, Icy Wind, Mist, Avalanche, Taunt, Mirror Shot, Acid Armor, Ice Beam, Hail, Mirror Coat, Blizzard

Vanillite → Vanillish → Vanilluxe

TYPE: WATER

With its gills and fins, Vaporeon has adapted to an aquatic life. It can control its watery habitat with ease.

How to say it: vay-POUR-ree-on

Height: 3' 03" **Weight:** 63.9 lbs.

Possible Moves: Helping Hand, Tackle, Tail Whip, Sand Attack, Water Gun, Quick Attack, Water Pulse, Aurora Beam, Aqua Ring, Acid Armor, Haze, Muddy Water, Last Resort, Hydro Pump

REGIONS
KALOS (COASTAL), KANTO

VAPOREON

Bubble Jet Pokémon

Eevee → Vaporeon

VENIPEDE

Centipede Pokémon

REGIONS
KALOS (CENTRAL), UNOVA

TYPE: BUG-POISON

Venipede uses the feelers at both ends of its body to explore its surroundings. It's extremely aggressive, and its bite is poisonous.

How to say it: VEHN-ih-peed

Height: 1' 04"
Weight: 11.7 lbs.

Possible Moves: Defense Curl, Rollout, Poison Sting, Screech, Pursuit, Protect, Poison Tail, Bug Bite, Venoshock, Agility, Steamroller, Toxic, Rock Climb, Double-Edge

VENOMOTH

Poison Moth Pokémon

REGION
KANTO

TYPE: BUG-POISON

When they become active after dark, Venomoth are often drawn to streetlamps. It isn't the light that attracts them, but the promise of food.

How to say it: VENN-oh-moth

Height: 4' 11"
Weight: 27.6 lbs.

Possible Moves: Silver Wind, Tackle, Disable, Foresight, Supersonic, Confusion, Poison Powder, Leech Life, Stun Spore, Psybeam, Sleep Powder, Gust, Signal Beam, Zen Headbutt, Poison Fang, Psychic, Bug Buzz, Quiver Dance

REGION
KANTO

VENONAT

Insect Pokémon

TYPE: BUG-POISON

Venonat's large, sensitive eyes pick up even the tiniest movement. The stiff hair that covers its body protects it from harm.

How to say it: VENN-oh-nat

Height: 3' 03" **Weight:** 66.1 lbs.

Possible Moves: Tackle, Disable, Foresight, Supersonic, Confusion, Poison Powder, Leech Life, Stun Spore, Psybeam, Sleep Powder, Signal Beam, Zen Headbutt, Poison Fang, Psychic

VENUSAUR

Seed Pokémon

REGIONS
KALOS (CENTRAL), KANTO

TYPE: GRASS-POISON

When Venusaur is well nourished and spends enough time in the sun, the flower on its back is brightly colored. The blossom gives off a soothing scent.

How to say it: VEE-nuh-sore

Height: 6' 07"
Weight: 220.5 lbs.

Possible Moves: Tackle, Growl, Vine Whip, Leech Seed, Poison Powder, Sleep Powder, Take Down, Razor Leaf, Sweet Scent, Growth, Double-Edge, Petal Dance, Worry Seed, Synthesis, Petal Blizzard, Solar Beam

MEGA VENUSAUR

Seed Pokémon

TYPE: GRASS-POISON

Height: 7' 10"
Weight: 342.8 lbs.

TYPE: BUG-FLYING

Vespiquen controls the colony that lives in its honeycomb body by releasing pheromones. It feeds the colony with honey provided by Combee.

How to say it: VES-pih-kwen

Height: 3' 11" **Weight:** 84.9 lbs.

Possible Moves: Fell Stinger, Destiny Bond, Sweet Scent, Gust, Poison Sting, Confuse Ray, Fury Cutter, Pursuit, Fury Swipes, Defend Order, Slash, Power Gem, Heal Order, Toxic, Air Slash, Captivate, Attack Order, Swagger

REGIONS
KALOS (CENTRAL), SINNOH

VESPIQUEN

Beehive Pokémon

Combee Vespiquen

TYPE: GROUND-DRAGON

Vibrava's wings aren't strong enough to fly very far, but it can vibrate them to produce ultrasonic waves that can give anyone listening a bad headache.

How to say it: VY-BRAH-va

Height: 3' 07" **Weight:** 33.7 lbs.

Possible Moves: Sonic Boom, Sand Attack, Feint Attack, Sand Tomb, Mud-Slap, Bide, Bulldoze, Rock Slide, Supersonic, Screech, Dragon Breath, Earth Power, Sandstorm, Hyper Beam

REGIONS
HOENN, KALOS (MOUNTAIN)

VIBRAVA

Vibration Pokémon

Trapinch Vibrava Flygon

VICTINI
Victory Pokémon

REGION
UNOVA

MYTHICAL POKÉMON

TYPE: PSYCHIC-FIRE

According to myth, Victini can bring victory in any kind of competition. Because it creates unlimited energy, it can share the overflow with others.

How to say it: vik-TEE-nee

Height: 1' 04" **Weight:** 8.8 lbs.

Possible Moves: Searing Shot, Focus Energy, Confusion, Incinerate, Quick Attack, Endure, Headbutt, Flame Charge, Reversal, Flame Burst, Zen Headbutt, Inferno, Double-Edge, Flare Blitz, Final Gambit, Stored Power, Overheat

Does not evolve

REGIONS
KALOS (MOUNTAIN), KANTO

VICTREEBEL

Flycatcher Pokémon

TYPE: GRASS-POISON

Victreebel uses its long vine like a fishing lure, swishing and flicking it to draw prey closer to its gaping mouth.

How to say it: VICK-tree-bell

Height: 5' 07"
Weight: 34.2 lbs.

Possible Moves: Stockpile, Swallow, Spit Up, Vine Whip, Sleep Powder, Sweet Scent, Razor Leaf, Leaf Tornado, Leaf Storm, Leaf Blade

REGION
HOENN

VIGOROTH

Wild Monkey Pokémon

TYPE: NORMAL

Vigoroth just can't sit still! If it spends too much time inactive, it gets stressed out and goes on a rampage. It doesn't sleep very well.

How to say it: VIG-er-roth

Height: 4' 07" **Weight:** 102.5 lbs.

Possible Moves: Scratch, Focus Energy, Encore, Uproar, Fury Swipes, Endure, Slash, Counter, Chip Away, Focus Punch, Reversal

VILEPLUME

Flower Pokémon

REGIONS
KALOS (CENTRAL), KANTO

TYPE: GRASS-POISON

Many people are terribly allergic to the poisonous pollen Vileplume gives off. The petals of its flower are truly enormous.

How to say it: VILE-ploom

Height: 3' 11"
Weight: 41.0 lbs.

Possible Moves: Mega Drain, Aromatherapy, Stun Spore, Poison Powder, Petal Blizzard, Petal Dance, Solar Beam

VIRIZION

Grassland Pokémon

REGION
UNOVA

LEGENDARY POKÉMON

TYPE: GRASS-FIGHTING

According to legend, Virizion can move so swiftly that its opponents are left bewildered. Its horns are lovely and graceful—and as sharp as blades.

How to say it: vih-RY-zee-un

Height: 6' 07" **Weight:** 440.9 lbs.

Possible Moves: Quick Attack, Leer, Double Kick, Magical Leaf, Take Down, Helping Hand, Retaliate, Giga Drain, Sacred Sword, Swords Dance, Quick Guard, Work Up, Leaf Blade, Close Combat

Does not evolve

VIVILLON

Scale Pokémon

REGION
KALOS (CENTRAL)

TYPE: BUG-FLYING

The colorful patterns on Vivillon's wings are determined by the Pokémon's habitat. Vivillon from different parts of the world have different wing patterns.

How to say it: VIH-vee-yon

Height: 3' 11" **Weight:** 37.5 lbs.

Possible Moves: Powder, Sleep Powder, Poison Powder, Stun Spore, Gust, Light Screen, Struggle Bug, Psybeam, Supersonic, Draining Kiss, Aromatherapy, Bug Buzz, Safeguard, Quiver Dance, Hurricane

Scatterbug Spewpa Vivillon

VOLBEAT

Firefly Pokémon

REGIONS
HOENN, KALOS (CENTRAL)

TYPE: BUG

When night falls, Volbeat flashes the light on its tail in different patterns to send messages to others. It follows the sweet scent of Illumise.

How to say it: VOLL-beat

Height: 2' 04"
Weight: 39.0 lbs.

Possible Moves: Flash, Tackle, Double Team, Confuse Ray, Moonlight, Quick Attack, Tail Glow, Signal Beam, Protect, Helping Hand, Zen Headbutt, Bug Buzz, Double-Edge

Does not evolve

VOLCARONA

Sun Pokémon

REGION
UNOVA

TYPE: BUG-FIRE

The scales that cover Volcarona's six wings are like embers, and it scatters them to engulf the battlefield in flames. Its fire shines as bright as the sun.

How to say it: vol-kah-ROH-nuh

Height: 5' 03"
Weight: 101.4 lbs.

Possible Moves: Ember, String Shot, Leech Life, Gust, Fire Spin, Whirlwind, Silver Wind, Quiver Dance, Heat Wave, Bug Buzz, Rage Powder, Hurricane, Fiery Dance

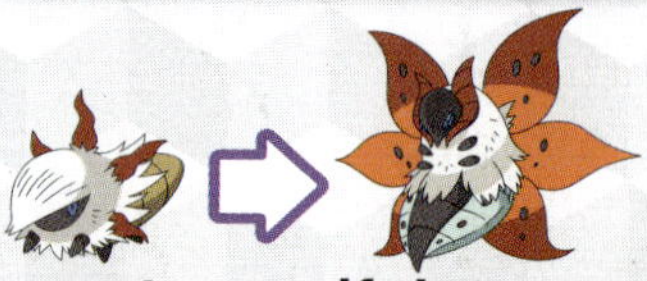

Larvesta → Volcarona

VOLTORB

Ball Pokémon

REGIONS
KALOS (MOUNTAIN), KANTO

TYPE: ELECTRIC

Voltorb looks a lot like a Poké Ball, and it was first spotted at a Poké Ball factory. What's the connection? Nobody knows.

How to say it: VOLT-orb

Height: 1' 08" **Weight:** 22.9 lbs.

Possible Moves: Charge, Tackle, Sonic Boom, Eerie Impulse, Spark, Rollout, Screech, Charge Beam, Light Screen, Electro Ball, Self-Destruct, Swift, Magnet Rise, Gyro Ball, Explosion, Mirror Coat

Voltorb → Electrode

REGION
UNOVA

VULLABY

Diapered Pokémon

TYPE: DARK-FLYING

Vullaby's wings aren't yet big enough to carry it through the air. The bones it wears around its lower half are gathered by Mandibuzz.

How to say it: VUL-luh-bye

Height: 1' 08" **Weight:** 19.8 lbs.

Possible Moves: Gust, Leer, Fury Attack, Pluck, Nasty Plot, Flatter, Feint Attack, Punishment, Defog, Tailwind, Air Slash, Dark Pulse, Embargo, Whirlwind, Brave Bird, Mirror Move

Vullaby Mandibuzz

REGION
KANTO

VULPIX

Fox Pokémon

TYPE: FIRE

Vulpix starts its life with a single tail that splits into six as it grows. The fire inside its body is constantly burning.

How to say it: VULL-picks

Height: 2' 00"
Weight: 21.8 lbs.

Possible Moves: Ember, Tail Whip, Roar, Quick Attack, Fire Spin, Confuse Ray, Imprison, Flame Burst, Safeguard, Will-O-Wisp, Payback, Flamethrower, Captivate, Inferno, Grudge, Extrasensory, Fire Blast

Vulpix Ninetales

WAILMER
Ball Whale Pokémon

REGIONS
HOENN, KALOS (COASTAL)

TYPE: WATER

Wailmer is so round because it stores seawater inside its body. It can use this water to inflate itself for higher bounces, or shoot the water from its nostrils.

How to say it: WAIL-murr

Height: 6' 07"
Weight: 286.6 lbs.

Possible Moves: Splash, Growl, Water Gun, Rollout, Whirlpool, Astonish, Water Pulse, Mist, Rest, Brine, Water Spout, Amnesia, Dive, Bounce, Hydro Pump, Heavy Slam

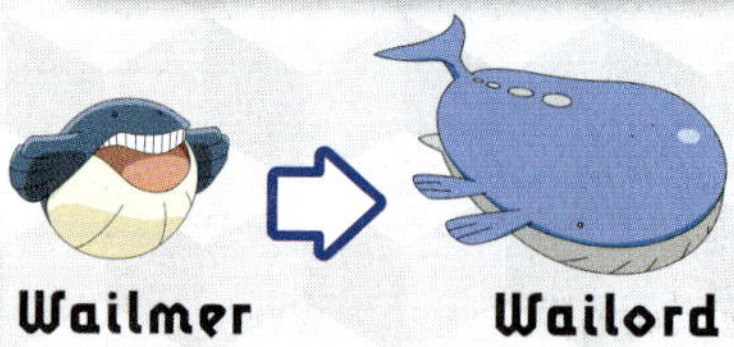

WAILORD
Float Whale Pokémon

REGIONS
HOENN, KALOS (COASTAL)

TYPE: WATER

The enormous Wailord makes its home in the open sea, where it swims with its mouth open to gather food. Sometimes it leaps out of the water, crashing back down with a massive splash.

How to say it: WAI-lord

Height: 47' 07" **Weight:** 877.4 lbs.

Possible Moves: Splash, Growl, Water Gun, Rollout, Whirlpool, Astonish, Water Pulse, Mist, Rest, Brine, Water Spout, Amnesia, Dive, Bounce, Hydro Pump, Heavy Slam

WALREIN

REGION
HOENN

Ice Break Pokémon

TYPE: ICE-WATER

Walrein's giant tusks are capable of smashing through icebergs. Its thick blubber keeps it warm in frigid seas and is great for fending off hits in battle.

How to say it: WAL-rain

Height: 4' 07"
Weight: 332.0 lbs.

Possible Moves: Crunch, Powder Snow, Growl, Water Gun, Encore, Ice Ball, Body Slam, Aurora Beam, Hail, Swagger, Rest, Snore, Ice Fang, Blizzard, Sheer Cold

Spheal → Sealeo → Walrein

WARTORTLE

REGIONS
KALOS (CENTRAL), KANTO

Turtle Pokémon

TYPE: WATER

The fur on Wartortle's tail darkens with age. Its shell bears the scratches of many battles.

How to say it: WOR-TORE-tul

Height: 3' 03"
Weight: 49.6 lbs.

Possible Moves: Tackle, Tail Whip, Water Gun, Withdraw, Bubble, Bite, Rapid Spin, Protect, Water Pulse, Aqua Tail, Skull Bash, Iron Defense, Rain Dance, Hydro Pump

Squirtle → Wartortle → Blastoise → Mega Blastoise

WATCHOG

Lookout Pokémon

REGIONS
KALOS (MOUNTAIN), UNOVA

TYPE: NORMAL

Watchog can make its stripes and eyes glow in the dark. Its tail stands straight up to alert others when it spots an intruder.

How to say it: WAH-chawg

Height: 3' 07" **Weight:** 59.5 lbs.

Possible Moves: Rototiller, Tackle, Leer, Bite, Low Kick, Bide, Detect, Sand Attack, Crunch, Hypnosis, Confuse Ray, Super Fang, After You, Psych Up, Hyper Fang, Mean Look, Baton Pass, Slam

WEAVILE

Sharp Claw Pokémon

REGIONS
KALOS (MOUNTAIN), SINNOH

TYPE: DARK-ICE

In the snowy places where they live, Weavile communicate with others in the area by leaving carvings in tree trunks. They work together to hunt for food.

How to say it: WEE-vile

Height: 3' 07" **Weight:** 75.0 lbs.

Possible Moves: Embargo, Revenge, Assurance, Scratch, Leer, Taunt, Quick Attack, Feint Attack, Icy Wind, Fury Swipes, Nasty Plot, Metal Claw, Hone Claws, Fling, Screech, Night Slash, Snatch, Punishment, Dark Pulse

REGIONS
KALOS (CENTRAL), KANTO

WEEDLE

Hairy Bug Pokémon

TYPE: BUG-POISON

Weedle's sense of smell is excellent. With its large red nose, it can sniff out the leaves it likes best.

How to say it: WEE-dull

Height: 1' 00" **Weight:** 7.1 lbs.

Possible Moves: Poison Sting, String Shot, Bug Bite

Weedle → Kakuna → Beedrill → Mega Beedrill

REGIONS
KALOS (MOUNTAIN), KANTO

WEEPINBELL

Flycatcher Pokémon

TYPE: GRASS-POISON

The hooked stem behind its head lets Weepinbell hang from a tree branch to sleep. Sometimes it falls to the ground during the night.

How to say it: WEE-pin-bell

Height: 3' 03" **Weight:** 14.1 lbs.

Possible Moves: Vine Whip, Growth, Wrap, Sleep Powder, Poison Powder, Stun Spore, Acid, Knock Off, Sweet Scent, Gastro Acid, Razor Leaf, Slam, Wring Out

Bellsprout → Weepinbell → Victreebel

WEEZING

Poison Gas Pokémon

REGION KANTO

TYPE: POISON

Rotting food gives off a noxious gas that attracts Weezing. Its twin bodies take turns inflating and deflating to keep its poisonous gases churning.

How to say it: WEEZE-ing

Height: 3' 11"
Weight: 20.9 lbs.

Possible Moves: Poison Gas, Tackle, Smog, Smokescreen, Assurance, Clear Smog, Self-Destruct, Sludge, Haze, Double Hit, Explosion, Sludge Bomb, Destiny Bond, Memento

WHIMSICOTT

Windveiled Pokémon

REGION UNOVA

TYPE: GRASS-FAIRY

Where the winds whirl, Whimsicott appear, slipping into homes through the tiniest cracks and playing tricks on people. The white fluff they leave behind sometimes gives them away.

How to say it: WHIM-zih-kot

Height: 2' 04"
Weight: 14.6 lbs.

Possible Moves: Growth, Leech Seed, Mega Drain, Cotton Spore, Gust, Tailwind, Hurricane

REGIONS
KALOS (CENTRAL), UNOVA

WHIRLIPEDE

Curlipede Pokémon

TYPE: BUG-POISON

Covered in a sturdy shell, Whirlipede doesn't move much unless it's attacked. Then it leaps into action, spinning at high velocity and smashing into the attacker.

How to say it: WHIR-lih-peed

Height: 3' 11" **Weight:** 129.0 lbs.

Possible Moves: Defense Curl, Rollout, Poison Sting, Screech, Pursuit, Protect, Poison Tail, Iron Defense, Bug Bite, Venoshock, Agility, Steamroller, Toxic, Venom Drench, Rock Climb, Double-Edge

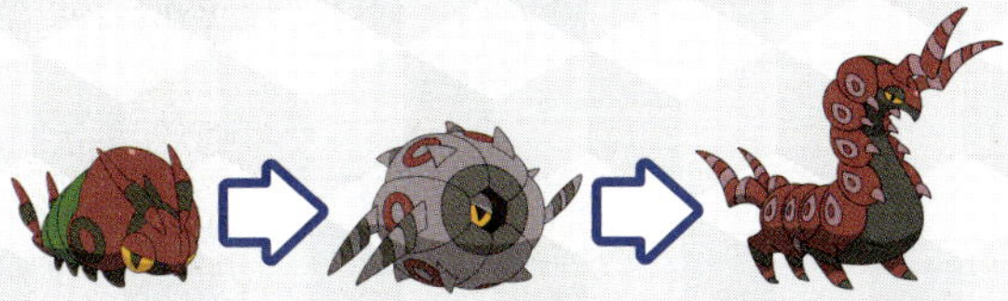

Venipede → Whirlipede → Scolipede

REGIONS
HOENN, KALOS (MOUNTAIN)

WHISCASH

Whiskers Pokémon

TYPE: WATER-GROUND

If you get too close to a pond where a Whiscash lives, it might thrash so violently to protect its territory that it sets off an earthquake. It can also sense when a regular earthquake is coming.

How to say it: WISS-cash

Height: 2' 11" **Weight:** 52.0 lbs.

Possible Moves: Zen Headbutt, Tickle, Mud-Slap, Mud Sport, Water Sport, Water Gun, Mud Bomb, Amnesia, Water Pulse, Magnitude, Rest, Snore, Aqua Tail, Earthquake, Future Sight, Fissure

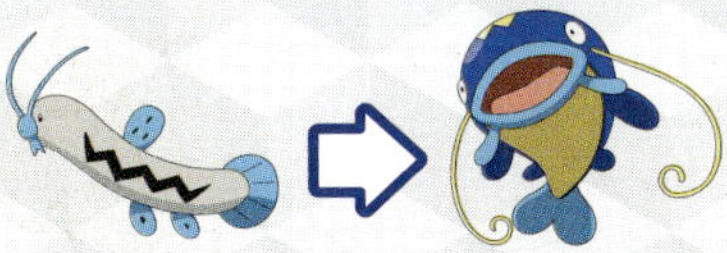

Barboach → Whiscash

WHISMUR

Whisper Pokémon

REGIONS
HOENN, KALOS (CENTRAL)

TYPE: NORMAL

When Whismur isn't in trouble, the noises it makes are very quiet. As soon as danger approaches, it sounds an earsplitting wail.

How to say it: WHIS-mur

Height: 2' 00"
Weight: 35.9 lbs.

Possible Moves: Pound, Uproar, Astonish, Howl, Supersonic, Stomp, Screech, Roar, Synchronoise, Rest, Sleep Talk, Hyper Voice

Whismur Loudred Exploud

WIGGLYTUFF

Balloon Pokémon

REGIONS
KALOS (MOUNTAIN), KANTO

TYPE: NORMAL-FAIRY

A protective coating of tears covers Wigglytuff's enormous eyes, keeping the dust away. It can suck in air to inflate its flexible body until it resembles a balloon.

How to say it: WIG-lee-tuff

Height: 3' 03"
Weight: 26.5 lbs.

Possible Moves: Double-Edge, Play Rough, Sing, Disable, Defense Curl, Double Slap

Igglybuff Jigglypuff Wigglytuff

REGIONS
HOENN, KALOS (COASTAL)

WINGULL

Seagull Pokémon

TYPE: WATER-FLYING

With its long wings, Wingull can catch updrafts from the sea and glide across the sky as if on skates. It hides food and other treasures in various places.

How to say it: WING-gull

Height: 2' 00"
Weight: 20.9 lbs.

Possible Moves: Growl, Water Gun, Supersonic, Wing Attack, Mist, Water Pulse, Quick Attack, Roost, Pursuit, Air Cutter, Agility, Aerial Ace, Air Slash, Hurricane

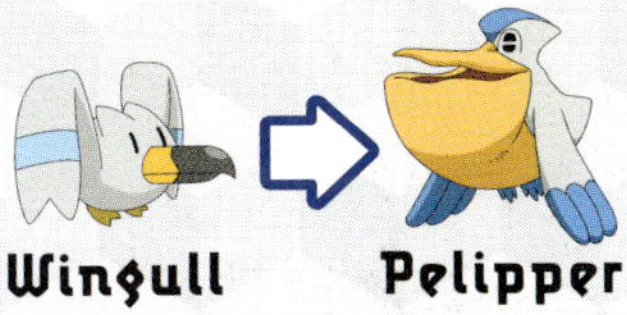

TYPE: PSYCHIC

Relying on its powers of endurance, Wobbuffet prefers not to attack—unless a foe goes after its tail. Then, it unleashes a powerful counterstrike.

How to say it: WAH-buf-fett

Height: 4' 03"
Weight: 62.8 lbs.

Possible Moves: Counter, Mirror Coat, Safeguard, Destiny Bond

REGIONS
JOHTO, KALOS (COASTAL)

WOBBUFFET

Patient Pokémon

WOOBAT

Bat Pokémon

REGIONS
KALOS (COASTAL), UNOVA

TYPE: PSYCHIC-FLYING

When Woobat attaches itself to something, it leaves a heart-shaped mark with its nose. The nose is also the source of its echolocation signals.

How to say it: WOO-bat

Height: 1' 04"
Weight: 4.6 lbs.

Possible Moves: Confusion, Odor Sleuth, Gust, Assurance, Heart Stamp, Imprison, Air Cutter, Attract, Amnesia, Calm Mind, Air Slash, Future Sight, Psychic, Endeavor

WOOPER

Water Fish Pokémon

REGIONS
JOHTO, KALOS (MOUNTAIN)

TYPE: WATER-GROUND

Though Wooper usually live in the water, they sometimes come ashore to look for food. To protect their bodies, they cover themselves with a sticky substance that is poisonous to the touch.

How to say it: WOOP-pur

Height: 1' 04" **Weight:** 18.7 lbs.

Possible Moves: Water Gun, Tail Whip, Mud Sport, Mud Shot, Slam, Mud Bomb, Amnesia, Yawn, Earthquake, Rain Dance, Mist, Haze, Muddy Water

REGIONS
KALOS (CENTRAL), SINNOH

WORMADAM (PLANT CLOAK)

Bagworm Pokémon

TYPE: BUG-GRASS

The cloak it wore as Burmy becomes a permanent part of Wormadam's body. Its appearance is determined by its surroundings at the time of Evolution.

How to say it: WUR-muh-dam

Height: 1' 08" **Weight:** 14.3 lbs.

Possible Moves: Tackle, Protect, Bug Bite, Hidden Power, Confusion, Razor Leaf, Growth, Psybeam, Captivate, Flail, Attract, Psychic, Leaf Storm

Burmy (Female Form) Wormadam

REGIONS
KALOS (CENTRAL), SINNOH

WORMADAM (SANDY CLOAK)

Bagworm Pokémon

TYPE: BUG-GROUND

If you want a Bug- and Ground-type Wormadam, make sure your Burmy has a Sandy Cloak! Once Burmy evolves, there's no going back.

How to say it: WUR-muh-dam

Height: 1' 08" **Weight:** 14.3 lbs.

Possible Moves: Tackle, Protect, Bug Bite, Hidden Power, Confusion, Rock Blast, Harden, Psybeam, Captivate, Flail, Attract, Psychic, Fissure

Burmy (Female Form) Wormadam

WORMADAM (TRASH CLOAK)

Bagworm Pokémon

REGIONS
KALOS (CENTRAL), SINNOH

TYPE: BUG-STEEL

Looking for a Wormadam with awesome Steel-type moves? You'll need to evolve a Burmy with a Trash Cloak.

How to say it: WUR-muh-dam

Height: 1' 08" **Weight:** 14.3 lbs.

Possible Moves: Tackle, Protect, Bug Bite, Hidden Power, Confusion, Mirror Shot, Metal Sound, Psybeam, Captivate, Flail, Attract, Psychic, Iron Head

Burmy (Female Form) Wormadam

WURMPLE

Worm Pokémon

REGION
HOENN

TYPE: BUG

With the spikes on its tail, Wurmple strips away tree bark to get at the delicious sap underneath. The spikes also come in handy when fending off an attacker.

How to say it: WERM-pull

Height: 1' 00" **Weight:** 7.9 lbs.

Possible Moves: Tackle, String Shot, Poison Sting, Bug Bite

Silcoon Beautifly

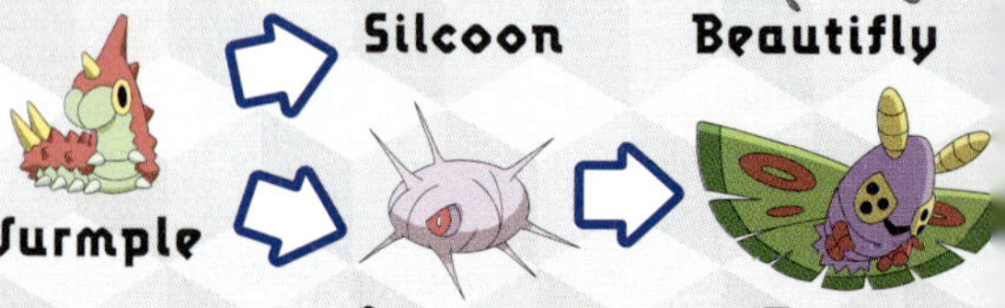

Wurmple Cascoon Dustox

REGIONS
HOENN, KALOS (COASTAL)

WYNAUT

Bright Pokémon

TYPE: PSYCHIC

If a Wynaut is smacking its tail against the ground that means it's angry, regardless of the big smile on its face.

How to say it: WHY-not

Height: 2' 00" **Weight:** 30.9 lbs.

Possible Moves: Splash, Charm, Encore, Counter, Mirror Coat, Safeguard, Destiny Bond

XATU

Mystic Pokémon

REGION
JOHTO

TYPE: PSYCHIC-FLYING

Some people believe Xatu can see the future, and they respect its mystical powers. When it stands still for hours on end, they say it's petrified by terrible visions.

How to say it: ZAH-too

Height: 4' 11" **Weight:** 33.1 lbs.

Possible Moves: Peck, Leer, Night Shade, Teleport, Lucky Chant, Miracle Eye, Me First, Confuse Ray, Tailwind, Wish, Psycho Shift, Future Sight, Stored Power, Ominous Wind, Power Swap, Guard Swap, Psychic

LEGENDARY POKÉMON

REGION
KALOS (MOUNTAIN)

XERNEAS

Life Pokémon

TYPE: FAIRY

Xerneas's horns shine in all the colors of the rainbow. It is said that this Legendary Pokémon can share the gift of endless life.

How to say it: ZURR-nee-us

Height: 9' 10" **Weight:** 474.0 lbs.

Possible Moves: Heal Pulse, Aromatherapy, Ingrain, Take Down, Light Screen, Aurora Beam, Gravity, Geomancy, Moonblast, Megahorn, Night Slash, Horn Leech, Psych Up, Misty Terrain, Nature Power, Close Combat, Giga Impact, Outrage

Does not evolve

YAMASK

Spirit Pokémon

REGION
UNOVA

TYPE: GHOST

The mask that Yamask carries is said to represent its face from a former life. Sometimes, remembering that former life makes it very sad.

How to say it: YAH-mask

Height: 1' 08"
Weight: 3.3 lbs.

Possible Moves: Astonish, Protect, Disable, Haze, Night Shade, Hex, Will-O-Wisp, Ominous Wind, Curse, Power Split, Guard Split, Shadow Ball, Grudge, Mean Look, Destiny Bond

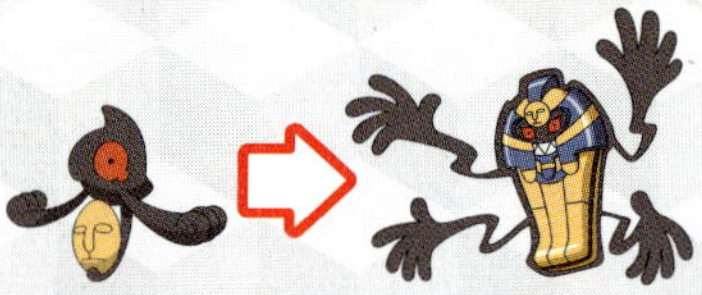

YANMA

Clear Wing Pokémon

REGIONS
JOHTO, KALOS (COASTAL)

TYPE: BUG-FLYING

With its compound eyes, Yanma can see in every direction without moving its head. It can make quick stops and turns during flight.

How to say it: YAN-ma

Height: 3' 11"
Weight: 83.8 lbs.

Possible Moves: Tackle, Foresight, Quick Attack, Double Team, Sonic Boom, Detect, Supersonic, Uproar, Pursuit, Ancient Power, Hypnosis, Wing Attack, Screech, U-turn, Air Slash, Bug Buzz

REGIONS
KALOS (COASTAL), SINNOH

YANMEGA

Ogre Darner Pokémon

TYPE: BUG-FLYING

With four wings on its back and two more on its tail to keep it balanced, Yanmega is capable of extremely high-speed flight. It can carry a full-grown person through the air.

How to say it: yan-MEG-ah

Height: 6' 03" **Weight:** 113.5 lbs.

Possible Moves: Bug Buzz, Air Slash, Night Slash, Bug Bite, Tackle, Foresight, Quick Attack, Double Team, Sonic Boom, Detect, Supersonic, Uproar, Pursuit, Ancient Power, Feint, Slash, Screech, U-turn

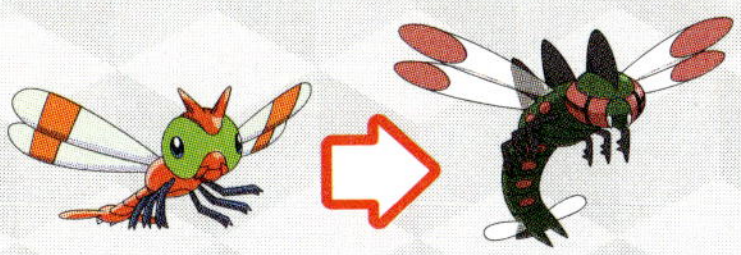

Yanma Yanmega

YVELTAL
Destruction Pokémon

REGION
KALOS
(MOUNTAIN)

LEGENDARY POKÉMON

TYPE: DARK-FLYING

When Yveltal spreads its dark wings, its feathers give off a red glow. It is said that this Legendary Pokémon can absorb the life energy of others.

How to say it: ee-VELL-tall

Height: 19' 00" **Weight:** 447.5 lbs.

Possible Moves: Hurricane, Razor Wind, Taunt, Roost, Double Team, Air Slash, Snarl, Oblivion Wing, Disable, Dark Pulse, Foul Play, Phantom Force, Psychic, Dragon Rush, Focus Blast, Sucker Punch, Hyper Beam, Sky Attack

Does not evolve

ZANGOOSE

REGIONS
HOENN, KALOS (COASTAL)

Cat Ferret Pokémon

TYPE: NORMAL

Zangoose slashes at opponents with its sharp claws extended. These Pokémon constantly feud with Seviper.

How to say it: ZANG-goose

Height: 4' 03"
Weight: 88.8 lbs.

Possible Moves: Scratch, Leer, Quick Attack, Fury Cutter, Pursuit, Slash, Embargo, Crush Claw, Revenge, False Swipe, Detect, X-Scissor, Taunt, Swords Dance, Close Combat

Does not evolve

ZAPDOS

REGIONS
KALOS (COASTAL), KANTO

Electric Pokémon

TYPE: ELECTRIC-FLYING

When Zapdos is hit by a bolt of lightning, its power increases. This Legendary Pokémon can bend electricity to its will.

How to say it: ZAP-dose

Height: 5' 03"
Weight: 116.0 lbs.

Possible Moves: Roost, Zap Cannon, Drill Peck, Peck, Thunder Shock, Thunder Wave, Detect, Pluck, Ancient Power, Charge, Agility, Discharge, Rain Dance, Light Screen, Thunder

LEGENDARY POKÉMON

Does not evolve

ZEBSTRIKA

Thunderbolt Pokémon

REGION
UNOVA

TYPE: ELECTRIC

A herd of Zebstrika running at top speed gives off a noise like thunder. If they get angry, their manes shoot off lightning.

How to say it: zehb-STRY-kuh

Height: 5' 03" **Weight:** 175.3 lbs.

Possible Moves: Quick Attack, Tail Whip, Charge, Thunder Wave, Shock Wave, Flame Charge, Pursuit, Spark, Stomp, Discharge, Agility, Wild Charge, Thrash

Blitzle Zebstrika

LEGENDARY POKÉMON

REGION
UNOVA

ZEKROM

Deep Black Pokémon

TYPE: DRAGON-ELECTRIC

Legends say Zekrom helps those who pursue their ideals. It surrounds itself with thunderclouds to travel unseen, and its tail can generate electricity.

How to say it: ZECK-rahm

Height: 9' 06" **Weight:** 760.6 lbs.

Possible Moves: Thunder Fang, Dragon Rage, Imprison, Ancient Power, Thunderbolt, Dragon Breath, Slash, Zen Headbutt, Fusion Bolt, Dragon Claw, Imprison, Crunch, Thunder, Outrage, Hyper Voice, Bolt Strike

Does not evolve

ZIGZAGOON

TinyRaccoon Pokémon

REGIONS
HOENN, KALOS (CENTRAL)

TYPE: NORMAL

Zigzagoon's curiosity drives it to wander constantly and restlessly. It rubs the sturdy bristles on its back against trees to mark its territory.

How to say it: ZIG-zag-GOON

Height: 1' 04"
Weight: 38.6 lbs.

Possible Moves: Growl, Tackle, Tail Whip, Headbutt, Baby-Doll Eyes, Sand Attack, Odor Sleuth, Mud Sport, Pin Missile, Covet, Bestow, Flail, Rest, Belly Drum, Fling

Zigzagoon
Linoone

ZOROARK

Illusion Fox Pokémon

REGIONS
KALOS (MOUNTAIN), UNOVA

TYPE: DARK

Masters of deception, Zoroark are able to create entire landscapes out of illusions. In this way, they can scare or trick people away from their territory and protect their pack.

How to say it: ZORE-oh-ark

Height: 5' 03" **Weight:** 178.8 lbs.

Possible Moves: Night Daze, Imprison, U-turn, Scratch, Leer, Pursuit, Hone Claws, Fury Swipes, Feint Attack, Scary Face, Taunt, Foul Play, Night Slash, Torment, Agility, Embargo, Punishment, Nasty Plot

Zorua
Zoroark

ZORUA

Tricky Fox Pokémon

REGIONS
KALOS (MOUNTAIN), UNOVA

TYPE: DARK

Zorua can use the power of illusion to make itself look like a person or a different Pokémon. It sometimes uses the resulting confusion to flee from a battle.

How to say it: ZORE-oo-ah

Height: 2' 04"
Weight: 27.6 lbs.

Possible Moves: Scratch, Leer, Pursuit, Fake Tears, Fury Swipes, Feint Attack, Scary Face, Taunt, Foul Play, Torment, Agility, Embargo, Punishment, Nasty Plot, Imprison, Night Daze

ZUBAT

Bat Pokémon

REGIONS
KALOS (CENTRAL), KANTO

TYPE: POISON-FLYING

Sunlight isn't good for Zubat, so it stays hidden during the day. It prefers dark places like caves and old houses.

How to say it: ZOO-bat

Height: 2' 07"
Weight: 16.5 lbs.

Possible Moves: Leech Life, Supersonic, Astonish, Bite, Wing Attack, Confuse Ray, Swift, Air Cutter, Acrobatics, Mean Look, Poison Fang, Haze, Air Slash

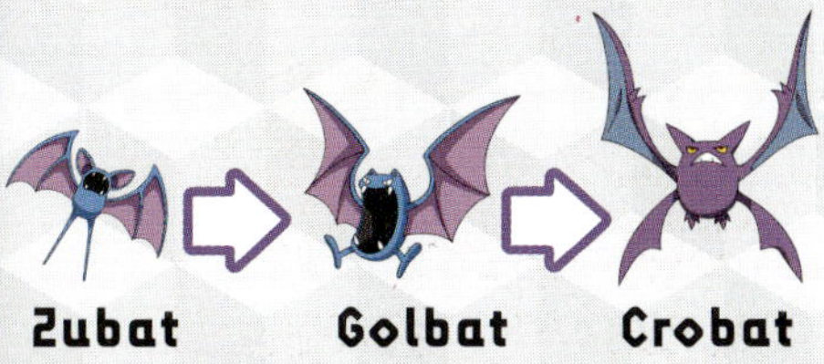

ZWEILOUS

Hostile Pokémon

REGIONS
KALOS (MOUNTAIN), UNOVA

TYPE: DARK-DRAGON

Zweilous has a ravenous appetite and exhausts the local food supply before moving on. Rather than working together, its two heads compete for food.

How to say it: ZVY-lus

Height: 4' 07" **Weight:** 110.2 lbs.

Possible Moves: Double Hit, Dragon Rage, Focus Energy, Bite, Headbutt, Dragon Breath, Roar, Crunch, Slam, Dragon Pulse, Work Up, Dragon Rush, Body Slam, Scary Face, Hyper Voice, Outrage

Deino → Zweilous → Hydreigon

ZYGARDE

Order Pokémon

REGION
KALOS (MOUNTAIN)

LEGENDARY POKÉMON

TYPE: DRAGON-GROUND

Zygarde dwells deep within a cave in the Kalos region. It is said that this Legendary Pokémon is a guardian of the ecosystem.

How to say it: ZY-gard

Height: 16' 05" **Weight:** 672.4 lbs.

Possible Moves: Glare, Bulldoze, Dragon Breath, Bite, Safeguard, Dig, Bind, Land's Wrath, Sandstorm, Haze, Crunch, Earthquake, Camouflage, Dragon Pulse, Dragon Dance, Coil, Extreme Speed, Outrage

Does not evolve